SPECIAL FORCES IN ACTION

SPECIAL FORCES IN ACTION ☆ ☆ ☆

MISSIONS, OPS, WEAPONS, AND COMBAT— DAY BY DAY

Kevin Dockery and E. Abbrecht

CITADEL PRESS
Kensington Publishing Corp.
www.kensingtonbooks.com

CITADEL PRESS books are published by

Kensington Publishing Corp.
850 Third Avenue
New York, NY 10022

All Kensington titles, imprints, and distributed lines are available at
special quantity discounts for bulk purchases for sales promotions,
premiums, fund-raising, educational, or institutional use. Special book
excerpts or customized printings can also be created to fit specific
needs. For details, write or phone the office of the Kensington special
sales manager. Kensington Publishing Corp., 850 Third Avenue, New
York, NY 10022, attn: Special Sales Department; phone 1-800-221-2647.

CITADEL PRESS and the Citadel logo are Reg. U.S. Pat & TM Off.

First printing: March 2004
10 9 8 7 6 5 4 3 2 1

Printed in the United States of America

Library of Congress Control Number: 2003112309

ISBN 0-8065-2520-7

Frontispiece: Crawling through the mud during training—a task
conducted by every would-be SEAL or UDT operator, both officer
or enlisted man, since the early days of World War II. And the action
looks to continue well into the future. U.S. NAVY

To my Father—
Frank R. Dockery,
who set an example and high standard
that I still strive to reach.

Thanks, Dad.

Contents

Introduction

This book began as a listing of significant events in the history of Naval Special Warfare—the SEALs and the Underwater Demolition Teams. They are the Navy component of the U.S. special operations forces, men who conduct unusual and unconventional missions, often right under the eyes and guns of the enemy. It quickly became obvious that no single special operations unit stands alone; all of their histories are intertwined with one another. So this book has been expanded to include significant dates and incidents of all of the special operations forces.

Our special operations forces trace their lineage back to the beginnings of the United States and earlier. The British fought against unconventional fighters in many small pitched battles as this country won its independence. During the dark days of World War II, the entire world was in danger of losing its independence. Unconventional fighters, guerrillas and commandos, had their genesis in the years the world teetered on the brink of total chaos.

The years following the war were unusual in that there were now weapons at hand that were considered so powerful that no one would consider facing them. People hoped war was a thing of the past. But the conflict of ideologies between the Communist East and the Free World of the West simply led to another way to conduct war. The "War of the Flea"—guerrilla and insurgent actions—became the byword of conflicts throughout the world. During the Korean War in the early 1950s, a number of special operations forces that had all but disappeared in the post–World War II era were resurrected and given new missions. Operating behind the lines, these men performed actions that had effects far greater than their numbers would have suggested possible.

When the United States entered the 1960s, a new president recognized that unconventional warfare would be the method of countries forcing their ideologies on smaller nations. In the early years of the decade, new units were founded within the United States military that would soon create a historic name for themselves. The forge where that name, that legend would be shaped was a small country in Southeast Asia. In the jungles and swamps of South Vietnam, the names of the Navy SEALs, the Green Berets, and others, became synonymous with small units creating havoc among the enemy. Areas where guerrillas and others had thought themselves safe were turned into killing zones by America's special operations forces.

When Vietnam ended, a new kind of war began that had been developing over centuries. Terrorism took battles to a completely unarmed, unsuspecting target—civilians. The special operations forces soon showed the terrorists that their actions would not go unpunished. When in the first year of the new millennium, terrorism conducted an attack against the homeland of freedom, the United States did not stand idly by. American special operations forces turned against the attackers and those who would give them shelter.

Day by day, the pages of this book list some of the actions of all of the U.S. special operations forces. These men conduct some of the most secret operations the world has ever known. Only a handful of these actions are ever revealed to the public: These men are the quiet professionals—they like it that way.

SPECIAL FORCES IN ACTION

JANUARY

In the Pacific off Pearl Harbor, Hawaii, the two Nasty-class fast patrol boats, PTF-3 and PTF-4, conduct a high-speed run. Though not armed with torpedoes, the PTFs are the descendants of World War II PT boats. U.S. Navy

January 01

1962 (USA)—SEAL Team One at the Naval Amphibious Base, Coronado, California, and SEAL Team Two at the Naval Amphibious Base, Little Creek, Virginia, are officially commissioned. Their name stands for the three environments in which the units will operate: sea, air, and land. The SEALs will be the primary unconventional warfare unit of the U.S. Navy.

Both teams are authorized initial manpower of ten officers and fifty enlisted men. The sole sources for the men of the SEAL teams are existing Underwater Demolition Teams (UDTs) and their replacement training units. To prevent the ranks of the UDTs from being depleted from the heavy initial draw of officers and enlisted men for the SEAL teams, the first musters were not of the complete complements, which was eventually achieved over several weeks.

On January 1, SEAL Team One holds the first muster of its men and officers at Coronado. The full complement of initial SEALs for SEAL Team One, the plankowners, are as follows:

Officers

Lieutenant David Del
   Guidice, commanding
   officer
Lieutenant James M.
   Kinney, executive officer
Abbett, Arthur W.
Fraser, Gary D.
Hawthorne, Rodman R.
Holts, Philip P.
Hunsaker III, Oscar W.
Pearson, Melvin E.
Routh, Alan C.
Stockholm, Jon R.

Enlisted Men

Abbot, Edwin D.
Abreu, Raymond N.
Adams, Floyd H.
Atkinson, Solomon D.
Beaver, Cecil M.
Betz, Clarence L.
Brown, Gordon C.
Campbell, Roy A.
Cobb, Lloyd T.
Curtis, J. H.
D'Errico, Andrew J.
Enoch, Barry W.
Eoff, Russell S.
Fisher, Robert F.

Fredrickson, Delmar
Gauthier, Ronald J.
George, Theodore E.
Gosselin, David J.
Gray, Roy M.
Hayes, Robert E.
Henry, Robert M.
Ledbetter, Arlando F.
Marriott, Carl D.
Mathison, Ted D.
McCleskey, Dale L.
McCormack, Dennis K.
Miller, Harry J.
Nelson, Charles E.

Enlisted Men

Niergarth, Charles E.	Perkins, James R.	Smith, Alwyn J.
Okesson, William F.	Perry, Francis H.	Spence, Thomas H.
Olivera, Vincent R.	Raschick, William E.	Sullivan, Robert F.
Parks, James L.	Raymond, Donald C.	Swider, John S.
Paul, Robert D.	Sick, Roger K.	Wagner, Robert K.
Peed, Jack B.	Skaggs, Arthur	Wilson, David A.
Perkins, Jack R.	Slempa, Peter P.	Yuill, Clarence C.

1990 (Panama)—Task Unit Papa, the largest single SEAL element of Operation Just Cause, the ousting of Panamanian dictator Manuel Noriega, disbands. The men are returned to the United States and SEAL Team Four the next day. They are the only SEAL element to suffer casualties during the operation when the Paitilla Airfield was taken. Task Unit Papa is part of Task Force White, the U.S. Naval Special Warfare component of the Joint Special Operations Task Force assigned to Just Cause.

1997 (Peru)—A small advance team from Detachment Delta is sent to Lima in reaction to the takeover of the Japanese ambassador's residence and the holding of almost 200 hostages. They are freed several weeks later when the building is attacked and most of the terrorists killed.

January 02

1968 (South Vietnam)—SEALs of the Eighth Platoon, SEAL Team Two, conduct operations against Viet Cong (VC) positions on May Island in the Bassac River, beginning shortly after sunrise. A VC defector leads the SEALs to the target. A short, fierce fire fight takes place as enemy contact is made with a small VC security group. The fight results in 6 enemy dead and the destruction of 2 structures and 600 pounds of rice.

1990 (Panama)—Some of the last SEAL groups who take part in Operation Just Cause, the U.S. invasion of Panama, end their deployment. The twenty-one men who make up Task Unit Whiskey (SEAL Team Two) return to the United States. Task Unit Foxtrot (the SEAL element assigned to secure the Pacific side of the Panama Canal) is also disestablished and the men return to their parent unit.

January 03

1944 (Britain)—The training of Jedburgh personnel begins in the United Kingdom.

1945 (Philippines)—At 1800 hours, the men of UDT Eight traveling off Mindoro, as part of Task Group 77.2, witness a Japanese kamikaze plane strike escort carrier USS *Omaney Bay* (CVE 9). Within twenty minutes of the attack, the order to abandon the *Omaney Bay* is given and the crew is picked up by other American vessels. In the attack, ninety-three men are listed as killed or missing and an additional sixty-five are wounded. A short time later, the order is given to sink the *Omaney Bay* with torpedoes from U.S. destroyers to prevent the burning ship from being a beacon to guide further Japanese planes. Seven of the survivors from the *Omaney Bay* are killed by Japanese kamikaze planes as they are being moved to safety. The Japanese use of organized kamikaze attacks against Allied ships began a few months before in late October 1944. It soon became a regular facet of the Pacific war. The men of UDT Eight, traveling aboard the USS *George E. Badger* (APD 33) to conduct operations at Lingayen Gulf, will spend the next eight days being ordered to stand watch at their battle stations during general quarters fifty-five times, often staying at their stations for more than eighteen hours straight.

January 04

1943 (USA)—The U.S. Army Psychological Warfare Group is established and attached to the Office of Strategic Services (OSS).

1962 (South Vietnam)—The USS *Cook* (APD 130), a World War II–era high-speed transport ship, with a detachment from UDT Twelve conduct hydrographic surveys along the South Vietnamese coast. Beach configurations, gradients, and composition, as well as the measurements of local tides and underwater obstacles, are assessed and reported. It had been noted by the commander of the Pacific Fleet that the information on the beaches and shorelines of South Vietnam were not available in sufficient detail to be used to tactically support amphibious landings where enemy forces are present.

1964 (South Vietnam)—Operation Sea Dog, a joint initiative between the South Vietnamese Army and Navy, begins as the tank landing ship *Cam Ranh*, motor gunboat *Phu Du*, and large infantry landing ship *Than Tien* bring on board an army battalion and head from Saigon to My Tho and the main target at Ilo Ilo Island. Personally commanded by the chief of staff of the South Vietnamese Navy, the raiding units include a detachment of South Vietnamese naval commandos, the Lien Doc Nguoi Nhai (LDNN), who have been undergoing training with U.S. Navy SEAL advisors.

January 05

1942 (USA)—Authority is given to Admiral Ben Moreell to create a new type of naval military construction unit, one that will not put civilian laborers in harm's way during the necessary building, modifying, and repairing of shore facilities required in combat zones. These men will supply necessary skilled labor to move forward the war and do construction right on the battlefield. The new units, called the Naval Construction Battalions, are soon known by a nickname developed from their initials CB. They are the Seabees and are given their motto: *Construimus Batuimus* ("We build, We fight").

The Seabees very quickly develop a reputation as men who can get almost any job done. Recruits for the new units are trained and experienced construction workers and engineers. Men are selected according to the level of their abilities, not their physical condition—and, in age, they range from eighteen to fifty. It isn't unusual, however, to meet a man in his sixties serving in the Seabees.

Besides construction men, the Seabees actively recruit hard-rock miners, quarrymen, blasters, and powdermen. By December 1942, all men in the Seabees are enlisted through the Selective Service System, which prevents the older men in their forties and fifties from being able to join the ranks.

Seabees become known as tough men and very hard workers. They are taught weapons handling to be able to defend themselves. During the war, it is not uncommon to see an armed Seabee working at the controls of a bulldozer, or even a captured enemy piece of equipment, repairing a roadway or landing strip.

Combined with their explosives skills, their toughness and abilities make the Seabees a primary source for volunteers when the Naval Combat Demolition Units (NCDUs), and later the UDTs, are first being formed.

1945 (Philippines)—Off Lingayen Gulf, Task Group 77.2, with the men of UDT Eight aboard the USS *George E. Badger* (APD 33), come under concerted attack by sixteen kamikaze planes and four escorts flying from the Japanese base at Mabalacat (Clark Field) on Luzon. The suicide planes crash into two heavy cruisers, an escort carrier, and a destroyer escort. They also cause near-misses on a number of other ships.

The men of UDT Eight help man battle stations as the kamikaze planes swoop down. UDT operators later said that they could see as many as three planes at a time beginning to dive at their ship. By the count of the UDT men, thirty-five Japanese aircraft were either shot down or crashed into a target within a half-hour.

1945 (Hawaii)—The men of UDT Thirteen complete their training at the Naval Combat Underwater Demolition Training and Experimental Base at Maui and receive their first orders. The UDT is assigned to the USS *Barr* (APD 39) and heads out to the Ulithi Islands in the central Pacific.

1961 (Soviet Union)—The statement by Soviet premier Nikita Krushchev that the Soviet Union will assist and recognize the legitimacy of "just wars of liberation and popular uprisings" gains an audience in the United States. President John F. Kennedy recognizes the Communist threat as a means of extending the Soviet influence through guerrilla wars. He immediately sets in motion plans to create American counterinsurgency forces—leading directly to the creation of the U.S. Navy SEALs and other special operations units.

January 06

1961 (USA)—The Twenty-fourth Special Forces Group is activated.

1967 (South Vietnam)—Formed to take ground action against enemy strongholds along the coast of South Vietnam, Operation Deckhouse V begins. South Vietnamese Special Landing Force Marines and Army of the Republic of Vietnam (ARVN) troops land amphibiously in the Mekong Delta after bombardment of the area by naval gunfire and shipborne rockets. Targeting the Than Phu Secret Zone on the shore of the South China Sea between the mouths of the Co Chien and Ham Luong Rivers, the operation maintains extensive surveys and reconnaissance of the area conducted by detachments from UDT Twelve.

1967 (South Vietnam)—Two SEAL squads from SEAL Team One are inserted by Mike boat to conduct patrols along the Rach Muoi Creek in South Vietnam's Rung Sat Special Zone. The SEALs uncover a small VC base camp and destroy it without enemy contact.

2002 (Afghanistan)—Special operations forces begin an eight-day mission in Afghanistan to search out and eliminate pockets of Taliban and al Qaeda fighters. The Special Operations Command (SOCOM) units, led by a SEAL platoon from Task Force K-Bar, enter the Zawar Kili cave complex. For twelve hours, SOCOM operators and SEALs scour more than seventy caves scattered throughout the length of a three-mile ravine near the Pakistani border. Caches of weapons, ammunition, supplies, and a wealth of intelligence materials are located. The intel materials collected include planning documents for terrorist attacks as well as tourist posters of landmarks in New York City and other locations around the United States. The SEALs and SOCOM operators face several days of dehydration, hunger, and exposure to subfreezing temperatures.

January 07

1945 (Philippines)—Preparing for the upcoming invasion of Lingayen Gulf, the men of UDT Eight conduct reconnaissance of White Beaches I and II. The total shore length of almost 2,000 yards is carefully investigated and surveyed by the UDT operators. The men of UDT Eight are given close fire support for their operations as two Landing Craft, Infantry (Guns) (LCI[G]) close to within 500 yards and open up with 40mm guns. The high-explosive cannon shells travel well over the heads of the swimmers and strike at targets along the dune line of the beach. No mines or obstacles are found by the UDT swimmers and they withdraw without losses.

1945 (Philippines)—The morning reconnaissance of Blue Beach 1 and 2 by UDT Ten is postponed because of turbid water and heavy swells. By afternoon, the situation improves enough for UDT Ten to complete its recon of the beach area 3,500 yards south of White Beach 3 at San Fabian. In spite of occasional mortar fire landing in the water, the recon is completed without casualties.

1945 (Philippines)—A thorough offshore bombardment of the beach and inland areas near White Beach 3 and the town of San Fabian on Lingayen Gulf paves the way for the reconnaissance by two platoons from UDT Fourteen. Under the cover of guns from two LCI(G)s as well as heavy fleet units, the first and third platoons from UDT Fourteen check the roughly 1,000-yard-long landing area. Only light sniper fire comes from the pounded beach and inland area to harass the UDT operators and they complete their mission without a loss.

1945 (Pacific)—UDT Twelve completes training and is deployed from the Naval Combat Demolition Training and Experimental Base at Maui aboard the USS *Bates* (APD 47). The APD stops at Pearl Harbor where provisions, the team's equipment, and tons of explosives are loaded. Along with UDT Thirteen, the USS *Barr* (APD 39), the battleship USS *Nevada* (BB 36), with its fourteen-inch guns, a veteran of Operations Overlord and Dragoon, the invasions of France in the Atlantic, and an amphibious force command ship leave Pearl Harbor. The convoy is bound for the Ulithi Islands, the staging area for the upcoming Iwo Jima operation.

1968 (South Vietnam)—Bravo squad of SEAL Team Two's Seventh Platoon is inserted on a night ambush patrol. It moves in to shore by SEAL Team Assault Boat (STAB) after being transported to its operational area by the much larger Mike boat. Two LDNNs accompany the SEALs on the operation. Only twenty feet away from where the SEALs are moving in to their insertion, two motorized sampans are spotted moving along the bank of the waterway. To prevent the mission from being compromised, the SEALs attempt to capture the sampans.

While running and under fire from the SEALs, the occupants of the sampans fire two red flares.

Their location hopelessly compromised, the SEALs decide to extract immediately. Moving to another location, the SEALs are inserted again onshore and set up a canal ambush along the bank. At 0135 hours, the SEALs successfully ambush another motorized sampan, this one carrying three Vietnamese males. The results of the operation are four VC killed in action with another two considered probable kills. Because of the tracers fired by the SEALs igniting the gasoline in the sampans, the small boats were quickly engulfed in flames and were unable to be searched.

1968 (South Vietnam)—Bravo Platoon of SEAL Team One conducts a daytime search-and-destroy operation near the Song Hau Giang River in Chau Doc Province. Moving through an area of thick coconut groves crisscrossed with numerous small streams, the SEALs come under fire from snipers and the Vietnamese subsector adviser leading the SEALs is wounded. During the eight-hour-long patrol, the operators come across a deserted VC base camp. They destroy 21 structures, 25 bunkers, and a 3,000-pound rice cache. In addition, the SEALs locate and destroy five booby traps, a motorized sampan, and forty hand grenades. One kilogram of documents is taken and forwarded to the Fourth Riverine Intelligence personnel for evaluation.

January 08

1962 (USA)—A week after its official commissioning, SEAL Team Two at the Naval Amphibious Base, Little Creek, Virginia, holds its first unit muster at 1300 hours on January 8. The first commanding officer of SEAL Team Two is Lieutenant John F. Callahan.

Lieutenant Roy H. Boehm, the officer of UDT Twenty-one, is tasked with SEAL staffing, equipping, and arranging qualification training for the SEAL concept on the East Coast. Working with UDT Twenty-one prior to the creation of the SEAL teams, Boehm developed a manpower pool with the East Coast UDT that is capable of conducting various unconventional warfare-type operations such as land operations, sabotage, and guerilla warfare. Many of these original UDT operators go on to be the plankowners of SEAL Team Two. Some of the plankowners come directly from the the most recent UDT Replacement training class, so as not to strip excessive manpower from the parent UDT. Others do not arrive at SEAL Team Two until several weeks later. The final complement of plankowners for SEAL Team Two is as follows:

Officers

Lieutenant John F.
   Callahan, commanding
   officer
Lieutenant Roy H. Boehm,
   executive officer
Ablitt, Gordon
DiMartino, Joseph
Doran, Georg W.
Graveson, David H.
Hager, Tex
Painter, William
Shapiro, Dante M.
   (Stephensen)
Wiggins, Charles C.

Enlisted Men

Andrews, James C. "Hoot"
Beal, Harry M.
Benzschawel, B.
Birtz, Pierre
Boesh, Rudolph E.
Boles, Wayne
Brozak, Richard
Bruhmuller, William
Bump, Charles
Burbank, William E., Sr.
Clark, A.D.
Dearmon, John W.
Finley, James F.
Fournier, Samuel R.
Fox, Ronald G.
Goines, William H.

Green, William T.
Iwaszczuk, Tom
Janecka, Stanley S.
Jessie, Charles W.
Johnson, Rex W.
Kelly, Michael D.
Kratky, Claudius H.
Kucinski, Louis A.
MacLean, James P.
Martin, Richard D.*
McCarty, Frederick*
McKeawn, Mike
Melochick, Melvin F.
Murphy, Tom
Nixon, Richard*
Peterson, Robert

*Assigned as Corpsmen

Ritter, John	Tegg, John D.	Wallace, Jim, Jr.
Schartz, Paul T.*	Tipton, James C.	Watson, James D
Stamey, Bobby G.	Tolison, James T.	Waugh, Leonard A.
Stone, Donald*	Tolison, Robert A.	Williams, Harry R.
Taylor, Joseph	Tornblom, Per Erik	

January 09

1945 (Philippines)—The landings at Lingayen Gulf on Luzon take place. For the first time, the UDTs have been operating as their own group with their own group commander. This organization allows a closer coordination of the teams for bombardment needs, target assignments, and intelligence reporting. Captain B. H. Hanlon is the assigned commander for the Underwater Demolition Teams, Amphibious Forces, Pacific and his flagship is the USS *Gilmer* (APD 11).

The invasion at Lingayen is conducted by two different attack forces: the Lingayen Attack Force landing to the south of Dagupan, and the San Fabian Attack Force landing in front and to either side of San Fabian to the north of Dagupan. UDTs Five, Nine, and Fifteen are assigned to the Lingayen Attack Force and beaches Crimson 1 and 2, Yellow 1 and 2, Green 1 and 2, and Orange 1 and 2. UDTs Eight, Ten, and Fourteen are assigned to the San Fabian Attack Force and beaches White 1, 2, 3, and Blue 1 and 2.

1967 (South Vietnam)—Fire Teams Five and Nine from SEAL Team One's Detachment Golf (the team's direct operations unit in South Vietnam) is inserted into the Rung Sat Special Zone to conduct a reconnaissance patrol while only a short distance from the shores of the South China Sea. Following near the south bank of the Rack Cat Loi Be Stream, the patrol finds a number of small fortifications and constructions. Crossing the stream, the SEALs continue their patrol until at and in the area of a hut they uncover a large cache (three tons) of rice, other materials, and fresh .30 caliber ammunition.

Noticing four VC approaching and surrounding the area from about twenty meters out, the SEALs recross the stream and move out along the bank. They enter the water and start silently swimming when they hear distinct Vietnamese voices coming from the shoreline.

Traveling at what they consider a safe distance from the voices, the SEALs call in their extraction boat and move out. With the location of the hut and supply cache known, the SEALs call an air strike on the area.

1975 (USA)—SEAL Team One receives the third of three Presidential Unit Citations for its actions during the Vietnam War. The citation reads:

> By virtue of the authority vested in me as President of the United States and as Commander-in-Chief of the Armed Forces of the United States, I have today awarded

THE PRESIDENTIAL UNIT CITATION (NAVY)
FOR EXTRAORDINARY HEROISM TO
SEAL TEAM ONE

For extraordinary heroism and outstanding performance of duty from 1 January 1970 to 7 December 1971 in connection with counterinsurgency operations against enemy forces in the Republic of Vietnam. Operating under the most adverse of conditions in a counter-guerrilla insurgency environment and always within enemy controlled or occupied areas, the various small detachments of SEAL TEAM ONE consistently displayed exceptional courage, professionalism and resourcefulness in the execution of hundreds of combat missions. These extremely hazardous missions included reconnaissance and intelligence collection operations, demolition raids, search and seizures, prisoner of war recovery operations, interdiction of enemy lines of communication, the capture and destruction of tons of Viet Cong supplies and armaments, the collection of vast amounts of intelligence on enemy plans and activities, and the liberation of forty-eight allied prisoners of war. The exemplary achievements of the officers and men of SEAL TEAM ONE attested to their esprit de corps and selfless dedication and were in keeping with the highest traditions of the United States Naval Service.

Richard Nixon

January 10

1969 (South Vietnam)—On patrol, Bravo Squad—from SEAL Team Two's Sixth Platoon—and a single south Vietnamese LDNN emplace specialized sensing equipment, two duffle bag devices that contain classified electronic sensors, near the Song Vam Co Dong River in Tay Ninh Province. As part of Operation Giant Slingshot, the SEALs are operating less than five miles from the Cambodian border along the blockade of the area known as the "Parrots Beak."

During the early morning installation of the second duffle bag device, the patrol uncovers four enemy ammunition caches. The SEALs spend almost three hours moving the captured munitions they find:

No.	Equipment
67	75mm recoilless rifle rounds
29	57mm recoilless rifle rounds
197	B-40 rockets
30	81mm mortar rounds
28,120	rounds of 7.62x39mm ammunition (AK-47)
24	hand grenades
1,615	quarter-pound blocks of Composition Three (C3) plastic explosive
6	ponchos
1	gas mask

All but 7,400 rounds of AK-47 ammunition, which the SEALs retain for their team's use, are turned over to the army.

January 11

1945 (Philippines)—A second Japanese suicide weapon is used against the Allied task forces as they approach Lingayen Gulf. These are the maru-ni explosive (suicide) motorboats, which carry hundreds of pounds of high explosives, often refuzed naval depth charges, in their wooden hulls.

Early in the morning, members of UDT Nine aboard the USS *Belknap* (APD 34) spot two Japanese swimmers, apparently survivors of an earlier suicide boat attack, clinging to floating pieces of wreckage.

A boat party of men from UDT Nine and the *Belknap*'s crew is quickly organized and put into one of the ship's boats to approach the swimmers. In spite of all attempts by the UDT operators and seamen to convince the Japanese to surrender, the Japanese refuse. When one of the swimmers tries to throw a grenade into the boat, the navy men open fire, killing the Japanese. Then the UDT operators and the *Belknap* crewmen, after examining the bodies for any items of intelligence value, continue to search the area. By the end of the day, now joined by a second boat, eleven Japanese swimmers are killed, none being willing to surrender as each put up a fight to the end.

1968 (South Vietnam)—A squad from Bravo Platoon, SEAL Team One, conducts a bunker search in the Mekong Delta. Operating from Binh Thuy, the squad, on the southern bank of the Bassac River in Bay Xuyen Province, patrols between 150 and 200 meters to the north. It discovers a VC bunker that is housing a five-man VC rocket squad. The first VC charges out of the bunker, firing an AK-47 rifle, mortally wounding Seaman Roy Keith. The rest of the squad continues to attack the bunker, killing the four VC occupants. A fifth VC is listed as a probable kill as he is struck by the SEALs' fire but manages to get away from them into the grassland. From the VC bodies and the bunker, the SEALs capture one Russian AK-47, two Chinese AK-47 rifles, over a hundred rounds of AK-47 ammunition, a B-40 rocket launcher, three B-40 rounds, and numerous documents.

1969 (South Vietnam)—SEAL Team Two's Sixth Platoon, operating out of Nha Be, moves along the Long Tau shipping channel. The SEALs are being transported at night by a Mike boat while they tow along a Light SEAL Support Craft (LSSC). The smaller and much quieter LSSC will be used for the final insertion and later extraction of the SEALs. Then, the LSSC suddenly capsizes, knocking the coxswain unconscious and throwing him into the water. He is dragged down by his heavy flak jacket and pulled under the Mike boat.

In disregard for his own safety, Joseph M. Silva of Sixth Platoon dives into the water. In spite of the eight-knot current in the river and the complete lack of visibility in the murky, dark water, the unconscious crewman is found and brought to the surface. For his quick actions, Silva is later awarded the Navy and Marine Corps Medal.

1970 (South Vietnam)—Lieutenant (j.g.) John C. "Bubba" Brewton of Tenth Platoon, SEAL Team Two, dies of wounds suffered in an operation in the Mekong Delta. In spite of having been wounded in the arm and back, Lieutenant Brewton continued to lead his SEALs against a numerically superior enemy force. Calling in helicopter gunship support for his beleaguered unit, Brewton sustained another wound. He is the last SEAL Team Two combat loss of the Vietnam War.

January 12

1945 (Philippines)—In the morning, with UDT Nine on board, the USS *Belknap* (APD 34) holds position at its screening station protecting the ships of the invasion fleet from enemy aircraft and submarines. The *Belknap* is suddenly struck amidship by a Japanese kamikaze. The resulting explosion destroys the two forward landing craft (Landing Craft, Personnel, Ramped) used by the UDTs. The forward stack is also largely blown away in the initial blast. The three-inch ready ammunition stored in the galley deckhouse is caught in the exploding wreckage and causes heavy casualties among the ship's crew and the UDT.

Quickly brought under control by the efforts of the *Belknap*'s crew and UDT Nine operators, the *Belknap* is assisted by the USS *Newman* (APD 59) in the recovery efforts. A second APD is also sent. The *Belknap* is towed to shallow water and anchored in a western beach area where the dead are buried at sea in the afternoon.

Losses to UDT Nine from the single kamikaze attack are one officer and seven men killed. Three men are missing and thirteen are wounded. It is the single largest loss to a UDT so far in the war and the largest number of casualties to the teams since the Normandy invasion.

1967 (South Vietnam)—Intelligence is gathered from captured documents taken during Operation Charleston in December 1966. It indicates that VC in the southern Rung Sat Special Zone are using a number of specific freshwater wells for resupply. Subsequent aerial photography helps pinpoint and confirm the wells. Two six-man units of SEALs from SEAL Team One, Detachment Golf, are inserted by helicopter and conduct a demolition raid on eight wells near the hamlet of Thanh Thoi. The wells are completely destroyed with high explosives.

January 13

1945 (Philippines)—Plans for the inclusion of UDT Nine in another operation are canceled after the kamikaze attack from the previous day. The team is down to twelve officers and forty-seven enlisted men from nearly a hundred men originally, with practically no equipment that survived the kamikaze attack. UDT Nine and its small amount of undamaged gear are transferred to the USS *Sands* (APD 13). That night, the *Sands* is ordered to leave the area and return to Leyte Gulf.

January 14

1969 (South Vietnam)—SEAL Team One's Charlie Platoon, along with an LDNN and enemy defector (Hoi Chanh) guide are inserted on a patrol in Vinh Long Province to kill or capture twelve VC reported to be in the area. Moving into the target area in their LSSC, the SEALs come across a VC sampan with three Vietnamese males aboard. The Hoi Chanh guide identifies the three as VC and the SEALs open fire. The small boat overturns and the VC start swimming to the bank, followed by the SEALs.

Signalman First Class David Wilson, the fourth man coming off the boat, steps onto the bank, triggering a hidden booby trap. The blast of what was later determined to be a 105mm howitzer round, kills Wilson and wounds another SEAL in the patrol. The explosion blasts a four-foot-diameter crater three and a half feet deep in the mud of the canal bank. Immediately recovering their teammates, the SEALs move to an outpost so a medevac can be called.

Of the three VCs from the sampan, the SEALs later learn that one had been an assistant district chief and the other a finance cadre. Such enemy personnel are highly valued as prisoners by the SEALs since they can be excellent sources of intelligence for an area.

1969 (USA)—As one of his last acts in office, President Lyndon B. Johnson awards the Presidential Unit Citation to SEAL Team One. Lieutenant Commander Franklin W. Anderson, the commanding officer, and seventeen men from SEAL Team One attend the award ceremony at the White House. All of the men have served in Vietnam during the time period covered by the citation. The citation reads:

The President of the United States takes pleasure in presenting the
PRESIDENTIAL UNIT CITATION to

SEAL TEAM ONE

For service as set forth in the following

CITATION:

For exceptionally meritorious and heroic service from 16 July 1966 to 31 August 1967, in the conduct of naval unconventional warfare operations against the Viet Cong in the Republic of Vietnam. Although often required to carry out their operations in treacherous and almost impenetrable mangrove swamps against overwhelming odds, SEAL TEAM ONE personnel maintained an aggressive operating schedule and were highly successful in gathering intelligence data and in interdicting Viet Cong operations. On one occasion, a six-man fire team ambushed one junk and two sampans, accounting for seven Viet Cong dead and the capture of valuable intelligence data. During this daring ambush, all members of the fire team remained in exposed, waist-deep mud and water in order to obtain clear fields of fire. As a result of their constant alertness and skillful reading of Viet Cong trail markers, patrols of SEAL TEAM ONE succeeded in discovering numerous well-concealed Viet Cong base camps and supply caches, and capturing or destroying over 228 tons of Viet Cong rice as well as numerous rivercraft, weapons, buildings, and documents. The outstanding esprit de corps of the men of this unit was evidenced on 7 October 1966 when a direct hit by an enemy mortar round wounded sixteen of the nineteen men aboard the detachment's armed LCM, and again on 7 April 1967 when three members of the SEAL TEAM ONE LCM were killed and eleven were wounded in a fire fight with Viet Cong positioned along the banks of a narrow stream. On both occasions, SEAL TEAM ONE men who were able, even though seriously wounded, returned to their positions and continued to fire their weapons until the boat was out of danger, thereby helping to save the lives of their comrades. The heroic achievements of SEAL TEAM ONE reflects the outstanding professionalism, valor, teamwork, and selfless dedication of the unit's officers and men. Their performance was in keeping with the highest traditions of the United States Naval Service.

★ ★ ★ ★ ★

January 15

1951 (Korea)—The guerrilla section Eighth Army G3 is established.

A trio of SEALs armed and equipped for desert warfare. The tan-and-brown-pattern camouflage uniforms help the SEALs more easily blend in to the desert environment. The weapons carried by the SEALs can quickly deal with any enemy force unlucky enough to detect them. U.S. NAVY

January 16

1945 (Philippines)—The USS *Sands* (APD 13) arrives at Leyte Gulf with the remaining team members of UDT Nine. With almost half its complement of men casualties, UDT Nine is ordered to return to Maui where it will take charge of training at the Naval Combat Underwater Demolition Training and Experimental Base after a brief island leave. With no direct transport available, UDT Nine transfers ships twice, ultimately arriving at Pearl Harbor in February.

1967 (South Vietnam)—A small, deserted VC camp is found by two fire teams from SEAL Team One's Detachment Golf. The SEALs are inserted into the patrol area that is located at the far southern end of the Rung Sat Special Zone by a slick, an unarmed helicopter. They find a canal in good condition that is navigable at high tide, running east to west through the area. During the patrol, the SEALs come across a small VC base camp that has been destroyed by a previous military action. Two huts are found a short distance from the destroyed camp that are filled with unhusked rice. The SEALs estimate the rice cache to be about seventeen and a half tons.

Calling in for a supply drop, 160 pounds of high explosives are brought in to the SEALs by helicopter. With them, the SEALs destroy the huts and the rice cache and recommend that the area be rechecked in the future.

1969 (South Vietnam)—Detachment Bravo is a group of specially trained SEALs who advise the Provincial Reconnaissance Units (PRUs). The PRUs are paramilitary units assigned to work in a specific province to gather intelligence on and eliminate the VC leadership and infrastructure. The PRUs are made up of South Vietnamese, Chinese, even ex-VC and North Vietnamese Army regulars who have deserted and come to South Vietnam. Leading these PRUs and arranging for their supply and pay are U.S. military advisors. In the Fourth Corps area in the far south end of South Vietnam, the vast bulk of the PRU advisors come from the SEALs Detachment Bravo.

1979 (Iran)—The Shah of Iran leaves Iran, relinquishing control of the government to the Islamic fundamentalist revolutionaries.

1991 (Middle East)—With the start of air attacks against Iraqi and Kuwaiti targets, Operation Desert Shield ends and Operation Desert Storm begins.

During that first day of attacks, 122 Navy Tomahawk cruise missiles are launched. The air strike is the largest the world has seen since World War II.

1964 (Vietnam)—Military Assistance Command, Vietnam/Studies and Observations Group (MACV/SOG) is formed in Saigon.

January 17

1943 (USA)—The first classes of the Amphibious Scout and Raider School (Joint) begin at the U.S. Naval Amphibious Training Base at Fort Pierce, Florida, their new location. As a joint service school, the Scouts and Raiders train units from navy personnel, the Forty-fifth Army Infantry Division, the Twenty-eighth Infantry Division, the Navy Demolition Unit, the Sixth Beach Battalion, the Second Ranger Battalion, the Thirty-first Infantry Division, units of Norwegians and Fighting French, the Fourth Army Infantry Division, the Fifth Ranger Battalion, and the Seventy-Seventh Army Infantry Division. In addition, units from the U.S. Marine Corps, the Fourth Amphibian Engineer Brigade, and a detachment of the Fourth Army Infantry Division undergo classes here.

1967 (USA)—The U.S. Navy Test Station orders eight Stoner 63 light machine guns for combat to be tested by SEAL detachments in Vietnam. Within a few weeks, the guns are in combat use by SEALs. The Stoner 63 is a complete weapons system, unique in the field of small arms. By changing components such as barrels, feed mechanisms, sights, and trigger groups, a single Stoner 63 receiver can be assembled as a carbine, a rifle, a magazine-fed machine gun, or three different types of belt-fed machine guns. It is as the belt-fed machine gun that the SEALs become most familiar with the Stoner system. The new design is the only lightweight, belt-fed, automatic weapon available that fires the same 5.56mm round as the M16 rifle.

The design of the Stoner still has developmental problems at this time. Later, these problems will be revised, but the SEALs lavish attention on the maintenance of the weapon that is demanded. The Stoner quickly becomes a favorite weapon of the SEALs, almost a trademark of theirs during the Vietnam War until the early 1980s.

1953 (USA)—The first Special Forces course 1-53 ends at the U.S. Army Psychological Warfare School.

1991 (Kuwait)—The phrase "Party in 10" is transmitted over the radio exactly ten seconds before 0238 hours. The phrase, coming from one of the AH-64A Apache gunships of Task Force Normandy, indicates that a swarm of AGM-114 Hellfire missiles have been launched and will impact in ten seconds. Task Force Normandy is made up of eight armed U.S. Army Apache gunships, a ninth backup Apache, a combat-rescue–equipped UH-60A Blackhawk helicopter, and two U.S. Air Force Enhanced Pave Low MH-53J helicopters. The missile racks of Task Force Normandy have just fired the opening shots of Operation Desert Storm, eliminating two Iraqi radar stations.

January 18

1968 (South Vietnam)—SEAL Team Two's Sixth Platoon divides into two squads to conduct ambushes and patrols on an island in the Song Co Chein River in the northeastern edge of Vinh Long Province. Squad 6A is inserted by the STAB that was used to move the SEALs quietly inland from the Mobile Support Team (MST) landing craft transport boat.

Moving inland, the squad settles in a dry area and sets up a perimeter to wait until first light. After dawn, Squad 6A patrols for several hundred yards and captures one VC guerrilla armed with several hand grenades and ammunition. The squad hears a number of signal shots being fired by enemy forces and detects a large amount of movement in the area around them. The squad calls in the extraction boat and moves to a small canal where it pulls out of the area with the prisoner.

Squad 6B moves 1,000 meters further down river before inserting by the STAB and patrolling north. Coming to a point calculated to be about 200 meters from Squad 6A's position, Squad 6B sets up an ambush position. As it waits in position, the SEALs of Squad 6B hear gunfire from the direction of the other squad.

The STAB comes up a small canal to reach the SEALs of Squad 6A and supports them with its firepower as the squad is extracted. As the squad begins to extract, the VC open up with a hasty ambush that they set up on either side of the canal. The SEALs board quickly while under enemy fire. In the exchange, Gunner's Mate First Class Arthur Williams is hit as a round glances off the stock of his weapon, strikes him under the arm, and lodges in his spine.

The STAB pulls out as the SEALs return fire and tend to their injured teammate. A Seawolf helicopter gunship light fire team comes in and gives cover from the air for the squad. The Seawolf also medevacs the wounded SEAL when the squad reaches a point of relative safety. Squad 6B calls for extraction after the ambush firing stops. Later examination shows seven hits on the armored engine covers of the STAB as well as a single round in the boat's hull.

Gunner's Mate Williams, severely wounded by the bullet in his spine, is eventually sent back to the United States for treatment. While in the Portsmouth Naval Hospital near Norfolk, Virginia, he is expected to recover but will be at least partially paralyzed. Months after being hit, he suddenly takes a turn for the worse and succumbs to his wound. He is the first SEAL Team Two fatality of 1968.

1968 (South Vietnam)—Operating in South Vietnam for only six days, Detachment Golf of UDT Twelve conducts a test of the Aqua Dart river reconnaissance system in the field. This is unusual in that the commanding officer of UDT Twelve, Lieutenant Commander Robert Cordon, is in South Vietnam observing it. Such a high-ranking officer is not usually found in the field on a simple equipment test. The Aqua Dart system is a panoramic camera mounted on a small, high-speed, water-craft, that is capable of taking pictures through 360 degrees of arc.

The test is being conducted in a river with a Landing Craft, Medium (LCM) providing support and a platform for the observers. Suddenly, a VC unit opens fire. Lieutenant Commander Gordon is killed when a B-40 rocket strikes and explodes against the LCM. He is the only active UDT Twelve operator killed during the Vietnam War.

1991 (Persian Gulf)—SEALs assist in the attack and capture of several offshore Iraqi-held oil platforms in the Durra oil field. The platforms have been used as sites for hand-held, shoulder-launched antiaircraft missiles the Iraqis fire at Coalition aircraft. U.S. Navy warships shell and U.S. Army OH-58D helicopter gunships strike at these oil platforms before the SEALs arrive. Along with twenty-three Iraqi prisoners, communications equipment, guns, and intelligence documents are captured by the SEALs. The Iraqis, severely shaken by the violence and power of the air attack and naval gunfire, offer little resistance when the SEALs land—a preview of what much of the ground war will be.

January 19

1945 (Philippines)—The USS *George E. Badger* (APD 53) with UDT Eight on board, leaves the Lingayen Gulf area and is bound for the Ulithi Islands for several weeks of relaxation and recuperation.

1951 (Korea)—The UDT One conducts beach reconnaissance off the coast of Korea. Until January 19, there has been no resistance. Then, a group from UDT One completes a survey of a location on the west coast of Korea and prepares to leave the beach. It is reembarking onto a Landing Craft, Vehicle, Personnel (LCVP) when the boat is taken under fire by the enemy on shore. One officer and a single enlisted man are killed and one additional officer and four enlisted men are wounded. Civilians in the area who were questioned earlier reported no enemy soldiers in the area for several days. The need for a security force to oversee UDT operations of this nature is stressed in the UDT after-action report of the incident.

1969 (South Vietnam)—Conducting a patrol in Dinh Tuong Province during the early evening, seven SEALs from Alfa Platoon, SEAL Team One, come across a large offensive bunker hidden in a canal bank. The squad also notices a light moving back and forth on the opposite side of the canal. Reacting, the SEALs quickly set up an ambush. The SEALs begin to hear troop movement off to their left. Then, sampans come into sight on the canal and are beached in front of a hooch about 100 meters to the left of the ambush site. As they watch, the SEALs see lights flashing from the hooch. Several motorized sampans are then heard coming up the canal, entering the kill zone of the ambush. The SEALs open fire.

The first sampan, having only a single occupant, is immediately taken when the ambush is initiated. A set of web gear and a number of personal effects are found. The second sampan, occupied by three males, is sunk and a third boat with three or four males drifts upstream unable to be retrieved, although four bodies are seen in the water.

Calling in their extraction boat, an LSSC, the SEALs leave the area under cover of their landing craft. Soon, however, the third sampan is seen drifting with the current and the SEALs notice a large box in the slender boat. A round from a 40mm grenade launcher is fired at the sampan and causes a large secondary explosion in the drifting sampan, sending a blast twenty meters into the air, and destroying the large box.

Return fire then starts coming at the SEALs from both banks of the canal. As the SEALs and the landing craft pull out, a strike from both Seawolf helicopter gunships and Patrol Boats, River (PBRs) from the nearby Song Tien Giang River are called in on the surrounding VC.

January 20

1967 (South Vietnam)—Providing blocking for the U.S. Army, the SEALs of Detachment Golf work with other units of the Operation Game Warden river forces. The mission: the SEALs are to use their armed Mike boat and smaller Mark 4 Landing Craft, Personnel, Large to prevent VC from escaping from a river island as the army units sweep part of the Rung Sat Special Zone, a heavily overgrown area of mangrove swamps to the southeast of Saigon, between the capital city and the South China Sea.

As the heavily armed and armored Mike boat approaches a village, VC forces open fire from a number of positions with automatic and antitank weapons. The SEALs and the crew of the Mike boat put out a heavy volume of fire, driving back the VC attackers. Three SEALs are wounded and an ARVN officer is killed in the ambush.

Continuing their sweep of the area, the army units kill four VC and capture a number of caches of food, ammunition, demolitions, clothing, and documents while clearing the village and surrounding swamp of VC. In addition, the army forces secure 360 detainees. Preliminary intelligence reports indicate that most of the males among the detainees are active VC.

1991 (Asia)—The Third Special Forces Group (Airborne) is deployed to Southwest Asia.

1991 (Iraq)—The British Special Air Service (SAS) begins operating in the Iraqi desert to locate SCUD launchers. It continues its presence by locating and "painting" targets with laser designators throughout the Persian Gulf War.

January 21

1968 (South Vietnam)—SEAL Team Two suffers its first loss of the war when Aviation Machinist's Mate Second Class Eugene Fraley is killed while preparing a booby trap for field emplacement. The booby trap was one that had been supplied to the teams from the development units at China Lake, California, to be filled with explosives.

1969 (South Vietnam)—Delta Platoon of SEAL Team One is assigned to the Coastal Surveillance Group (CTF 115) headquartered at Cam Rahn Bay. The SEALs are to assist the Operation Market Time forces that will curtail the waterborne flow of supplies and personnel from North Vietnam to the south.

Part of Delta Platoon is nicknamed the "Kerrey Raiders" of Market Time because of one of its platoon officers, Lieutenant (j.g.) Joseph "Bob" Kerrey.

1969 (South Vietnam)—A detachment of swimmers from UDT Eleven begins operations off the submarine USS *Tunny* (LPSS 282) in South Vietnamese waters. The team will use submarine-launched Swimmer Delivery Vehicles (SDVs) to conduct hydrographic recons. The operation of the SDVs is conducted successfully, but some mechanical failures on board the *Tunny* cause the submarine to return to Subic Bay in the Philippines for repairs.

1970 (USA)—Chief Hospital Corpsman Donel C. Kinnard, attached to UDT Twelve's Detachment Golf, receives the Navy Cross for actions during the Vietnam War. Kinnard is the first UDT operator to receive the citation, which reads in part:

> *For extraordinary heroism while engaged in armed conflict against enemy forces in the Republic of Vietnam on 20–21 January 1970. During this period, Chief Petty Officer Kinnard was serving with Underwater Demolition Team Twelve, Detachment Golf, and operating with the Second Battalion, Fifth Mobile Forces Command during a sweep and clear mission in the Ca Mau peninsula. On one occasion, Chief Petty Officer Kinnard was singled out as a target by an enemy force while he was attempting to beach a damaged sampan from which three of the enemy had leaped into the water and escaped. His courageous action resulted in the capture of the sampan and enemy weapons. On another occasion, when his unit was subjected to intense enemy rocket, machine-gun and automatic-weapons fire, Chief Petty Officer Kinnard was wounded in the arms and legs by shrapnel from an enemy hand grenade. He immediately hurled several hand grenades across a canal into enemy positions. During the ensuing battle, he was suddenly attacked by one of the enemy who had crept up behind him. After several minutes of fierce hand-to-hand struggle, Chief Petty Officer Kinnard succeeded in overcoming his attacker who was later identified as a North Vietnamese Army Lieutenant. By his personal courage and inspiring devotion to duty, Chief Petty Officer Kinnard contributed materially to the success of a vital mission and upheld the highest traditions of the United States Naval Service.*

★ ★ ★ ★ ★

January 22

1946 (USA)—The Central Intelligence Agency (CIA) is created.

1968 (South Vietnam)—Eight Platoon of SEAL Team Two and Bravo Platoon of SEAL Team One combine men from their forces to conduct a demolition operation. Having built a blockage on the Rach Ong Tam Canal, the VC are trying to prevent movement of U.S. Riverine forces. The SEALs will blast the blockage free to allow PBRs access to a suspected VC hospital area on Cu Lao Dung Island in the Bassac River.

Two PBRs and two squads of SEALs set up security around the banks of the canal while another squad lays 300 pounds of Composition Four (C-4) explosive on the blockage. The blast successfully clears thirty yards of water, thus opening up a major VC communication/liaison route to PBR patrols.

1968 (South Vietnam)—In the southwest corner of the Giao Duc District of Dinh Tuong Province, along two canals, SEAL Team Two's Sixth Platoon splits into squads to cover two ambush positions. The operation starts less than an hour before midnight on January 22 and finishes almost five hours later. Even for the SEALs, the results of one of the ambushes is unusual.

After waiting several hours in position for its first ambush, Squad 6A spots an unlighted sampan with four occupants moving up the canal. Taking the sampan under fire, the SEALs eliminate all occupants. A half-hour after the first sampan is taken under fire, Squad 6A ambushes a second unlighted sampan, killing both occupants. The squad then moves to a rendezvous point to wait for extraction.

Nearby, Squad 6B reacts to the sudden actions of an estimated seven VC on the north bank of the canal. The VC are reacting to the first ambush by Squad 6A and are firing in that squad's general direction. As Squad 6B establishes a hasty ambush, an estimated group of four VC on the south side of the canal open fire. The VC on the south side of the canal, however, aren't reacting to the SEALs, they are firing at the seven VC on the north side of the canal. The SEALs hold their fire and listen to the VC shoot at each other. Some of the VC fire is effective as the SEALs hear a number of cries from wounded personnel.

Just a few minutes after the first ambush initiated by Squad 6A, Squad 6B opens fire on a sampan with a single occupant in the canal as well as on a VC on the north bank. While the SEALs of Squad 6B pull out to rendezvous with Squad 6A, they hear enemy movement in the area. The SEALS take a single VC under fire shortly before they meet up with Squad A.

After a second ambush setup fails to make contact with the enemy, the platoon calls in its extraction and pulls out of the area. Attempts to locate the ambushed sampans are blocked by the low water in the canal, preventing the SEALs' STAB from being able to enter the area. Seawolf gunships provide air cover for the extraction and the sampan search.

1968 (South Vietnam)—On an overnight ambush patrol, a squad from SEAL Team One's Alfa Platoon joins forces with a detachment of five men from the Australian SAS. The combined force is inserted by climbing down a rope ladder hanging from a hovering helicopter. It is going into a mangrove swamp on the southern bank of the Rach Ong Trac River in the Nhon Trach District of Bien Hoa Province, an area near the northern edge of the Rung Sat Special Zone.

The SEALs and SAS have been waiting in position for eleven hours when three sampans with eight to twelve VC aboard come out of the mouth of a small stream some 300 meters north of the ambush site. After the SEALs and SAS trigger their ambush, a recovered sampan with two Vietnamese bodies in it along with web gear and hand grenades is captured. The uniforms on the bodies indicate that they are North Vietnamese Army regulars operating with the VC in the local area.

The SEALs and SAS leave the area by Mike boat. Later, that same boat takes several sampans under fire as it encounters them in the Thai Vai River. No friendly civilians are supposed to be in the area and that makes it easy for large groups of VC to operate without being seen. The SEALs suspect that there is a VC base camp up the small stream.

The SEALs and the SAS of both Australia and New Zealand operate together a number of times throughout the Vietnam War. All three units normally work as small groups of five men or so acting as the eyes and ears of the much larger regular forces. The like manner of operating made the SEALs and SAS natural allies in the operations against the Communist insurgents in Southeast Asia.

January 23

1943 (Far East)—A Group, OSS Detachment 101, makes its first jump into enemy-held Burma.

1951 (Korea)—Plan ABLE is published; defined are partisan guerrilla activities in North Korea.

1968 (Korea)—The USS *Pueblo* (AGER 2), an intelligence gathering vessel operating off the coast of North Korea, is attacked and seized by the North Koreans. The ship operates in the Sea of Japan, fifteen miles from the coast of Korea and technically in international waters. The mission of the *Pueblo* is to monitor and collect Soviet and North Korean message traffic, as well as to observe and analyze activity at several North Korean naval ports.

North Korean–armed patrol boats and MiG jet fighters attack and seize the *Pueblo*, killing one of its eighty-three crewmen as well as wounding its captain and several of its crew. The ship is taken to a secured position in Wonsan Harbor and the crew held prisoner. For eleven months, the *Pueblo*'s eighty-two surviving crewmembers are held captive and the United States examines a number of plans to destroy the ship before the Communists have a chance to dismantle and move the sophisticated electronics on board.

One of the plans involves the USS *Tunny* (LPSS 282), a Gato-class diesel-electric submarine that has been converted for use as an amphibious transport submarine by special warfare personnel. The *Tunny* is well known to the men as the UDTs have operated off the boat in Vietnam for years. The current plan calls for the *Tunny* to take a detachment of UDT operators within range of the location of the *Pueblo*. There, the UDT combat swimmers can raid the captured ship and destroy the classified equipment if not the *Pueblo* itself. The plan is disapproved after concerns are voiced as to just what the North Koreans might do to the captive crewmen of the *Pueblo* and how the action could jeopardize their possible release.

1991 (Persian Gulf)—Of the three active combat, search, and rescue (CSAR) operations of Desert Storm, only one takes place over water. A pilot bails out of a damaged U.S. Air Force F-16 over the northern Persian Gulf. Aboard the USS *Nicholas* (FFG 47), a U.S. Navy SH-60B helicopter equipped for CSAR missions lifts off with two SEALs on board and relocates the pilot six miles off the coast of Kuwait. Acting as rescue swimmers, the SEALs enter the water and attach a rescue harness to the pilot. The hovering helicopter winches all three men on board and returns to the *Nicholas*. From liftoff to landing, the mission takes thirty-five minutes. The pilot is cold from his immersion, but otherwise unharmed.

January 24

1964 (South Vietnam)—The Special Operations Group (SOG) is established by the Military Assistance Command, Vietnam (MACV). SOG will be a joint force from all branches of the U.S. military and is to take over the CIA's covert military programs in Vietnam. Under the command of a U.S. Army full colonel, SOG soon grows into the largest clandestine military unit since the end of World War II and the OSS. Army Special Forces, Navy SEALs, and Air Force Air Commandos are all part of the personnel of SOG. Also included in the personnel roster are a large number of indigenous personnel from all over Southeast Asia as well as a number of CIA officers. Included in the organization of SOG as well is the Naval Advisory Detachment (NAD) manned with SEAL officers and men.

Within a few months, the identification of SOG changes. The initials remain the same, but the meaning is changed to Studies and Observations Group as a security measure.

1991 (Persian Gulf)—An Iraqi minesweeper is spotted leaving Qaruh Island, a small barren island off the Kuwaiti shore, early in the morning. After the ship is attacked by U.S. warships and helicopters, a party of SEALs and other sailors board and strip all intelligence value from the ship before it is sunk by gunfire from the USS *Curtis Wilbur* (DDG 54).

During the attack on the minesweeper, OH-58D helicopters come under small arms fire from Qaruh Island. The helicopters strike at emplacements and gun positions on the island with 2.75-inch rockets and heavy machine gun fire. A short time later, an examination of a video tape of the attack shows an Iraqi raising a white flag on the island. A composite SEAL platoon is put together from SEAL elements on three navy ships and the island is taken, with twenty-nine Iraqis becoming prisoners. SEAL Ensign John Pugh raises the flags of Kuwait and the United States at 1707 hours. The operation results in the first liberation of occupied Kuwaiti soil and nets a treasure trove of intelligence material on Iraqi naval minelaying and mine field locations.

January 25

1943 (USA)—Joint Scout and Raider training officially starts in Florida at Fort Pierce Amphibious Training Base for the first time. The base is not yet officially commissioned, however, and some of the physical training of the original contingent of students consists of assembling the base itself.

1968 (South Vietnam)—SEAL Team Two's Sixth and Seventh Platoons, along with four LDNNs, six PBRs, two Monitors, four Assault Support Patrol Boats (ASPBs), and four Seawolf helicopter gunships, conduct a daylight village search as part of Operation Wind Song I. SEAL platoons are inserted along the Mo Cay Canal in the Mo Cay District of Kien Hoa Province from an ASPB. They burn or destroy fifty bunkers, forty structures, ten pounds of medical supplies, and five tons of rice and capture five pounds of documents. During the operation, fifty-one Vietnamese males are detained and later turned over to the Mo Cay district chief for processing. One VC tax collector is determined to be among the detainees. When the SEALs extract and insert on the other side of the canal for an additional area search, they discover numerous punji pits; however, there are no SEAL casualties. During the search of the area, the SEALs engage an unknown number of VC. Later, five dead VC are accounted for in an agent's report from the area.

January 26

1943 (USA)—The U.S. Naval Amphibious Training Base on South Hutchensen Island at Fort Pierce, Florida, is officially commissioned. Captain G. Gulbranson of the U.S. Navy, the commanding officer of the new Joint Scout and Raider School at Fort Pierce, reads his orders before an assembly of the six Scout and Raider officers at 1000 hours.

1952 (Korea)—The 8240th Army Unit infiltrates ninety-seven guerrillas into North Korea.

January 27

1970 (South Vietnam)—Chief Shipfitter Guy E. Stone of UDT Twelve is awarded the Navy Cross. The award citation reads:

For extraordinary heroism on 17 January 1970 during operations against the enemy in the Republic of Vietnam. Engaged in clearing a graveyard of booby traps for a detachment of Underwater Demolition Team TWELVE during a bunker-destruction sweep near the Vinh Dien River, Chief Petty Officer Stone suddenly discovered eight of the enemy hidden in the grass. The hostile troops opened fire with automatic weapons and began hurling hand grenades. Yelling a warning to the other members of his team, Chief Petty Officer Stone, without a weapon at that moment, took cover behind a mound and began to direct the fire of his companions. Subsequently, in the face of the hostile fire, he raced to within fifteen feet of the enemy and hurled three grenades into their midst. Observing two of the enemy soldiers retreating, he again exposed himself to hostile fire to borrow a weapon from a team member and shoot the fleeing soldiers, accounting for a total of six enemy dead and two captured. Chief Petty Officer Stone's instinctive reactions saved two United States and two Vietnamese Naval personnel in his team from certain death. His exceptionally courageous and heroic actions and selfless efforts on behalf of his team members were in keeping with the highest traditions of the United States Naval Service.

★ ★ ★ ★ ★

January 28

In Vietnam, the Mike boat was a converted Mark 6 Landing Craft, Medium (LCM). The large, boxy craft is armored and heavily armed to perform as a Heavy SEAL Support Craft (HSSC). This bow-on picture of an early version shows the Mike boat with several .50 caliber machine guns along its sides. On the overhead cover, placed over the central troop decks, is an M40 106mm recoilless rifle. Only three boats of this type are made during the war, and they are constantly being modified. These include mounting miniguns in gun tubs, 81mm mortars, and a variety of machine guns and grenade launchers to line the boat's sides.

The Vietnam-era SEAL "Mike" boat. Modified to better act as a heavy SEAL support craft (HSSC), the Mike boat is built from the LCM (landing craft, medium), the last letter of the original designation resulting in the Mike name. Fifty-caliber machine guns behind armored shields protrude from the sides of the boat. An M40 106mm recoilless rifle is secured on the "overhead" covering the central troop well of the craft. U.S. Navy

January 29

1944 (Pacific)—Operation Flintlock, the invasion of Kwajalein Atoll in the Marshall Islands, begins under Rear Admiral Marc A. Mitscher's Task Force Fifty-eight, a Fast Carrier Force. Planes and ships bomb and shell targets on Roi, Namur, Maloelap, and Wotji Islands. Land-based aircraft also attack Jaluit and the Mille Islands.

Kwajalein is the largest coral atoll in the world, consisting of ninety-seven islands and islets strung out along a reef that covers 839 square miles and surrounds a lagoon. The atoll is sixty-six miles long in a roughly northwest to southeast direction and is twenty miles wide at its greatest width. The only islands in the atoll that are considered large enough to support a military presence are the main island of Kwajalein, Roi, and Namur at the northern end, as well as Ebadon at the western end. The main Japanese air base of the atoll is on Roi-Namur; the main naval base is on Kwajalein Island.

To help ensure the success of the landings of Operation Flintlock, UDTs have been rushed into existence by the operation commander, Vice Admiral Richmond Kelly Turner. UDT One is assigned to Task Force Fifty-two under Vice Admiral Turner and is used in the initial Kwajalein attack. UDT Two is assigned to Task Force Fifty-three under Rear Admiral Richard Conolly for use in attacking Roi-Namur. This is to be the first combat use of UDTs.

January 30

1945 (Philippines)—The Sixth U.S. Army Ranger Battalion, Mucci's Rangers, conducts a deep behind-the-lines raid to take control of a Japanese prisoner of war (POW) camp. The camp is at Cabanatuan on the island of Luzon and many of the POWs have survived years of hellish existence under their brutal Japanese captors. The Rangers, reinforced by men from the U.S. Army's Alamo Scouts as well as Filipino guerrillas, raid the camp before the Japanese can execute the prisoners. They rescue 500 Allied POWs, some of whom had survived the Bataan Death March and the building of the Burma railway.

1968 (South Vietnam)—On the first day of Tet, the Southeast Asian Lunar New Year, the VC and North Vietnamese launch a massive offensive against key cities and positions throughout South Vietnam. It catches the U.S. and South Vietnamese troops and leadership unaware and breaks the negotiated truce for the holidays. The coordinated series of attacks begins shortly after dawn on January 30 and, according to a broadcast from Hanoi, is intended to "punish the U.S. aggressors." Thousands of VC attack villages, towns, and cities throughout the south, acting en mass as regular troops for the first time. SEAL detachments and units in all of South Vietnam go into action along with all other U.S. forces to defend bases, towns, and local population centers.

1991 (Kuwait)—As part of a major plan to convince the Iraqis that the land war portion of Operation Desert Storm is going to take a different path, Central Command (CENTCOM) orders a number of close-in reconnaissance missions. They are to be conducted by the SEALs of Navy Special Warfare Task Group One. The first of what will be fifteen separate operations begins on January 30. The actions will continue for over two weeks.

1991 (Persian Gulf)—SEALs and a detachment from SEAL Delivery Vehicle Team One begin the first of six operations to search for moored sea mines in the area of the northern Persian Gulf. The SEAL Delivery Vehicle (SDV) assigned to the mine search is the Mark IX, a flat, two-man underwater vehicle with a sophisticated integral sonar system. The Kuwaiti barge *Sawahil*, having escaped Kuwait as the Iraqis invaded, serves as a support and transport craft for the SEALs and their SDV. The equipment of the *Sawahil* includes a crane that can easily launch and recover the SDV. This is the first combat use of the Mark IX SDV.

BARNDANCE #   8-18

DATES: 30-31 Jan 68

WT Ø97 Ø66
WT Ø52 Ø58
COORD: WT Ø94 Ø6Ø
TIMES: 3Ø2ØØØH - 31Ø53ØH

1. UNITS INVOLVED: Seal 8th Platoon, LDNN Advisor, Scout Dog, PRU Advisor
                               3 PRU guides, Interpreter, PBR sec 535, LTJG Marcinko

2. TASK: Patrol along border crossing corridor.

3. METHOD OF INSERTION: PBR   EXTRACTION: PBR

4. TERRAIN: Open fields, Wood lines

5. TIDE: ———   WEATHER: Clear

6. MOON: New

7. ENEMY ENCOUNTERED: VC Platoon

8. CASUALTIES: None

9. NAMES OF SEALS INVOLVED: Marcinko   Boyce   Kucinski

    Scollise   Nixon   Saunders   Humphries   Risher

  Schwalenberg   Engraff   Drady   Thornton   Silver

10. RESULTS: Verified intelligence report that possible 500 VC were collecting near border. Contact proved they were protecting something
of value. This was at Ø4ØØH. Ø34ØH Chau Phu was over run.
Unknown VC total strength.

11. REMARKS/RECOMMENDATIONS: S/A Chau Phu required we submit fire support
plan. When we needed support I was advised I couldn't get a
fire mission. Also I was told a shotgun would fly over every
two hours for radio check, no shotgun. My only support was 2
PBR's from RivSec 535. 4 clicks away.

    INCLUDE INTELLIGENCE INFORMATION GATHERED, MATERIAL FOUND, DESTROYED,
CAPTURED, ETC.

13 Feb 68

January 31

1944 (Pacific)—The first ever UDT combat operation takes place. Landings begin at Roi-Namur in the Kwajalein Atoll under the command of Lieutenant Commander John T. Koehler, when UDT Two sends in its Stingray radio-controlled explosives-filled boats at first light to begin Operation Flintlock. At the target Roi Red Beaches 1 and 2 as well as Green Beaches 1 and 2 on Namur, the drone boats become almost as great a menace to the U.S. fleet ships as they fail to stay under control. The UDT operators themselves move in toward the beaches in rubber boats under the cover of darkness and check the depths of the water over the reefs. No obstacles are found and the way is clear for the marines to land.

Rear Admiral Richard Conolly orders his ships to close in to point-blank range to give naval gunfire support for the marines and, for such powerful and accurate protection, he becomes known as "Close-in Conolly" for the rest of the war.

1944 (Pacific)—At Kwajalein Island, Vice Admiral Richmond Kelly Turner orders UDT One to conduct a daylight reconnaissance mission of the reefs off the landing beaches. Several groups of UDT operators move in toward the beach in standard LCVPs. The men feel unable to recon the reef from inside the boats due to the number of coral heads in the water. Ensign Lew Luehrs and Chief Bill Acheson strip off their fatigues to expose their swimming trunks. In spite of orders to the contrary, the two men enter the water and swim in to the reef for a better view. They are the first UDT operators to swim in on an operation. Due to the information gathered by the men of UDT One about the terrain, the landing crafts used at Kwajalein are changed from LCVPs to Landing Tracked Vehicles (LTVs) that can climb over the coral heads.

1967 (South Vietnam)—Second and Third Platoons of SEAL Team Two arrive in South Vietnam to begin direct combat actions. The two platoons are the first sent from the U.S. East Coast and are used as manpower in Detachment Alfa. The two platoons comprising two officers and ten enlisted men have undergone more than six months of predeployment training at Little Creek, Virginia, and other sites, as well as two weeks of training and updates with SEAL Team One at the Naval Amphibious Base, Coronado, California.

BARNDANCE #   0-19
DATES: 31 Jan 68

COORD: WS 135 835
TIMES: 0700H - 1800H

1. UNITS INVOLVED: Seal 8th Platoon, LDNN Advisor, Scout Dog, PRU Advisor,
   PBR RivSec 535, LTJG Marcinko
2. TASK: Protect U.S. citizens in Chau Phu, which was under VC attack.

3. METHOD OF INSERTION: PBR   EXTRACTION: PBR

4. TERRAIN: Streets, Rooftops, Doorways

5. TIDE: ———   WEATHER: Clear

6. MOON: ———

7. ENEMY ENCOUNTERED: Approximately 2 reinforced platoons

8. CASUALTIES: 1 USN KIA (Seal) 1 USN WIA (Seal)

9. NAMES OF SEALS INVOLVED: Marcinko   Boyce   Kucinski

   Scollise   Nixon   Saunders   Humphries   Risher

   Schwalenberg   Drady   Engraff   Thornton   Silver

10. RESULTS: Liberated 1 U.S. nurse, U.S. citizens from Cords compound,
    secured MSS office. PIC, National police guarded the PRU
    armory and maintained security on the Embassy House. 2 VC
    KIA (BC), unknown number of VC WIA

11. REMARKS/RECOMMENDATIONS: It took 2 hrs and 20 minutes for medivac of
    Risher. Nixon HM1 had to perform a field tracheotomy to keep
    him alive. Special Forces units remained in thier compound
    while Seals/PRU fought for the city. Although the men performed
    unquestionably, this is not our job. Thornton was wounded
    above left eye from frag when a round struck the wall next to
    him.

RAS 13 Feb 68

INCLUDE INTELLIGENCE INFORMATION GATHERED, MATERIAL FOUND, DESTROYED,
CAPTURED, ETC.

FEBRUARY

SEALs move ashore during an exercise on the coast of Spain. The kneeling man *(front left)*, one of the swimmer scouts, is wearing a wet suit for protection from the cold water. The rest of the unit is wearing standard camouflage uniforms. U.S. NAVY

February 01

1944 (Pacific)—Vice Admiral Richmond Kelly Turner initiates the landings on Kwajalein Island. The first wave hits Red Beach 1 at 0930 hours with Red Beach 2 being landed on at 0931 hours.

1944 (Italy)—The First Special Service Force assumes responsibility for the Anzio flank.

1964 (USA)—Boat Support Unit One (BSU One) is established in Coronado, California. It is to be part of the Naval Operations Support Group, Pacific, to specifically work with Navy Special Warfare Units. BSU One includes 24 officers and 140 enlisted men and will build or modify a number of small craft used extensively in Vietnam, such as the HSSC and the Mike boat: Both are heavily armed and armored landing craft.

1969 (USA)—The Long Range Reconnaissance Patrol units formed in Vietnam are designated Ranger companies. The two new Ranger units so formed are Company A at Fort Benning, Georgia, and Company B at Fort Carson, Colorado. Both companies are part of the Seventy-Fifth Ranger Regiment and the Rangers now take on the mission of a Long Range Reconnaissance Ranger Company.

1979 (Iran)—The Ayatollah Khomeini returns to Iran after exile. He becomes the religious leader and de facto ruler of the country.

February 02

1946 (USA)—UDT Ten is decommissioned at Fort Pierce where it helped tear down the base following the end of World War II.

1967 (South Vietnam)—Fire Teams Seven, Eight, Nine, and Ten of SEAL Team One Detachment Golf operate in the Rung Sat Special Zone. They are working from Mike boat and an additional Landing Craft, Personnel, Large. Fire Team Ten is inserted for patrol to the site of a rice cache that has previously been destroyed by SEALs on another mission. At a site only a mile away, the SEALs find a number of large bunkers. During the mission, an ambush takes four sampans under fire, making a probable kill of five VC. Because of many friendly units operating in the area, on the second day the SEALs are called back to base. The recall is to prevent a possible friendly-fire incident, with units who might mistake the SEALs for enemy forces. Before returning, the SEALs recover clothing, medical supplies, Chicom hand grenades, fish nets, and other materials from a VC camp site.

February 03

BARNDANCE # A-917 SEAL TEAM 1 : DET G ; A PLT.

DATE(S) 1/03/69 OTHER UNITS: MST-2 DET LTJG ANGELA
MSG REF (S): 020315 Z FEB 69 PBR 573 -LTJG SPERBER
LDNNS , GONG, TICH

NAMES OF PERS: MR BLISS, ENOCH, GARDNER, WELCH,
CRAWFORD, HORST, BEAMAN, BRATLAND, GIENG
GONG .

MISSION TASK: CAPTURE 3 VC LIVING IN HOOTCH
POINTED OUT BY VN AGENT FROM PBR.

INTEL/INFO SOURCE(S): VN FISHERMAN AGENT, PBRS.

INSERTION: TIME: 03.0430H METHOD: PBR AMS COORD: WS 887405

EXTRACTION: TIME: 03.0745H METHOD: PBR AMS COORD: WS 883404

TERRAIN: FIELDS, TREELINES, HOOTCHES ON CANAL
WEATHER: CLEAR TIDE: HIGH MOON: FULL.

OTHER MISSION NARRATIVE: INSERTED AND PATROLLED
TO VC HOOTCH, NO ONE HOME. SET
AMBUSH IN HOOTCH. CAUGHT ONE
VC APPROACHING HOOTCH. TOOK ONE FLEEING
VC UNDER FIRE. EXTRACTED.

RESULTS OF ENEMY ENCOUNTERED: 1 VC KIA (BC), 1 VC POW

FRIENDLY CASUALTIES: NONE

REMARKS (SIGNIFICANT EVENTS, GENERAL RESULTS, ETC.) POW SAYS
HE WILL LEAD US TO VC VILLAGE
CHIEFS HOUSE TOMORROW NIGHT.

RECOMMENDATIONS/LESSONS LEARNED: OUTSTANDING - WAY TO
OPERATE!

DD COPY DIST:
(FORM REV. 8/68) BARNDANCE # A-917

February 04

BARNDANCE # ___5-83___   SEAL TEAM _2_ ; DET. _A_ ; _5_ PLT.

DATE(S): ___4 FEB69___   OTHER UNITS: SEALS, PBR 123 SM1 PORTER,
                                        PBR 124 SM1NILES, AGENT, INTERPRETER

MSG REF(S): _____

NAMES OF PERS: LTJG MURPHY, MC CARTHY, GIRARD, SUTHERLAND, ASHTON, KEENER,
MC CUTHAN, JAUNZEMS, MIHN

MISSION TASK: PATROLL

INTEL/INFO SOURCE(S): AGENT

INSERTION: TIME: 0100   METHOD: LSSC   AMS COORD: _____

EXTRACTION: TIME: 0315 METHOD: LSSC   AMS COORD: _____

TERRAIN: POPULATED
WEATHER: CLEAR   TIDE: LOW   MOON:

BRIEF MISSION NARRATIVE: INSERTED AT XS327408. HAD 2 PBR'S AND LSSCPUT A BLOCKADE
AROUND ISLAND. SEALINF OFF ALL TRAFFIC.COMMENCED HOUSE TO HOUSE SEARCH. UNCOVERED
1 VC IN SPIDERHOLE. USING HIM AS GUIDE CONTINED SEARCHING ISLAND. FOLLOWED FOOT
PRINTTRAIN INTO HEAVY BUSH AT EDGE OF ISLAND. ATTEMPTED TO GET VC TO COME OUT
TOOK BUSHES UNDER FIRE. 4 VC KIA IN SPIDER HOLE. PICKED UP 13 MALES VN IN
HOUSESEARCH EXTRACTED.

RESULTS OF ENEMY ENCOUNTERED: 4 VC KIA 1 VC wia 13 MALE DETAINEES. SEAL
AMMO EXPENED 400RDS 7.62 #))RDS 5.56 4 OFFENSIVE GRENADES. DETAINEES WILL BE
CLASSIFIED BY NILO AND TURNED OVER TO MU THO POLICE.

FRIENDLY CASUALTIES: NONE

REMARKS (SIGNIFICANT EVENTS, OPEVAL RESULTS, ETC.):

RECOMMENDATIONS/LESSONS LEARNED:

                                                    5-83

BD COPY DIST:

(FORM REV. 8/68)   BARNDANCE # _____

February 05

1945 (Pacific)—Having been in training at Maui since December 7, UDT Seventeen finally receives orders to ship out. After spending more than a week loading explosives and supplies aboard its transport, the team embarks on the USS *Crosley* (APD 87). UDT Seventeen is assigned to the Western Islands Attack Force to deal with the Kerama-Retto Islands during Operation ICEBERG, the invasion of Okinawa.

1969 (South Vietnam)—A squad from SEAL Team Two's Fifth Platoon sets up an ambush overlooking a trail and the Rach Miou Ba Canal in Kien Hoa Province. Inserted on the My Tho River, it patrols for about a kilometer. The SEALs stop two sampans coming into their area and detain the occupants. As one Vietnamese man comes along the trail, the SEALs stop him and the accompanying LDNN squad questions him. The man agrees to point out a house that the VC have made accessible by building a bridge of sampans across the waterway.

Spotting several VC in the vicinity of the house as they reach it, the SEALs take the enemy under fire. During the engagement, five VC are killed and a bunker in the house is destroyed. The SEALs recover two weapons, ammunition, fifteen pounds of valuable intelligence documents and letters, and three pounds of medical supplies. A later examination of the documents show that the SEALs have taken down a probable VC postal drop.

February 06

1945 (Europe)—The Headquarters and Headquarters Detachment, First Battalion, Third Regiment, First Special Service Force, is officially disbanded. The American and Canadian troops who made up the unit created a legend known by their nickname "The Devil's Brigade."

1967 (South Vietnam)—SEAL Team One, Detachment Golf's Fire Team Nine is inserted into an ambush site on the south bank of the Bong Gienge Lon using the SEAL Support Boat (SSB). The fire team sets up an ambush site on the south bank of the Bong Gienge Lon, later reporting that it considers both streams as being excellent for future ambush sites—they have good fields of fire with a clear view of possible enemy approaches, good concealment, and are dry positions to wait in.

At 2130 hours, the security element back at the SSB spots a sampan approaching from the south along the bank of the Soi Rap. As the sampan noses into the stream, waves lap against the sides of the SSB, making an odd sound and warning the sampan's occupants. Immediately suspicious, the VC in the sampan withdraw from the area. The SEALs call in their PBR support to supply cover and withdraw from the ambush site.

1991 (Iraq)—The first of twelve Special Forces cross-border operations into Iraq begins.

February 07

1967 (South Vietnam)—At 1830 hours, Detachment Golf's Fire Team Nine is inserted by a PBR into an ambush site on the east bank of the Soi Rap. The team will conduct an all-night ambush. The SEALs set up their position on the south side of a small canal, near its mouth, so that they can cover both the canal and the Soi Rap. The location is good for an ambush—the fire team has good fields of fire, good concealment, and good visibility. What it doesn't have are targets. During the night, the SEALs hear a sampan engine running to the southeast of their position, but nothing comes into their kill zone. The mission reports negative contact and the SEALs are extracted by a PBR at 0530.

1967 (Vietnam)—Special Forces Lieutenant George K. Sister performs the actions that result in his posthumous award of the Congressional Medal of Honor.

1968 (Vietnam)—Green Berets and Montagnards hold a camp against massive attacks and inflict heavy casualties on their attackers. By the time the rescue helicopters arrive, all but one of twenty-four Green Berets and hundreds of Montagnards are dead, wounded, or missing.

February 08

1954 (USA)—On the West Coast at Coronado, California, UDTs One, Three, and Five respectively become UDTs Eleven, Twelve, and Thirteen. On the East Coast at Little Creek, Virginia, UDTs Two and Four respectively become UDTs Twenty-One and Twenty-Two. The UDT redesignation will prevent confusion with World War II predecessors.

From the experiences and development of the UDTs during the Korean War, the missions of the units are expanded to include, in no specific order:

Demolition of obstacles
Clearance of harbors or channels
Destruction of facilities or supplies during a withdrawal
Limpeteer attacks against ships at anchor, including the penetration
    of bays, harbors, or rivers to accomplish this task
Mine clearance
Guidance of assault waves through cleared gaps of defenses during
    landings
Lifeguard duties during military maneuvers on or near the water
Improvement of channels and anchorages through demolitions and the
    marking of same
Inland penetrations to conduct reconnaissance or demolition operations
Insertion, extraction, or resupply of raiders, saboteurs, guerrillas, or agents
    behind enemy lines

February 09

1969 (South Vietnam)—A squad from Sixth Platoon of SEAL Team Two's Detachment Alfa conducts a reconnaissance patrol at the southern end of Bien Hoa Province. The patrol locates a salt cache containing three 135-pound bags of salt. As the patrol continues, the SEALs stop and set up an observation/listening post overlooking a trail in the jungle. The SEALs observe two men moving east on the trail. At about 0420 hours, the SEALs discover five more VC also moving south on the trail, several of whom are carrying weapons. Five minutes later, seven more armed VC are found moving along the trail and joining up with the five men seen earlier.

The SEALs continue watching the area, but no further VC are spotted. Finally, at 0630 hours, the SEALs abandon their position and continue on their patrol. They move east for about sixty-five meters when they see two VC in the distance, again moving south. Further patrolling leads the SEALs to sight another Vietnamese, this one evading them as he moves south. The SEALs are taken under fire by a friendly unit but take no casualties.

The patrol continues to its extraction point and links up with its support units several hours later. Two SEALs are transported by helicopter back to the location of the salt cache. The rest of the unit goes in and checks the area, this time with much heavier support immediately available to back it up. Four sampans are found along with a 100-pound watermine, a large container of explosives set up to be floated toward a ship or other target.

The final results of the mission are a salt cache destroyed, one VC killed in action, and a quarter-ton of rice and other supplies captured. The four sampans are also taken by the SEALs and the mine is destroyed.

February 10

1945—After several months of training at the Maui base, UDT Twelve completes its preparations and reaches its complete complement of thirteen officers and eighty-five enlisted men. The UDT loads aboard the USS *Bates* (APD 47) for transport to the Ulithi Islands, the staging area for the upcoming Operation Detachment. UDT Twelve joins with UDTs Thirteen, Fourteen, and Fifteen to conduct weeks of intense rehearsals for the upcoming operation. On February 10, the UDTs leave Ulithi and join with the fleet heading for the invasion of Iwo Jima.

February 11

An example of the high-speed transport (APD) class of ship used by the UDTs from World War II through most of the Vietnam War. The early APD transports were usually made by converting old "four-stacker" destroyers from the 1920s and earlier. U.S. Navy

February 12

1961 (USA)—Retired Admiral Richmond Kelly Turner dies in Monterey, California. Admiral Turner commanded many of the actions during the island-hopping campaign in the central Pacific. His far-seeing reaction to the losses at Tarawa resulted in his ordering the creation of the UDTs for operations in the Pacific during World War II.

February 13

1967 (South Vietnam)—Detachment Charlie of UDT Twelve continues hydrographic surveys along the South Vietnamese coast as directed. Operating from the submarine USS *Tunny* (LPSS 282), the men of the detachment are conducting a predawn launch of a motorized Inflatable Boat, Small (IBS) from the deck of the surfaced submarine. The submarine is off the coast of the Second Corps area, near Sa Huynh. The weather is deteriorating, but the UDT operators continue with their mission, anchoring the IBS outside of the surf zone—it will act as a command boat. From that point, a pair of swimmer scouts go onto the beach.

In the darkness with a squall building up, the command boat is hit by a breaker that is later estimated to be twenty feet high. The huge breaker capsizes the command boat, throwing the three occupants into the water. The UDT operators jump into the water and struggle in to shore, while a second rubber boat is rocked by the surf and tries to ride the waves out. The men in the second boat fire emergency flares to let the *Tunny* know that the situation is deteriorating considerably.

The *Tunny* launches a third rubber boat to go to the aid of the others near the shore. The submarine also radioes for additional assistance from the nearby Landing Ship, Tank (LST) *Westchester County*. The LST sends aid in the form of a smaller landing craft to help search for and recover the UDT men in the water.

The UDT men tossing in the surf manage to make their way to shore and link up with the swimmer scouts. Making several attempts to swim out through the surf, the UDT operators eventually link up with the other rubber boat still at sea. The *Tunny* moves in to within 1,300 yards of the shoreline and drops anchor in an attempt to pick up the UDT men. The swimmers are recovered, the last one being picked up by the landing craft sent from the LST. The hydrographic survey of the target beach is eventually obtained and the planned missions go ahead.

February 14

1945 (Pacific)—UDT Thirteen arrives off Iwo Jima aboard the USS *Barr* (APD 39). Once in position, the UDT is ordered to put up a navigation light on Higashi Iwa, a small islet about 4,000 yards offshore of Iwo Jima's eastern side. In spite of taking heavy fire, which is quickly silenced by the guns of the *Barr*, three officers and fifteen men from UDT Thirteen are assigned the mission of emplacing the light; they successfully complete their operation without taking any casualties.

1968 (South Vietnam)—Two SEALs from Eighth Platoon, SEAL Team Two, conduct a reconnaissance mission along the Cambodian border in the Seven Mountains region. Seeking to to evaluate enemy strength in the post-Tet situation, the SEALs wear black uniforms and carry foreign weapons as they walk or use local transportation to pass through the area. They are later reported by another intelligence source that saw "two Russian advisors" in the area.

1991 (Saudi Arabia)—SEALs in the Persian Gulf begin to train thirteen Kuwaitis in maritime infiltration techniques. The intent is to infiltrate the Kuwaitis onto a targeted beach south of Kuwait City. There, the Kuwaitis will make direct contact with resistance forces inside occupied Kuwait. The training continues for six days.

February 15

1945 (USA)—UDT Twenty-seven is formed at Fort Pierce, Florida. UDT Twenty-three is detached from the base and reports to San Bruno, California, for further transportation to Maui.

1951 (Korea)—Task Force William Able arrives in Paengyong to coordinate partisan operations in North Korea.

BARNDANCE #____8-34
DATES:____14-18 Feb 68

COORD
TIMES 141500H- 18220H

1. UNITS INVOLVED: SEAL Element 8th PLT (2 MEN)

2. TASK: Collect Intell in 7 mountain region

3. METHOD OF INSERTION: Slick   EXTRACTION: Slick

4. TERRAIN: Mountains

5. TIDE: _____   WEATHER: Clear

6. MOON: _____

7. ENEMY ENCOUNTERED: Observed a total of over 400 VC. No engagement

8. CASUALTIES: None

9. NAMES OF SEALS INVOLVED: Marcinko   Humphries

10. RESULTS: Verified with US eyes VC strength, movement, strongholds and
               tactics

11. REMARKS/RECOMMENDATIONS: Dressed in black pajamas and sterilized equipment
                element passed and was reported as two Russian Advisors. Bold
                actions as this can net worthwhile results.

                Intell study follows

     INCLUDE INTELLIGENCE INFORMATION GATHERED, MATERIAL FOUND, DESTROYED,
     CAPTURED, ETC.

1991 (Persian Gulf)—A group of SEALs and a detachment from SEAL Delivery Vehicle Team One are working in the northern Persian Gulf to complete a sweep for sea mines using the Mark IX SDV. Operating from the Kuwaiti barge *Sawahil*, the SEALs examine areas for moored sea mines using the sonar suite on board the SDV. Six mine searches are conducted, beginning on January 30, and cover six sectors. The areas searched add up to twenty-seven square miles of the gulf; no mines are found.

1991 (Kuwait)—A detachment of SEALs from Naval Special Warfare Task Group One complete fifteen close-in recon operations of the Kuwati shoreline. At one point, Lieutenant Tom Deitz and two other SEALs swim to the shore and lay observing and gathering information as to which beach would be the best target for the final deception operation of February 23 ordered by CENTCOM.

February 16

1945 (Pacific)—UDT Fourteen arrives off Iwo Jima aboard the USS *Bull* (ADP 78).

1964—The first thirty-four Alpha (34A) operations against North Vietnam under the code name Timberlake takes place. The 34A operations are to be a naval variation of the OPS 34 penetrations into North Vietnam. The Swift and Nasty boats supplied to the South Vietnamese for these operations will go into North Vietnamese waters with specially trained South Vietnamese crews. In the first operation, an LDNN crew is sent to attack the North Vietnamese naval base at Quang Khe, destroying the Chinese-built P6 Swatow-type motor gunboats there as well as the ferry on Cape Ron.

1965 (South Vietnam)—A Communist trawler is spotted in South Vietnamese waters by a U.S. Army helicopter. The boat is in Vung Row Bay, just south of Qui Nhon in Binh Dinh Province. The trawler is one of many purpose-built by North Vietnam for running supplies to the South. The 50- to 100-ton-capacity trawlers are part of the 125th Sea Transportation Unit of the North Vietnamese Navy.

Infiltration of seaborne Communist supplies into South Vietnam are not confirmed as fact until the chance discovery of the Vung Row Bay trawler. Ultimately, South Vietnamese Skyraider aircraft locate and sink it. But a large part of the ship's cargo has already been landed and is stacked on shore. After several days of attempts to reach the area of the on-shore supplies, South Vietnamese troops land and secure the area.

The amount of supplies found in an area the size of three football fields is staggering. These include over 1 million rounds of small arms ammunition, 3,500 to 4,000 rifles and submachine guns, 500 pounds of TNT, 2,000 rounds of mortar ammunition, 1,500 grenades, and other supplies and munitions weighing in the neighborhood of 100 tons. Divers led by a U.S. Navy SEAL officer dive on the wreck of the trawler and recover even more supplies and intelligence documents.

1967 (South Vietnam)—Operation Deckhouse VI is launched, landing marines on the shore in First Corps. The intent is for the marines to throw the Communist forces in the area off balance by their sudden appearance, which they do. The landing follows the charts built from hydrographic information gathered by Detachment Charlie of UDT Twelve.

February 17

1945 (Pacific)—Captain B. H. "Red" Hanlon, Commander, Underwater Demolition Teams, Amphibious Forces, Pacific, and his staff direct the operations of the UDTs at Iwo Jima. Lieutenant Commander Draper Kauffman directs the UDTs' beach operations as commander of the UDT. The eastern landing beaches of Iwo Jima are scheduled to be examined at 1100 hours and the western beaches will be reconned that same day, D minus 2, at 1630 hours.

UDT Twelve conducts the recon of Red Beaches 1 and 2 on the eastern side and Brown Beaches 1 and 2 on the western side. To aid in the elimination of mines on the swims, the UDT operators wear canvas belts, with each belt holding ten Mark 1 demolition destructors and Mark 136 demolition outfits, small waterproof charges that will detonate a mine.

UDT Thirteen conducts the recon of Green Beach 1 on the east side of Iwo Jima and Purple Beach 1 on the west side. Both beaches are about 500 yards long and each almost in the shadow of Mount Suribachi. Extremely heavy enemy fire pours down on the UDTs in the water, severely damaging the gun-equipped landing craft that has come in close to support them. In spite of the incoming fire, the UDTs complete their operation without sustaining any casualties.

Platoons One and Three from UDT Fourteen make the reconnaissance of the team's assigned beaches on the east side of Iwo Jima. Platoons Two and Four conduct the western beach recons of Yellow Beaches 1 and 2. Swimmers in the water only take relatively light small arms fire from Japanese snipers off the eastern beaches. UDT Fifteen undertakes the recon of the northernmost landing beaches.

1968 (South Vietnam)—A SEAL advisor leads a sixty-man PRU into action against the VC in Ba Xuyen Province. The PRU engages a large enemy unit, resulting in twenty VC killed and another twenty-three VC wounded. The PRU loses a single man.

The mission of the PRUs is to eliminate the VC infrastructure in a given province. To do this, the PRUs need intelligence, the kind of intelligence that they can get from their own sources among the people of the province and the prisoners they take. A successful PRU takes more enemy troops prisoner than it kills, as is evidenced by the above operation.

February 18

1945 (Pacific)—The heavy fire support given to the UDTs off Iwo Jima lead Japanese general Tadamichi Kuribayashi to believe that the main landing has begun. To counter this action, he deploys his hidden batteries of cannon, which had remained untouched and unknown by the Allies during a two-month bombardment of the island. The uncovering and employment of these guns make them a target for the fleet and is considered the only major mistake made by the Japanese general in his defensive tactics on Iwo Jima. If the guns remained undiscovered until the actual amphibious landings, they would have caused heavy casualties among the Allied forces.

1945 (Pacific)—UDT Thirteen successfully reestablishes the navigation light it had emplaced earlier on the islet of Higashi Iwa off Iwo Jima.

1945 (Pacific)—Aboard the USS *Blessman* (APD 48), UDT Fifteen completes its reconnaissance mission. The APD then steams out to take up a position for screening duty away from Iwo Jima and much of the invasion fleet. The *Blessman* moves at a flank speed of 20 knots to take up its screening position. The bow wave of the ship causes the phosphorescent waters off Iwo Jima to glow eerily in the night. The commanding officer and several other officers from UDT Fifteen leave the ship and brief the marine officers in the fleet on the conditions they can expect going in to the beaches the next day.

A Japanese "Betty" bomber, Type-1 2EB, spots the *Blessman* and makes a single bomb run on the ship; the bulk of the UDT men are relaxing in the enlisted men's mess at this time of the evening. Of the two 500-pound bombs the plane drops, one is a near miss and the other explodes into the middle of the ship on level with the mess deck.

The sudden blast rips the *Blessman* open, immediately starting fires. The *Blessman* is not only carrying the ammunition it needs to feed its own guns, it also has thirty tons of high explosives in the aft explosives magazine.

Casualties are brought out from below decks while other portions of the ship's crew and the UDT operators try to conduct damage and fire control. No power is available to run deck pumps or any other fire fighting apparatus. The men of the UDT organize a bucket brigade, lifting water up from over the side to throw on the flames.

The fire is contained from the fantail of the ship, where the wounded are laid out in the most stable and least damaged part of the ship. The fantail is also where the explosives locker is located.

When the USS *Gilmer* (APD 11) pulls alongside the *Blessman*, that ship is also at risk. If the explosives in the magazine go off, two ships can be eliminated in an instant. But the *Gilmer*, with Lieutenant Commander Draper Kauffman aboard, pulls up alongside and runs fire hoses over to the *Blessman*. With the means at hand to fight the raging fires, the crew of the *Blessman* and the UDT operators demonstrate the pride of the navy.

Several UDT officers and some of its operators go down into the burning aft hold of the *Blessman* to fight the fires that threaten to destroy both ships. With paint on the bulkhead already blistering with heat, the fire is pushed back by the UDT men.

Eventually, the fire is extinguished and the *Blessman* saved. The incident costs forty-two men and thirty-four wounded. The UDT itself loses eighteen men with twenty-three wounded. It is the single largest loss to a UDT, or later SEAL team, ever.

1966 (South Vietnam)—BSU One has proven itself a very successful concept and is expanded in size. It is also made a commissioned unit on this date. By 1967, BSU One will have increased in size to where it is manned by 36 officers and 310 enlisted men.

1975 (USA)—President Gerald Ford signs Executive Order 11905. The order puts restrictions on the activities of any of the intelligence services of the United States, cutting back on covert operations and outlawing the use of assassination by any government employee against foreign leaders and heads of state.

February 19

1945 (Pacific)—Operation Detachment, the invasion of Iwo Jima, begins; H hour is at 0900. Thousands of rounds of high-explosive shells are fired onto the island by the surrounding fleet. Almost 2,000 rounds of monstrous sixteen-inch rounds are launched by the battleships aiding the preinvasion bombardment. Of the much smaller, and more common, five-inch guns found all through the fleet, 31,000 rounds are fired.

All the ammunition slammed into the volcanic island is in support of the nearly 30,000 men who land on the beaches that day. The marines face a Japanese garrison of about 21,000—deeply dug in and completely accepting that the fight will be to the last man. Eight square miles of the island have been turned into fortifications. Overlooking it all is the cone-shaped 600-foot high Mount Suribachi. The U.S Marines will plant a flag on top of that volcano four days from the time of the landings.

1945 (Pacific)—On the eastern invasion beaches of Iwo Jima, platoons from UDT Thirteen aid the beachmaster in directing the incoming waves of landing craft. They also conduct important salvage work to try and keep the beaches open.

February 20

These SEALs insert to shore from their ridged hull inflatable boats (RIBs). This type of landing operation is normally conducted at night, under the cover of darkness—a situation much preferred by the SEALs to operating in daylight.
U.S. Navy

February 21

1963 (South Vietnam)—The USS *Weiss* (APD 135) is sent to conduct operations with Detachment Bravo, which consists of twenty-nine enlisted men and five officers from UDT Twelve. The U.S. fleet wants further intelligence on the offshore waters and beach areas of South Vietnam. In addition to the UDT detachment, a team from the Third Marine Reconnaissance Battalion joins the mission aboard the *Weiss*. The operations are not considered to be high risk, but the UDT operators are armed for their own protection. The marine detachment will conduct inland security for the surveys. Operations begin to survey beaches at Danang, Qui Nhon, Cape Vung Tau, and Bac Lieu on February 21.

1944 (Britain)—Jedburghs, uniformed personnel that are air dropped into occupied Europe, begin operational training in the United Kingdom.

1991 (Saudi Arabia)—A dress rehearsal is conducted by the SEALs with the Kuwaiti nationals they have been training with the last week. The Kuwaitis will infiltrate occupied Kuwait by water. The operation is given the green light to go ahead the next night.

1991 (Saudi Arabia)—At around 0300 hours, an MH-60 helicopter crashes into a sand dune during severe zero-visibility flying conditions at the Al Ar Airfield. Killed in the crash are four pilots and crew from the 160th Special Operations Aviation Regiment and three operators from Special Forces Detachment Delta.

February 22

1991 (Kuwait)—Five Kuwaitis attempt an infiltration of occupied Kuwait. SEAL swimmer scouts recon the shoreline of the target area, a pier south of Kuwait City. The Kuwaitis move to the pier after being given the go ahead by the SEALs. In spite of their best efforts, the Kuwaitis are unable to link up with resistance forces at the pier.

Finally, the Kuwaiti infiltration team signals for extraction by the SEALs and it moves out from the pier. The SEALs meet up with the Kuwaiti team about 500 meters from the shore and the mission is aborted. Later examination of the beach and pier area after the liberation of Kuwait is completed shows undetected beach obstacles. In addition, the SEALs learn of there having been a much greater volume of Iraqi troops in the area during the time of the infiltration attempt.

February 23

1991 (Kuwait)—During the night, SEALs take two high-speed boats from al-Mishab to an area off the shore of southern Kuwait. Switching to rubber boats, they silently paddle to within swimming distance of the shore near Mina Saud. Eight SEAL combat swimmers, led by Lieutenant Tom Deitz, slip into the water about 500 yards from shore and conduct what is a classic UDT demolition swim. Each SEAL is towing a twenty-pound haversack of C-4 explosives. The haversacks have timers set to 0100 hours local time of the next morning, February 24. Slipping right up to the surf zone of the beach, the SEALs emplace their charges, arm them, and swim back to their boats.

The SEALs also release floating timed high-explosive charges from the boats as well as emplace orange marker buoys, as if marking the landing lanes for a beach. By the time the beach charges detonate, the SEALs are back onboard the high-speed boats. They run the boats the length of the beach, strafing the area with machine guns and grenade launchers. The Iraqis take the bait and consider the beaches attacked by the SEALs to be the site of a Coalition amphibious landing. Several major Iraqi division elements are diverted from their positions to cover the expected landings.

February 24

1945 (Pacific)—On Iwo Jima, a few men from UDT Thirteen climb up the slopes of Mount Suribachi and aid in placing a navigation light on the side of the volcano. It is the day after the marines have raised the famous flag—and there are no photographers available.

1991 (Kuwait)—G day, the ground war to liberate Kuwait, begins. At 0400 hours local time, U.S. and Coalition ground forces cross the border into Kuwait and southern Iraq. Meanwhile, Third Battalion, 160th Special Operations Aviation Regiment, rescues three Special Forces troopers deep inside Iraq.

February 25

1966 (USA)—SEAL Team Two participates in Operation White Geese as a unit; it runs from February 25 to March 1. The team divides into seven assault teams and conducts extensive penetration raids against the U.S. Coast Guard facility at Cape Hatteras, North Carolina.

1991 (Persian Gulf)—A Chinese-made HY-2 Silkworm missile is launched by Iraq against the USS *Missouri* (BB 63). U.S. Navy surveillance aircraft immediately detect the launch and sound a warning. The British destroyer *Gloucester* is in the screening force protecting the *Missouri* and it launches two Sea Dart missiles that intercept the incoming Silkworm. A second Silkworm missile is launched by Iraq and falls into the Persian Gulf without hitting any target. The navy directs an immediate air strike against the Iraqi missile launch site, obliterating it.

February 26

A captured Iraqi Silkworm missile, captured near Kuwait City, is transported aboard a U.S. Army vehicle. U.S. NAVY

February 27

1991 (Kuwait)—Precautionary measures are planned to deal with Iraqi "stay-behind" forces who might remain behind as the main Iraqi army retreats and as U.S. and Coalition troops take back Kuwait City. Political considerations are also important. The marines are moving so fast that they have to be held back so that the first regular troops in Kuwait City are Arab Coalition forces.

When the allies are on the outskirts of Kuwait City, Operation Urban Freedom is put into effect where special operations forces conduct a take down of the U.S. embassy compound in Kuwait City. SEALs and troopers from the Third Special Forces Group (Airborne) form a convoy of heavily armed SEAL Fast Attack Vehicles that quickly approach and surround the compound. An assault force ropes down from helicopters onto the roofs of the embassy compound and performs a search for Iraqis and booby traps. Neither are found and the embassy is placed back in U.S. hands.

February 28

1944 (USA)—The first draft of NCDUs to take part in Operation Dragoon, the invasion of southern France (at that time known as ANVIL), leave Fort Pierce, Florida. The twelve NCDUs, comprising sixty men and officers, depart Norfolk some time later, eventually arriving in Salerno, Italy, to train for their upcoming operation.

1991 (Persian Gulf)—Kuwait is liberated, the Operation Desert Storm ground war ends, and Third Special Forces Group (Airborne) personnel secure the U.S. Embassy in Kuwait City.

February 29

(USA)—Because of required extensive training in advanced parachuting skills, a large number of SEALs enjoy sport parachuting. In addition, the SEALs have created a number of demonstration jump teams. The Leap Frogs are the present-day Navy SEAL demonstration jump team and they conduct jumps all over the country at various public events. There is even a commercial demonstration jump team made up of retired SEALs—the Elite Frogs.

A member of the SEAL demonstration jump team jumps the colors in. Colored smoke streams behind the man as he guides his parachute in for a precision landing in front of a large crowd.
KEVIN DOCKERY

MARCH

A SEAL sniper, posed for the photograph, takes aim with his McMillan M88 .50-caliber sniper rifle. The massive clamshell muzzle break visible on the end of the barrel helps reduce the recoil produced by the huge cartridge the weapon fires. If this was an actual firing position, the sniper would be much more concealed and difficult to locate. USSOCOM PAO

March 01

1968 (South Vietnam)—Spotrep reports—which are higher command reports on an operation—often tell a good deal of different information of a SEAL operation than the Barndance cards—which are individual reports maintained by a SEAL platoon on every operation it conducts during a tour of duty in Vietnam—can. The information in a Spotrep can also include the results of intelligence analysis of the information or material gathered from the original operation. This analysis takes time and the Spotreps usually run anything from a few days to several weeks or more after the original operation has been conducted.

March 02

1945 (Pacific)—After a kamikaze strike against their APD, UDT Nine, reduced to twelve officers and forty-seven men, is returned to Maui. UDT Nine will be assigned to take charge of the training of the base staff at the Naval Combat Underwater Demolition Training and Experimental Base—but not until after the operators have had some rest and relaxation.

1969 (South Vietnam)—A squad from SEAL Team Two's Fifth Platoon is conducting a patrol along the Song My Tho River in the Cai Lay district of Dinh Tuong Province. The squad is inserted silently by sampan and patrols to a hooch. The LDNN officer accompanying the SEALs, is armed with an AK-47 and dressed as a VC, speaks to an old woman at the beach. She tells him where she thinks he will find other VC.

Following the old woman's directions, the SEALs and the LDNN officer patrol and find another hut. Next to the building are two unarmed VC working. As the SEALs try to slip past the hooch, they are spotted by the two men who try to escape. The commotion causes the SEAL squad to open fire early, but still with devastating results.

The two VC workers are taken under fire and killed. Seven other armed VC run from the front of the hooch and into the SEAL's fire. Another VC runs from the rear of the hut but is stopped by a SEAL running rear security for the squad. The squad collects a considerable quantity of weapons and ammunition, destroys three sampans found at the side of the house, and calls for extraction.

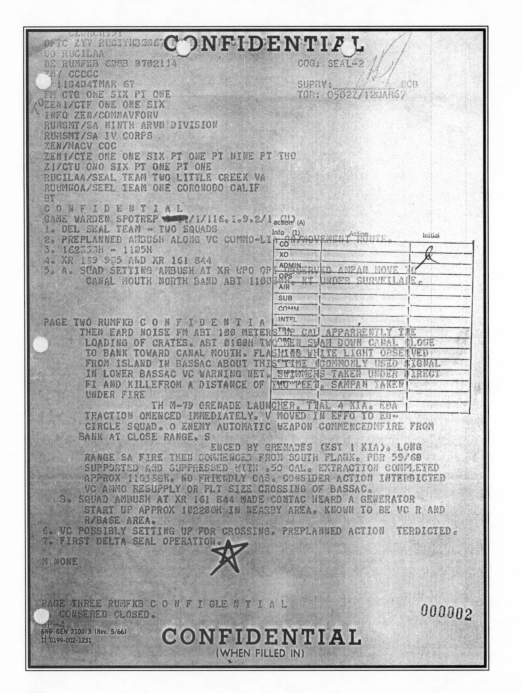

OFTC ZYY RUCIYHB3G2G7

CO RUCILAA
DE RUMFKB C26B 9702114
ZNY CCCCC
   110404TMAR 67
FM CTG ONE SIX PT ONE
ZEN1/CTF ONE ONE SIX
INFO ZEN/COMNAVFORV
RUMSMT/SA NINTH ARVN DIVISION
RUMSMT/SA IV CORPS
ZEN/MACV COC
ZEN1/CTE ONE ONE SIX PT ONE PT NINE PT TWO
ZI/CTU ONO SIX PT ONE PT ONE
RUCILAA/SEAL TEAM TWO LITTLE CREEK VA
RUUMNOA/SEEL TEAM ONE CORONODO CALIF
BT
C O N F I D E N T I A L
GAME WARDEN SPOTREP ▒▒▒/1/116.1.9.2/1 (U)
1. DEL SEAL TEAM - TWO SQUADS
2. PREPLANNED AMBUSH ALONG VC COMMO-LI ON/MOVEMENT ROUTE.
3. 162333H - 1105H
4. XR 139 905 AND XR 161 844
5. A. SCAD SETTING AMBUSH AT XR WPO OP OBSERVED SAMPAN MOVE TO
      CANAL MOUTH NORTH BAND ABT 1100   KT UNDER SURVEILANE.

COG: SEAL-2
SUPRV: _____ DCB
TOD: O502Z/12MAR67

	Info (1)	Action (A)	Action	Initial
CO				
XO				𝒸
ADMIN				
OPS				
AIR				
SUB				
COMM				
INTEL				

PAGE TWO RUMFKB C O N F I D E N T I A
         THEN EARD NOISE FM ABT 100 METERS TRAP CAL APPARRENTLY THE
         LOADING OF CRATES. ABT 0100H TWO MEN SWAM DOWN CANAL CLOSE
         TO BANK TOWARD CANAL MOUTH. FLASHING WHITE LIGHT OBSERVED
         FROM ISLAND IN BASSAC ABOUT THIS TIME (COMMONLY USED SIGNAL
         IN LOWER BASSAC VC WARNING NET. SWIMMERS TAKEN UNDER DIRECT
         FI AND KILLEFROM A DISTANCE OF TWO FEET. SAMPAN TAKEN
         UNDER FIRE
                  TH M-79 GRENADE LAUNCHER. TTAL 4 KIA. EBA
         TRACTION OMENCED IMMEDIATELY. V MOVED IN EFFO TO EN-
         CIRCLE SQUAD. O ENEMY AUTOMATIC WEAPON COMMENCEDNFIRE FROM
         BANK AT CLOSE RANGE. S
                  ENCED BY GRENADES (EST 1 KIA). LONG
         RANGE SA FIRE THEN COMMENCED FROM SOUTH FLANK. PBR 59/69
         SUPPORTED AND SUPPRESSED WITH .50 CAL. EXTRACTION COMPLETED
         APPROX 110158H. NO FRIENDLY CAS. CONSIDER ACTION INTERDICTED
         VC AMMO RESUPPLY OR PLT SIZE CROSSING OF BASSAC.
      B. SQUAD AMBUSH AT XR 161 844 MADE CONTAC HEARD A GENERATOR
         START UP APPROX 102200H IN NEARBY AREA. KNOWN TO BE VC R AND
         R/BASE AREA.
6. VC POSSIBLY SETTING UP FOR CROSSING. PREPLANNED ACTION TERDICTED.
7. FIRST DELTA SEAL OPERATION.

N NONE

PAGE THREE RUMFKB C O N F I GLE N T I A L
   CONSERED CLOSED.
P-4
6ND GEN 2100/3 (Rev. 5/66)
II 0199-002-1231

000002

The operation nets ten VC killed with another VC considered probably wounded. The weapons and ammunition captured include three AK-47s, one M1 Carbine, two Chicom pistols, one Chicom hand grenade, five B-40 rockets, two B-40 boosters, two B-40 launchers, twelve AK-47 magazines, ten pistol magazines, one Chicom gas mask, two back packs, five sets of web gear, and the three sampans. The mission runs, from insertion to extraction, from 0610 hours to 0745 hours, all of an hour and fifteen minutes.

March 03

1992 (Yugoslavia)—The Muslim and Serbian population of Bosnia-Herzegovinia declare themselves, in a referendum, an independent country apart from Yugoslavia. The Bosnian Serbs demand a right to be part of Serbia and to have self-determination as a nation. The situation deteriorates when the Bosnian Serbs raise an army and take over 70 percent of Bosnia-Herzegovinia through force of arms, terrorism, and a policy of "ethnic cleansing" of the Muslim and Croatian population.

1995 (Somalia)—The U.S. withdrawal is completed.

March 04

1969 (Pacific)—UDT Thirteen, the newest UDT on the West Coast, relieves UDT Eleven in the western Pacific. UDT Thirteen is still undermanned and has been augmented by the Fifth Platoon from the East Coast's UDT Twenty-one. The two East Coast officers and twenty enlisted men add to the four other platoons of UDT Thirteen, bringing the unit up to strength for its deployment.

2002 (Afghanistan)—At 0300 hours local time, a pair of MH-47E Chinook helicopters land in the Shah-i-Kot Valley to drop off SEALs who will set up an observation point as part of Operation Anaconda. Landing zone Ginger is not expected to to be hot. However, as many as three rocket-propelled grenades (RPGs) strike one of the landing Chinooks, with one round entering the passenger compartment and severing a hydraulic line that spews fluid throughout the compartment filled with SEALs. None of the rockets detonate, but the helicopters scramble to gain altitude and leave the area. The rear deck hatch is open and one member of the team on board falls out of the helicopter but is restrained from falling to the ground by his harness.

Aviation Boatswain's Mate (Aircraft Handling) SEAL First Class Neil C. Roberts sees the teammate fall and unharnesses himself to help the man struggling to climb back on board. As the team member is pulled back, no one notices that Roberts has fallen from the back of the helicopter and tumbled ten feet down to the ground. He is armed only with a pistol as the helicopter pulls away.

Turning on his infrared marker beacon, Roberts crawls to avoid the al Qaeda forces in the area and takes cover in a crevice about 200 feet from where he hit the ground. A Predator unmanned reconnaissance drone circles overhead and notes about sixty al Qaeda fighters surrounding Roberts's position. Roberts fights the al Qaeda with his pistol and grenades, but is soon overwhelmed.

At 0630 hours local time, a second pair of helicopters return to the last known position of Roberts. One helicopter is hit on the insertion and goes down. Twenty-one special operations troops exit the stricken helicopter and set up a perimeter in the face of heavy enemy fire. Within minutes, six are killed and eleven wounded. In spite of their situation, the rest of the team fights the enemy forces, keeping them at bay until nightfall when a rescue Chinook comes in and removes the wounded and dead. Seven bodies are recovered, including that of Roberts.

March 05

1968 (South Vietnam)—A SEAL squad inserts to an ambush site in the Tuyen Binh district of Kien Tuong Province to react to intelligence gathered from the PBRs. The SEALs spot twenty-five VC in a nearby field as a result of illuminating rounds, but they are unable to take the enemy force because the terrain is blocking a clear field of fire. To eliminate the VC, the SEALs call in an airstrike from Seawolf Light Helicopter Fire Team 72 and direct the fire to the VC's location. The SEALs are testing out a hearing device on the operation to help them detect enemy movement. Their only comment of the device is that it could be useful for listening posts.

March 06

1968 (South Vietnam)—Backed up by a Seawolf flight, PBRs, and having joined with a PRU element, Seventh Platoon of SEAL Team Two's Detachment Alfa continues conducting operations against the VC after the Tet offensive. Patrolling south of the Song Tien Giang River in the Chau Thanh district of Vinh Binh Province, the combined SEAL and PRU unit encounter a VC troop concentration of company strength or greater. The battle between the VC and the SEALs and PRUs lasts for seven hours. The constant air support of the Seawolves is credited with saving many lives. The PBRs bring fire to bear when targets become available to them. The operation is considered a maximum use of a navy team.

After the engagement, the enemy forces are identified as the 531st Company with elements of the 509th Company mixed in with them. By the SEALs' accounting, at least six VC have been killed. Another fifteen VC are considered probable kills and twenty are considered wounded. Casualties caused among the enemy forces by the Seawolves are unable to be estimated. Only a relatively small handful of weapons, grenades, and ammunition are captured by the SEALs after the engagement. Preliminary intelligence estimates after the battle indicate that the VC's 531st company no longer maintains an effective force strength—a result of the serious losses suffered during the failed Tet offensive.

March 07

1968 (South Vietnam)—Intelligence reports give the SEALs of Seventh Platoon, SEAL Team Two, a possible target. Reports describe a VC tax collector in the area and such a person would be a primary source of information on VC activities and strengths in an area. The platoon is inserted by PBR on the bank of the Song Cuo Dai River in the Giong Trom district of Kien Hoa Province. The terrain around the SEALs is open rice fields and small banana groves. After patrolling south, the SEALs set up an ambush site on the bank of the Rach Lac Canal. At 0500 hours, the SEALs see one male who successfully evades them. Ten minutes later, the SEALs have a single round of what is estimated to be an 81mm mortar impact fifty yards south of their position. The SEALs immediately shift the ambush site 200 yards east. At 0730 hours, the SEALs take a single VC under fire. They extract ninety minutes later. Locals confirm that a VC tax collector is working the water traffic in the area, but he evaded the SEALs this time.

March 08

1965 (South Vietnam)—The first U.S. combat regiments, the Third Marine Regiment and the Third Marine Division, land in Danang at 0800 hours. The two battalions total 3,500 men and as they come ashore, newsmen are filming the moment. They also face a sign that had greeted marines before. Hanging from two rubber boat paddles dug into the beach, the sign reads: "Welcome U.S. Marines—UDT 12."

The UDT operators from UDT Twelve have been working as part of the Naval Beach Group One on Red Beach 2 just north of Danang. The marines may have been a little more startled by the beautiful Vietnamese schoolgirls who hung garlands of flowers around the necks of the landing marines.

March 09

1945 (Philippines)—At Leyte, the six UDT making up Underwater Demolition Group Baker, UDTs Four, Seven, Eleven, Sixteen, Seventeen, and Twenty-One, conduct training and preparations for their part in the upcoming invasion of Okinawa. In the morning, the entire group conducts a rehearsal of its coming operations at Homohon Island in Leyte Gulf. Underwater Demolition Group Baker is part of Task Group 52.11, the Underwater Demolition Flotilla. The new organization is to coordinate operations and support for the UDTs involved in the upcoming invasions. Group Baker will be part of the Western Attack Force at Okinawa. Another Underwater Demolition Group, Group Able, is made up of four UDTs: UDTs Twelve, Thirteen, Fourteen, and Nineteen.

March 10

1961 (USA)—The acronym "SEAL" is used for the first time to name a new navy unit intended for unconventional warfare. Rear Admiral William Gentner Jr., the director of the Strategic Plans Division, approves the recommendations of an earlier meeting of the Unconventional Activities Committee, which states that the navy should be more involved with lower level (direct action) counter-guerilla operations. The proposed units to conduct these operations are to be called SEALs, a term coined in Rear Admiral Gentner's office. The SEAL acronym stands for the three environments the units will operate in: the sea, air, and land.

1962 (South Vietnam)—Two SEAL instructors arrive in Saigon to begin a six-month tour of duty. The SEALs will be instructing selected members of the South Vietnamese military on how to conduct clandestine maritime operations. It will be the first of a series of assignments of SEAL–South Vietnamese cooperation.

1968 (South Vietnam)—The Seventh Platoon of SEAL Team Two is contacted by a local Vietnamese willing to provide knowledge on the local VC. When he is questioned as to why he will give up such information, the Vietnamese civilian states that it is because the VC have killed his father.

On an ambush patrol, the Seventh Platoon contacts the man and has him lead them to a hooch containing three VC. Before the SEALs can set up the VC capture, a dog begins barking. The VC are taken under fire and killed before they escape.

The Vietnamese informant leads the SEALs to another hooch where a single female VC is quickly captured by the unit. It turns out that the woman is a communication liaison cadre who knows many other VC in her area. She offers to lead the SEALs to a VC tax collector. The three VC that have been killed by the SEALs are identified as the hamlet security chief and two of the hamlet cadre. The Vietnamese informant, whose identity had been protected throughout the operation by the SEALs, offers to give more information for future operations.

1987 (Persian Gulf)—President Ronald Reagan offers military aid and support for the government of Kuwait, whose ships in the gulf have been attacked. The request results in eleven Kuwaiti tankers being reflagged as American ships and escort protection is extended to them by the U.S. Navy. This action and others are conducted as part of Operation Earnest Will.

By August, two SEAL platoons, six Mark II patrol boats, four Mark II PBRs, two Seafox patrol boats, and a detachment from Special Boat Unit Eleven are deployed to the Persian Gulf. Also sent to the area are U.S. Army assets of two MH-6 helicopters, four AH-6 helicopters, and thirty-nine men as Operation Prime Chance I.

March 11

1965 (South Vietnam)—Task Force 115 is inaugurated in South Vietnam to conduct Operation Market Time. It will involve patrolling and securing the coastline of South Vietnam and interdicting infiltration of personnel and supplies from North Vietnam to the VC in the south. The commander of the Seventh Fleet inaugurates the new unit as a South Vietnamese coastal patrol operation. Effectively, the Market Time forces will be conducting a coastal blockade along all the South Vietnamese shoreline.

1967 (South Vietnam)—The first direct combat contact of the Vietnam War for SEAL Team Two, Second Platoon.

ZCALA956
TTCZYWV RUCILLA/8196 0620638-CCCC--RUCILAA
ZNY CCCCC ZOU RUCILLA RERUTE OF RUHSBB 578 B 0610327
F COMNAVSUPPGRULANT
Z O 0108052 MAR 68
FM CTU ONE ONE SIS PT ONE PT ZERO
TO ZEN1/ UVT ONE ONE IX
IN O ZEN1/7 A OURTY OUR PEVIAL ZONE
ZEN1/ SA IV CTZ
ZEN1/ SA CHAU DOC PROVINCE
ZEN1/ CTG ONE ONE SIX PT SIS
EN1/ CTG ONE ONE SIX PT ONE
ZEN/ CTU ONE NE SIX PT FUR PT ZERO
ZEN1/ CTU ONE ONE SIX PT SIS PT ONE
EN/ CTE ONE ONE SIS PT FOUR PT ZERO PT ONE
RJWJMSAAXCOMNAVOPSUPPGRUPAC
RUCILLA/ COMNAVSUPPGRULANT
ZEN1/ CTU ONE ONE SIX PT TWO PT ZERO
ZEN1/ UVTU ONE ONE IX PT THREE PT ZERO
ZEN/ COMNAVFORV
BT

INFO: CNOSGL_____ CP_
SUPVR ___ RI ___
TOR: 02/08052 MAR 68/GJB

8 - 1

CONFIDENTIAL
GAME WARDEN SPOTREP
1. ELGHTH PLATOON 2 MAN SEAL RECON ELEMENT, LTJG MARCINKO
2. INSERTED BY SLICK VIC VS 955630 14150074. PATROLLED NUI GIAI,
NUI CAM, NUI COTO AREAS. FREQUENT ENEMY ACTIVITY WAS OBSERVED, N

PAGE TWO RU SBB 578B C O N F I D E N T I A L
UNITS WERE LARGER THAN PLATOON SIZE. VC STRENGTH NOT NEAR IN-
TELLIGENCE ESTIMATED. VC OPERATING UNCHALLENGED THROUGHOUT 7
MOUNTAINS AREA IN PLATOON SIZE ELEMENTS OR LESS. RADIO STATIONS
IN MOUNTAINS JAN U. S. FREQUENCIES. EXTRAVTED ROM TRI TON Y
LIVK 18 FEB 68.
3. 141500 H TO 18 FEB 68.7
4. VS 959 614, VS 970 620, WS WPWP YWIN WS 030 634, WS 035594, US
010548, WS 009514.
5. NO U. S. VASUALTIES. VC CONTACT AVOIDED. INTELLIGENCE
GATHERED SUBMITTED TO CTF U116 INTELLIGENCE OFFICER.
BARNDANCE NO. 8-34.
6. CLOSED 7
80-4
BT

info (1)

CO	
XO	
ADMIN	
OPS	
AIR	
SUB	
COMM	
INTEL	
TRA	
ORD	
1ST LT	
ENG	
SUPPLY	
MEDICAL	

DUPE COPY

E 4 mar

NNNNN

5ND GEN 2100/3 (Rev. 5/66)
1] 0199-002-1231

43

March 12

1963 (South Vietnam)—While conducting a hydrographic survey mission to chart the offshore sea floor along the South Vietnamese coast, the men of Detachment Bravo, UDT Twelve, come under fire from an estimated twelve to fifteen VC. The attack takes place at high noon only five miles east of Vinh Chau in Bac Lieu Province of the Mekong Delta. The VC do not press forward with their attack, but the small arms fire makes extraction difficult for the marines and UDT operators on the beach. By 1500 hours, all shore personnel have safely returned to the USS *Weiss* (APD 135). Considering that the risk of making enemy contact has become too great for the information being gathered and that the ship was near the end of its mission anyway, command orders the operation ended and the APD returned to port.

1967 (South Vietnam)—Fire Teams Nine and Five of SEAL Team One are inserted by Mike boat deep into the Rung Sat Special Zone, in the Quang Xuyen district of Gia Dinh Province. The short mission begins at noon. The SEALs emplace twenty DST 115A listening devices in the Vam Sat, at a curve in the west bank of the Song Vam Sat River. The SEALs spot many bunkers in the area but no people. Using a placement sliderule to calculate just how to set up the devices in the most effective pattern, the SEALs complete their mission in twenty minutes and are extracted.

March 13

1968 (South Vietnam)—

> BARNDANCE # 7-66 COORD: XS 692 388

> DATES: 13-14 Mar 68 TIMES: 2200-0330

1. UNITS INVOLVED: SEAL 7th Plt, Seawolf 66/69, Outlaw 66/26, 2 USA 9th Div LRRP

2. TASK: Recon area for POW camp

3. METHOD OF INSERTION: Stab EXTRACTION: Helo

4. TERRAIN: Rice field, jungle

5. TIDE: Out WEATHER: Clear

6. MOON: Three/quarters

7. ENEMY ENCOUNTERED: At least 1, possibly 2 VC Battalions

8. CASUALTIES: Four USA WIA, 1 VN Interp WIA, 17 VC KIA (BC), 10 VC KIA (Prob)

9. NAMES OF SEALS INVOLVED: (Sqd 7A) Lt Peterson, HMC Riojas, ADJ1 Jessie, SK1 Burbank, RM2 Rowell, EM3 Constance, FN Keener, 2 VN LDNN, 2 US 9th Div LRRPs

   (Sqd 7B) Lt (jg) Yeaw, ICC Gallagher, AO2 Boynton, AE2 Ashton, PT2 Tuure, CS2 Matthews, Ming (Vn Interpreter),

10. RESULTS: Area heavily bunkered with fields of fire on all avenues of approach. Many barracks type structures in area.

11. REMARKS/RECOMMENDATIONS: Radios should be checked with support boats periodically as distance from beach increases

INCLUDE INTELLIGENCE INFORMATION GATHERED, MATERIAL FOUND, DESTROYED, CAPTURED, ETC.

GAME WARDEN SPOTREP 3/14/1/116.3.0/1(U)

1. SEAL Det Alfa Seventh Platoon, MST LCM, STAB, SEAWOLF 66/69 Lieutenant Commander Myers/Lieutenant Commander Gyler, OUTLAW 66/26, 2 LDNN, Vietnamese interpreter, 2 U.S. 9th Division Long Range Reconnaissance Patrol, Lieutenant Peterson.

2. 132200Hours 7th Platoon inserted at XS 692388 by STAB. Patrolled north to XS 703417. Squad 7B conducted area recon to northwest, Squad 7A to northeast. 140200H, 7A engaged two Viet Cong at XS 705423, heard many voices to east, evaded north being followed by approximately 50 VC. Set perimeter at XS 706426, called for Seawolf cover and slick [Outlaw 66/26] extraction. 140300H engaged approximately 20 VC approaching from the east. 140330H 7A extracted by slick following Seawolf strike. 140230H 7B encountered approximately 20 VC in barracks type structures at XS 702422, evaded south. Set perimeter at XS 703410, called for Seawolf strike and slick extraction, 140315H 7B extracted by slick following Seawolf strike

3. 132200H–140330H

4. –

5. 4 US Navy wounded in action by grenade fragments (Squad 7B) Vietnamese interpreter wounded in action grenade fragments, 16 VC killed in action (body count), 10 VC killed in action (probably). All VC armed, unable to carry out VC weapons due to WIA. Area heavily bunkered with fields of fire on all avenues of approach. Many barracks type structures in area. Barndance 7-66. Seawolf expended 10,700 rounds of 7.62mm, MST LCM expended 15 rounds 81mm Mortar ammunition—Seawolf spotting.

6. Closed

With these dry words giving little more than the facts and figures, the Barndance cards and Game Warden Spotreps tell of a harrowing mission conducted by the SEALs on a search for a possible POW camp. Barndance cards are individual reports kept by a SEAL platoon on every operation it conducts during a tour of duty in Vietnam. Spotreps are further reports on an operation, but are issued by the higher authority command the SEALs are supporting. They also often contain more information on an operation's support and the final results.

The above reports barely tell the story of SEAL Team Two's Seventh Platoon separating into two squads and penetrating several kilometers deep into VC-controlled territory. When both squads run into different groups of heavily armed VC, the SEALs fight and run.

Squad 7B enters a VC barracks and fights it out with the VC troops inside the building. An exploding VC grenade wounds half the unit, including a Vietnamese interpreter and platoon chief. The interpreter is so badly injured that he can't walk, so he in turn is carried for over 1,000 meters of VC-infested jungle and rice paddies by a SEAL who is less injured.

When they finally make their stand at a rice paddy, the SEALs of Squad 7B are prepared to sell themselves very dearly to the approaching VC forces. The timely arrival of the Seawolf gunships help drive the VC back until the U.S. Army helicopters can set down and extract the beleaguered SEALs.

For their actions that day, Michael Boynton, the SEAL who carried the wounded Vietnamese interpreter, is awarded the Silver Star. The Seventh's platoon chief, Robert Gallagher, who was so severely wounded that he was near death on the SEALs' return to base, is awarded the nation's second highest award for valor, the Navy Cross. The citation for the Navy Cross reads as follows:

For extraordinary heroism on 13 March 1968 while serving with SEAL Team Detachment ALFA engaged in armed conflict against the communist insurgent forces (Viet Cong) in the Republic of Vietnam. Senior Chief Petty Officer Gallagher served as assistant patrol leader for a SEAL night combat operation deep in an enemy battalion base area. His patrol penetrated 5,000 yards into the Viet Cong base camp, locating a large barracks area occupied by approximately 30 well-armed insurgents. Senior Chief Petty Officer Gallagher led three men into the barracks. When discovered by a Viet Cong sentry, the patrol came under heavy enemy fire. Although wounded in both legs, Senior Chief Petty Officer Gallagher accounted for five enemy Viet Cong killed. Discovering that his patrol leader was seriously wounded, Senior Chief Petty Officer Gallagher took command and led his patrol 1,000 yards through heavily occupied enemy territory to an open area where he radioed for helicopter support. He continually exposed himself to heavy enemy automatic weapons fire to direct friendly helicopter gunships and extraction ships. While assisting his patrol to the evacuation point, Senior Chief Petty Officer Gallagher was again wounded, but, despite his multiple wounds, succeeded in leading his men to a safe extraction. By his courage, professional skill, and devotion to duty, he was directly responsible for the safe withdrawal of his patrol and for killing a large number of the enemy in their own base area. His heroic achievements were in keeping with the highest traditions of the United States Naval Service.

March 14

1969 (USA)—Lieutenant Joseph R. Kerrey receives the Congressional Medal of Honor for his actions conducted on this date in Vietnam. The citation reads as follows:

For conspicuous gallantry and intrepidity at the risk of his life above and beyond the call of duty on 14 March 1969 while serving as a SEAL Team Leader during action against enemy aggressor (Viet Cong) forces in the Republic of Vietnam. Acting in response to reliable intelligence, Lieutenant (j.g.) Kerrey led his SEAL Team on a mission to capture important members of the enemy's area political cadre known to be located on an island in the bay of Nha Trang. In order to surprise the enemy, he and his team scaled a 350-foot sheer cliff to place themselves above the ledge on which the enemy was located. Splitting his team in two elements and coordinating both, Lieutenant (j.g.) Kerrey led his men in the treacherous downward descent to the enemy's camp. Just as they neared the end of their descent, intense enemy fire was directed at them, and Lieutenant (j.g.) Kerrey received massive injuries from a grenade which exploded at his feet and threw him backward onto the jagged rocks. Although bleeding profusely and suffering great pain, he displayed outstanding courage and presence of mind in immediately directing his element's fire into the heart of the enemy camp. Utilizing his radioman, Lieutenant (j.g.) Kerrey called in the second element's fire support which caught the confused Viet Cong in a devastating crossfire. After successfully suppressing the enemy's fire, and although immobilized by his multiple wounds, he continued to maintain calm, superlative control as he ordered his team to secure and defend an extraction site. Lieutenant (j.g.) Kerrey resolutely directed his men, despite his near-unconscious state, until he was eventually evacuated by helicopter. The havoc brought to the enemy by this very successful mission cannot be overestimated. The enemy who were captured provided critical intelligence to the allied effort. Lieutenant (j.g.) Kerrey's courageous and inspiring leadership, valiant fighting spirit, and tenacious devotion to duty in the face of almost overwhelming opposition, sustain and enhance the finest traditions of the United States Naval Service.

2002 (USA)—A posthumous Bronze Star is awarded to Aviation Boatswain's Mate (Aircraft Handling) SEAL First Class Neil C. Roberts for his actions during Operation Anaconda in the Shahikat Mountains of Afghanistan on March 4. The citation reads in part:

> On that evening, his unit was to conduct a clandestine insertion onto a 10,000-foot mountain peak to establish an overwatch position, for an indeterminate amount of time, protecting other U.S. forces participating in the operation.
>
> As the helicopter moved into position for the insertion, Petty Officer Roberts positioned himself on the helicopter ramp in order to expeditiously exit the helicopter, minimizing the threat to the aircraft and crew. Without notice, his CH-47 helicopter received three rocket-propelled grenades exploding through the body of the aircraft. Hydraulic lines showered the metal ramp with slippery fluid as the aircraft lurched violently from the unexpected assault.
>
> Petty Officer Roberts was thrown from the ramp of the helicopter, falling onto the al Qaeda-infested mountain top just feet below. He immediately maneuvered to make contact with rescue forces and establish a defensive position but, surrounded by overwhelming enemy force with superior fire power, Petty Officer Roberts died on the battlefield from fatal combat wounds.
>
> By his zealous initiative, courageous actions, and exceptional dedication to duty, Petty Officer Roberts reflected great credit upon himself and upheld the highest traditions of the United States Navy.
>
> The Combat Distinguishing Device is authorized.

March 15

1944 (Hawaii)—Vice Admiral Richmond Kelly Turner issues the basic letters (serial number 0034-C52/576/Ply—14 March and serial number 00370-S76/P16—15 March) that outline the basic organization of the training base at Maui and the UDTs. Following the intelligence that has been learned while undergoing Operation Flintlock with UDT One and Two, and working from a proposed organization plan put together by the commanding officer of UDT Two, the organization of the UDTs will undergo some changes and refinement.

For example, men from other services, such as the U.S. Army, will no longer be included in the basic manpower of a UDT. The difference in manner of operating and simple nomenclature from the other services proves to be of more difficulty than it is worth with the soldiers and marines who have been part of UDT One.

Teams will now consist of thirteen officers and eighty-five enlisted men, organized into five operating platoons and a headquarters platoon. The personnel that operate the remote-control drone boats will be dropped from the organization and UDT operators listed in their stead. The Naval Combat Underwater Demolition Training and Experimental Base will prepare the graduates who arrive from basic Naval Combat Demolition Unit (NCDU) training at Fort Pierce, Florida, to conduct the mission of the UDTs during World War II: "To reconnoiter and clear the approaches to prospective landing beaches."

March 16

1967 (South Vietnam)—Rear Admiral Norvell G. Ward, Chief of the Naval Advisory Group, Admiral Ulysses S. Grant Sharp, Commander in Chief Pacific, and General William C. Westmoreland, Commander of the U.S. Military Assistance Command in Vietnam, visit SEAL Team One's Detachment Golf. The high-ranking officers express their personal admiration for the missions that the SEALs are conducting throughout the Mekong Delta area.

March 17

1970 (USA)—

The President of the United States, Richard Nixon, takes pleasure in presenting the Silver Star Medal to:

RONALD JACK RODGER
BOATSWAIN'S MATE FIRST CLASS
UNITED STATES NAVY

for service as set forth in the following:

CITATION

For conspicuous gallantry and intrepidity in action while serving with friendly forces engaged in armed conflict with the North Vietnamese and VC Communist aggressors in the Republic of Vietnam on 17-18 March 1970. While attached to SEAL Team TWO, Detachment ALFA and operating out of Coastal Group THIRTY-SIX, Long Phu District, Ba Xuyen Province, Republic of Vietnam, Petty Officer RODGER was the senior U. S. Navy SEAL Advisor to eight Vietnamese SEALs on a night combat operation on Dung Island, a well established Viet Cong stronghold and sanctuary. He planned and coordinated the operation, acted as point man for the patrol and led his unit to the objective. After security was established and the strike element entered the hootch, a fire fight from point blank range ensued wherein a Vietnamese SEAL was seriously wounded in action. Petty Officer RODGER personally carried the wounded man to a nearby canal and while under intense automatic weapons fire, placed him in a sampan, paddled to the main river to a support boat and aided in placing the wounded man on the boat. While again under enemy fire, he proceeded back and successfully rescued the remainder of his men. Petty Officer RODGER's heroic actions in the face of enemy fire, courage, decisive actions, professional performance and devotion to duty were in keeping with the highest traditions of the United States Naval Service.

For the President
John J. Hyland
Admiral, U.S. Navy
Commander in Chief U.S. Pacific Fleet

★ ★ ★ ★ ★

2002 (USA)—SEAL Team Seven, part of Navy Special Warfare Group One, is commissioned at Coronado, California.

March 18

1967 (South Vietnam)—Fire Team Ten of SEAL Team One's Detachment Golf is inserted in two groups to conduct a straightforward body snatch and ambush mission. The groups, using a PBR as their insertion platform, are inserted 250 meters apart. During the night, one SEAL is forced to retreat from his position as a crocodile approaches him and refuses to be driven away. Finally, in desperation the SEAL shoots the crocodile in self-defense.

The noise of the shot, however, compromises the SEALs' ambush position, so they call for extraction. The other SEAL group waits at its ambush position until the tide goes out. In spite of the crocodile startling the SEALs, its approach may have been much better than if a VC unit had come in. The AR-15 carbine the SEAL fired had an obstruction in its barrel. When the fired round lodged in the barrel, the barrel burst from the pressure. No one is hurt, but the still newly adopted weapon has to be returned to the States and then on to the manufacturer for examination.

March 19

1967 (South Vietnam)—Fire Team Seven of SEAL Team One's Detachment Golf is inserted to conduct an ambush patrol with the additional intention of attempting a sniper attack. The mission lasts from 1800 hours the night before to 0600 hours. To give them an additional long range reach, the SEALs have taken along a 7.62mm bolt-action sniper rifle.

In spite of the half-moon illuminating the target area through clear weather until 0400 hours, the sniper rifle is not considered worth the trouble to carry. Not only does the precision weapon have to be carefully protected from the muddy, wet environment the SEALs often operate in, it doesn't work well at night with its standard telescopic sight, at least not any better than a simpler weapon with straightforward iron sights.

March 20

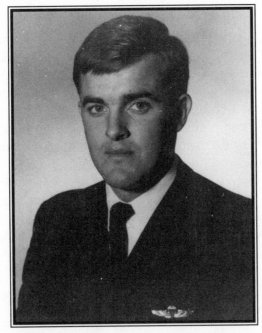

Lieutenant, Junior Grade, Joseph Robert Kerrey,
SEAL Medal of Honor recipient. U.S. NAVY

March 21

1967 (South Vietnam)—Special Forces Master Sergeant Charles E. Hosking Jr. performs the actions that result in his posthumous award of the Congressional Medal of Honor.

CITATION

For conspicuous gallantry and intrepidity in action at the risk of his life above and beyond the call of duty. M/Sgt. Hosking (then Sfc.), Detachment PA-302, Company A, greatly distinguished himself while serving as company adviser in the III Corps Civilian Irregular Defense Group Reaction Battalion during combat operations in Don Luan District. A Viet Cong suspect was apprehended and subsequently identified as a Viet Cong sniper. While M/Sgt. Hosking was preparing the enemy for movement back to the base camp, the prisoner suddenly grabbed a hand grenade from M/Sgt. Hosking's belt, armed the grenade, and started running towards the company command group which consisted of 2 Americans and 2 Vietnamese who were standing a few feet away. Instantly realizing that the enemy intended to kill the other men, M/Sgt. Hosking immediately leaped upon the Viet Cong's back. With utter disregard for his personal safety, he grasped the Viet Cong in a "Bear Hug" forcing the grenade against the enemy soldier's chest. He then wrestled the Viet Cong to the ground and covered the enemy's body with his body until the grenade detonated. The blast instantly killed both M/Sgt. Hosking and the Viet Cong. By absorbing the full force of the exploding grenade with his body and that of the enemy, he saved the other members of his command group from death or serious injury. M/Sgt. Hosking's risk of his life above and beyond the call of duty are in the highest tradition of the U.S. Army and reflect great credit upon himself and the Armed Forces of his country.

1968 (South Vietnam)—The extreme stress and demands of the Tet offensive bring out the best in the SEALs and other units. For the first time, the civilian authorities notice the special operations forces, since the offensive is the first time a majority of these authorities have come under direct personal threat from combat in Vietnam. The following memorandum illustrates what some of these civilian authorities think about the SEALs who came to their rescue during the pitched fighting of Tet.

OFFICER OF CIVIL OPERATIONS

AND

REVOLUTIONARY DEVELOPMENT SUPPORT

IV CTZ

CORDS-IDC-DEPCORDS   21 March 1968

MEMORANDUM FOR: Commander Naval Forces Vietnam

SUBJECT: Commendation for SEAL 8th Platoon

Navy Task Force 116

1. During the crucial phase of the initial Viet Cong Tet attack, a SEAL platoon from Navy Task Force 116, in conjunction with the Chau Doc PRU, was instrumental in thwarting the Viet Cong efforts to occupy and hold the capital city of Chau Doc province. In the early morning hours of 31 January 1968, the SEALs and the PRU were conducting a joint operation when they received a message that the provincial capital was under heavy attack by the Viet Cong. The SEALs and PRU returned immediately to the provincial capital, which by the time of their arrival was almost entirely occupied by the Viet Cong.

2. Working closely with the PRU, the SEALs, in vicious house-to-house fighting, succeeded in breaking the hold that the Viet Cong had established on the city. The SEALs and PRU, among other distinguished actions, liberated eight American members of the CORDS staff who were surrounded by the VC and under heavy VC fire. In a separate action, while fighting to clear the VC out of the Vietnamese Security Service Headquarters, one of the SEALs, AMH3 Clarence T. Risher, was killed by sniper fire and two other SEALs were wounded.

3. Throughout the entire engagement, every member of this platoon distinguished himself many times over by his cool professionalism and heroic action while under intense fire from the enemy. The members of the CORDS staff in Chau Doc have the deepest admiration for and profound gratitude to each member of this platoon of Navy SEALs. I wish to make it a matter of record that this Headquarters is highly appreciative of the valor and fighting spirit these men displayed during this particularly critical period.

> Sterling J. Cottrell
> Deputy for CORDS
> IV CTZ

March 22

Demonstrating a view that took a number of Viet Cong by surprise is Silver, one of the German Shepherd scout dogs employed in Vietnam by SEAL Team Two. U.S. NAVY

March 23

1969 (South Vietnam)—The citations for awards of high valor tell the facts of an individual's actions, but often details are missing. For example, Radioman Second Class Robert J. Thomas demonstrates fortitude and cool, deliberate skill when he performs the deeds that result in his being awarded the Navy Cross. His skills as a marksman are of great value during his actions as the only weapon available to him is the M1911A1 .45 automatic, the sidearm of one of the injured helicopter crewmen he is protecting. The citation reads as follows:

For extraordinary heroism on 23 March 1969 while serving with SEAL Team Detachment ALFA, Seventh Platoon, during combat operations against communist aggressor forces in the Republic of Vietnam. Embarked in a Seawolf helicopter on a visual reconnaissance and strike mission on Da Dung Mountain near the Cambodian border when the aircraft was struck by enemy ground fire and crashed in an exposed rice paddy, Petty Officer Thomas was thrown from the wreckage, sustaining multiple injuries. Fighting off the stunning effects of shock, he immediately moved to the aid of the helicopter crewmen who were still in the burning aircraft. Despite the intense flames and the heavy gunfire from both the mountain and a nearby tree line, Petty Officer Thomas managed to remove one of the crewmen to safety and, with the aid of another man who had been dropped onto the site by an accompanying helicopter, succeeded in freeing the trapped pilot from the flaming cockpit. Petty Officer Thomas then made a gallant attempt to rescue the two remaining men trapped beneath the twisted metal, discontinuing his efforts only when driven back by the exploding bullets and rockets of the burning helicopter. After moving the two previously rescued men to a greater distance from the crash site, Petty Officer Thomas realized that Viet Cong troops were steadily advancing on his position. He selflessly threw himself upon the body of one of the wounded men and began returning the enemy fire. His deadly accuracy accounted for at least one enemy dead and held the aggressors at bay until an Army rescue helicopter landed. By his valiant efforts and selfless devotion to duty while under hostile fire, Petty Officer Thomas upheld the highest traditions of the United States Naval Service.

March 24

1961 (USA)—The Twelfth Special Forces Group (Airborne) is activated.

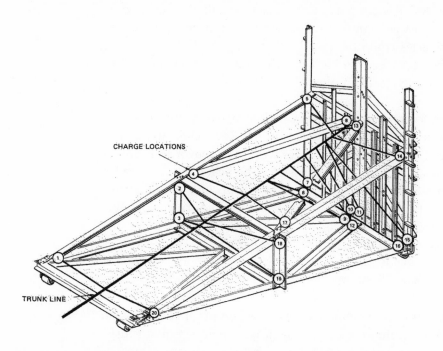

Still in the manuals today, this is the illustration for the placement of charges (Hagensen packs) to properly demolish Element C. The massive steel obstacle was the primary target for the NCDUs (naval combat demolition units) going in to Normandy Beach. The multi-ton obstacle stands ten feet tall, ten feet wide, and fifteen feet long. Element C, also called the Belgian Gate, could be connected together to form walls hundreds of yards long. U.S. NAVY

March 25

1943 (England)—The Beach Battalions in England are ready to report to the marshaling areas where they will gather in preparation for the upcoming invasion of Europe. The men of the NCDUs are part of the Beach Battalions, but there is still no official word as to just what mission they will have during the invasion. The knowledge that obstacles could be quickly placed by the Germans along any probable invasion beach causes the higher authorities to immediately consolidate the NCDUs for use in a unified plan of attack.

1945 (Pacific)—Operation Iceberg, the invasion of Okinawa, begins for the UDTs. The first reconnaissance missions are conducted on the Kerama-Retto Islands, which cover an area about seven-by-thirteen miles west of Okinawa and contain ten principle islands and a number of smaller islets. The beach reconnaissance operations for the Kerama-Retto will be conducted by Group Able of the Underwater Demolition Flotilla. Group Able consists of UDTs Twelve, Thirteen, Fourteen, and Nineteen. UDT Fourteen acts as the standby team during the Kerama-Retto operations. Aboard the USS *Bates* (APD 47), UDT Twelve arrives off the Kerama-Retto with the advance group and proceeds to conduct recons of beaches on Yakabi Shima, Zamami Shima, and Amuro Shima.

1945 (Pacific)—The large number of islands to be landed on in rapid succession in the Kerama-Retto group requires the UDTs to conduct recons simultaneously. UDT Nineteen aboard the USS *Knudson* (APD 101) conducts a preassault reconnaissance of Red Beach on Kuba Shima in the morning. In the afternoon, further recons are swum on the Gold, Yellow, and Blue invasion beaches of Aka Shima, Geruma Shima, and Hokaji Shima, respectively. The UDT operators receive some light weapons fire from the island as they conduct their operations, but no casualties are taken.

1945 (Pacific)—UDT Thirteen conducts a preassault reconnaissance of a Kerama-Retto island shortly after its transport, the USS *Barr* (APD 39), arrives on site. In the morning, the UDT Thirteen operators conduct their recon of the Orange Zebra Beach on the southern tip of Tokashiki Shima. In the afternoon, it completes a recon of the Purple Zebra Beach on the western side of Tokashiki Shima.

1966 (South Vietnam)—Detachment Charlie is augmented by additional elements of UDT Eleven making up Detachment Delta. The assignment of the Detachment Delta personnel make this the first time that a complete UDT (UDT Eleven) is deployed to Vietnam at the same time.

March 26

1945 (Pacific)—Men from UDT Twelve, both officers and enlisted, act as pilots for the U.S. Army's Seventy-seventh Division's landing craft. The army forces land to secure the western islands of the Okinawa group as a fleet anchorage for the invasion and support vessels prior to the invasion of Okinawa itself.

1945 (Pacific)—During the morning hours, personnel from UDT Nineteen help guide landing craft ashore at the Gold, Yellow, and Blue Beaches of Aka Shima, Geruma Shima, and Hokaji Shima, respectively. On Geruma Shima, UDT Nineteen operators blast an entrance through the trees facing Yellow Beach so that vehicles can more easily penetrate inland.

1945 (Pacific)—Group Baker UDTs Four, Seven, Eleven, Sixteen, Seventeen, and Twenty-one as part of the Underwater Demolition Flotilla assigned to the Western Attack Group for Operation Iceberg arrive at the Kerama-Retto Island groups.

1966 (South Vietnam)—Operation Jackstay, the first major joint action in the Rung Sat Special Zone, begins. This is the first joint UDT-SEAL and marine operation in the Vietnam War. The twelve-day effort will have U.S. Navy, Marine, and South Vietnamese forces attacking the VC hidden within the Rung Sat. The opening operation places personnel from UDT Eleven Detachments Charlie and Delta on the beach marking beacons at around 0300 hours to guide marine landing craft through the shallow, dangerous portions of the Saigon River.

After the landings, the UDT personnel conduct further operations including surveillance and minesweeping. The UDT operators also set up four-man units in blocking positions to prevent the escape of VC forces driven from their positions by the SEALs and other units. One group of UDT operators ambushes a VC junk and fights an extended fire fight with the occupants of the craft.

March 27

1945 (Pacific)—At Red Beach on Kuba Shima, one of the two westernmost islands of the Kerama-Retto group, personnel from UDT Nineteen help guide the invasion forces ashore without incident. The island has been evacuated by the Japanese and there is no resistance to the landings.

1945 (Pacific)—The USS *Crosley* (APD 87), with UDT Seventeen aboard, makes a reconnaissance run along the western beaches of Okinawa. UDT Seventeen is assigned the Green 1 and 2 Beaches, the northern part of the Hagushi area. The run by the *Crosley*, 5,000 yards from shore, allows the men of the UDT to see the beaches they will recon within a few days.

1955 (USA)—The 300th Special Forces Operational Detachment is activated.

March 28

1945 (Pacific)—UDT Seventeen aboard the USS *Crosley* (APD 87) is held at an assigned screening station outside the transport area at the Kerama-Retto group. Around 0630 hours, a Japanese aircraft suddenly appears and dives toward the *Crosley*. The guns of the *Crosley* fire at the kamikaze as it bores in to the ship full of UDT operators. A quick maneuver by the *Crosley* at the last moment causes the kamikaze to miss and plunge into the sea only thirty feet astern of the ship. There will be more kamikazes seen and engaged by the *Crosley* over the next several weeks.

1945 (Pacific)—A Japanese maru-ni explosive (suicide) motorboat unit is discovered on Tokashiki Shima in the Kerama-Retto group. The boat unit's commander and the majority of the boat pilots are reported to be on Okinawa for a training exercise when the invasion takes place. Without proper leadership, the suicide boats do not damage the U.S. fleet. Only a single attack takes place on the night of March 28 with one suicide boat dropping a 264-pound explosive charge (modified depth charge) about fifty feet from the USS *Terebinth* (AN 59).

The charge explodes, doing no damage to the ship, and the boat speeds away. During the search of the island, 250 explosive motorboats are found in various locations. If pilots had been available, the boats could have done significant damage to the fleet's forces.

1945 (Pacific)—By the late afternoon, the islands of the Kerama-Retto group are considered secured. In the taking of the group, the losses to the U.S. Army Seventy-seventh Division is thirty-one killed and eighty-one wounded. The U.S. Navy lost 124 killed or missing and 230 wounded. The vast bulk of these casualties are taken by aircraft bombings and kamikaze missions against navy craft. About 530 Japanese are killed and 121 captured.

1967 (Bolivia)—Major Ralph "Pappy" Shelton is deployed to train Bolivian recruits in counterinsurgency operations for campaign against Ernesto "Che" Guevara and his guerrilla band.

2002 (Afghanistan)—During a training mission in the early morning hours, Chief Hospital Corpsman SEAL Matthew J. Bourgeois is killed stepping on a land mine or other booby trap at an abandoned al Qaeda base near the airport in Kandahar. A second SEAL is injured in the blast. Chief Bourgeois is the thirty-first U.S. serviceman, but only the second SEAL, to die in Afghanistan since the ground action of Operation Enduring Freedom began on October 7, 2001.

March 29

1945 (Pacific)—UDT Nineteen conducts a demolition swim to blast channels in the reefs off Keise Shima for tracked amphibious vehicles and landing craft.

1945 (Pacific)—UDT Four places explosives to load and then fires the four-deep rows of posts it found blocking the landings at the Purple 1 and 2 and Orange 1 and 2 Beaches on the western coast of Okinawa. In spite of the huge number of posts, each one to be individually charged for demolition, UDT Four succeeds in loading and firing the posts in only two hours.

1945 (Pacific)—UDT Seven makes a reconnaissance of the Yellow 1, 2, and 3 Beaches on the western coast of Okinawa. The beaches are found to be relatively clear of obstacles except for Yellow 2. Yellow 2 Beach is found to have three rows of wooden posts, each six inches in diameter, driven into the reef about forty yards from the high water mark. The estimated 200 posts had been in place for some time according to the plant and animal growth noted by the UDT swimmers. The UDT swimmers report that the six-foot-tall posts do not appear to be able to block incoming landing craft. In spite of this, a decision is made to clear the post obstacles in a demolition swim the next day.

1945 (Pacific)—UDT Twelve conducts a demonstration reconnaissance of the beaches at Green Able 1 and 2 on the southern coast of Okinawa. The recons are part of the deception operation intended to confuse and distract the Japanese.

1945 (Pacific)—UDT Fourteen conducts a reconnaissance of the southernmost beaches of Okinawa. The action is a feint intended to help confuse the enemy as to just which will be the actual landing beaches.

1945 (Pacific)—UDT Sixteen swimmers conduct a reconnaissance of their assigned beaches on the western coast of Okinawa. Wooden post obstacles set in three rows are found embedded in the reefs off Red 3 and Blue 1 and 2 Beaches. The approximately 1,200 posts look to have been in place for some time and are all about eight inches in diameter and about six feet long.

1945 (Pacific)—UDT Seventeen conducts its reconnaissance swim at the same time as the rest of the UDTs assigned to Group Baker. It had been decided to conduct all of the UDTs' recons at the same time to minimize any single team's exposure to the enemy. About 200 wooden posts are discovered by the UDT swimmers during their recon of the 400-yard-wide reefs off the invasion beaches.

March 30

1945 (Pacific)—UDT Thirteen completes several days of work loading and blasting a channel so that heavy artillery can be landed on Keise Shima. The 155mm army guns will add to the preinvasion bombardment of the main island of Okinawa as well as give artillery support to the troops once they land on the island.

1945 (Pacific)—UDT Nineteen conducts demolition operations on the reef off Kamiyama Shima. After channels are cleared through the reefs, the UDT swimmers emplace buoys to mark the channels. Once the demolition and marking operations are complete, the USS *Knudson* (APD 101) and UDT Nineteen are assigned to a screening station as part of the antiaircraft screen for the fleet. They remain on station for two weeks until relieved April 15, suffering a near miss when a bomb landed only twenty-five yards from the ship.

1945 (Pacific)—UDT Seven conducts its demolition swim against the post obstacles it found earlier off Yellow 2 Beach. One block of tetryl high explosive is considered enough to demolish a single post. The demolition is successful, though one swimmer is injured by close-in friendly fire. In addition, the UDT swimmers suffer badly from cramps and exposure to the cold waters off Okinawa.

1945 (Pacific)—Continuing its feint actions to distract the enemy, UDT Fourteen returns to the same beaches it conducted a reconnaissance on the day before and goes on a demolition swim. Swimmers plant and fire a one-ton demolition charge on a reef off the beaches at the same time as the rest of the UDTs are conducting demolition and reconnaissance swims elsewhere on Okinawa.

1945 (Pacific)—While operating with UDT Eleven to conduct demolition swims against the post obstacles it had located earlier, UDT Sixteen loses one of its swimmers, Francis Joseph Lynch, when he's killed by enemy fire from Okinawa. In spite of their almost constant exposure to enemy fire during their recon and demolition swims, the UDTs suffer relatively few casualties when they're in the water—a point not lost on the UDT operators or their later descendants, the Navy SEALs.

March 31

1945 (Pacific)—A massive bombardment from navy gunfire, army artillery, and aircraft plaster Okinawa to soften the island's defenses against the incoming invasion forces.

1967 (South Vietnam)—Second Platoon of SEAL Team Two's Detachment Alfa moves to the U.S. PBR base at My Tho on the Song My Tho River in Dinh Tuong Province. The platoon will begin SEAL operations in the Mekong Delta region. It is the first of many SEAL platoons to follow and operate here. The platoon's unorthodox operations will prove very effective against the VC in the Delta region.

1995 (Haiti)—Operation Uphold Democracy becomes Operation Restore Hope as the UN mission takes over in Haiti.

APRIL

An Iranian oil platform is engulfed by flames during Operation Praying Mantis. The photograph is from the transport boat of the SEAL detachment that boarded and searched the platform. The silhouette of a SEAL's M16A1/M203 grenade launcher is visible *(left)*. U.S. Navy

April 01

1945 (Pacific)—The largest naval operation in the Pacific to date begins. More than 1,200 transport and landing ships hold over 450,000 army and marine personnel who will conduct the landings of Operation Iceberg, the invasion of Okinawa. Members of the UDTs who conducted the reconnaissance swims and demolition operations on the actual landing beaches on the west coast of the island help guide the assault waves in to shore.

1953 (Korea)—The 8240th Army Unit Rabbit I guerrilla warfare team infiltrates into North Korea.

1967 (USA)—Helicopter Attack Squadron (Light) Three, the Seawolves, is commissioned to provide Task Force 116 with its own air support and evacuation units. The Seawolves, flying borrowed Army UH-1B helicopter gunships, quickly become a force to be reckoned with in South Vietnam. As a navy unit, the Seawolves quickly become a favorite support unit of the SEALs in Vietnam. Their bravery and skill with heavily armed helicopters, coming in to save SEALs and other navy units when no one else could, make the stories of the Seawolves the stuff of legends in the annals of Naval Special Warfare.

1982 (USA)—The all-volunteer U.S. Army aviation unit that has been conducting intensive helicopter training to support special operations forces is designated the 160th Aviation Battalion. The men and their helicopters are quickly known throughout the special operations community as Task Force 160.

April 02

1945 (Pacific)—UDT Seven conducts further reconnaissance of the reefs off Yellow 3 Beach on the western shore of Okinawa. In an unusual move, the UDT swimmers move inland as the reconnaissance is continued according to orders, about 200 yards up the Bishi River. The river marks the operational boundaries between the marine's Third Amphibious Corps and the army's Twenty-fourth Corps. No obstacles or need for demolition work is found during the UDT recon.

1945 (Pacific)—UDT Sixteen begins postassault demolition operations off Okinawa. The primary action of the UDT is to blast channels through the reefs sufficient to allow Landing Craft, Tank (LCTs) and LCMs to clear the reefs and come in to the beaches to unload.

1961 (USA)—The Fourteenth Special Forces Operational Detachment (Area) is activated.

April 03

1961 (USA)—The Seventeenth Special Forces Group (Airborne) is activated.

The Hagensen charge was specifically designed to demolish the Element C obstacles on Normandy Beach. Here, that same charge is being placed by a UDT swimmer to destroy a steel hedgehog obstacle. U.S. NAVY

April 04

1944 (Mediterranean)—Operational Group One infiltrates Greece.

1945 (Pacific)—Proving the importance of the UDTs in amphibious operations, Admiral of the Fleet Chester W. Nimitz, the commander in chief of the Pacific Fleet, arrives at the UDT camp on Guam to inspect the camp and teams. At 1000 hours, Admiral Nimitz walks to where the men of UDTs Eight and Ten are standing and holds an informal talk with them. His tour of the camp and view of the men causes him to remark that it is "one of the finest groups of men it has been my pleasure to inspect." The admiral spends over an hour in the camp that was built by the men of UDT Eight with able assistance lent to them by the Seabees on the island.

2002 (Eastern Europe)—Retired Master Chief Boatswain's Mate SEAL Harry O'Connor is killed in Czechoslovakia while conducting an aerial stunt on the set of the movie *XXX*. Reportedly, the former SEAL struck a pillar of the Palacky Bridge while paragliding. A number of former SEALs work as movie extras, actors, and stunt men as well as hold down a variety of hazardous jobs after they leave the service. Many have careers as police officers, bail enforcers, and private investigators. A large number also go on to be accomplished artisans, teachers, writers, and simply office workers.

April 05

In this artist's rendition, the USS *Grayback* is releasing early-model SDVs (swimmer delivery vehicles) from her cavernous bow hangars—all while remaining underwater. U.S. Navy

April 06

1945 (Pacific)—For several days, UDT Seven conducts recons of beaches at White Baker, Purple Baker, and Brown Baker on Okinawa. All of the beaches are behind the front lines and considered to be in Japanese hands. The recons are to determine the capacity of the beaches to support the unloading of supplies.

1953 (Korea)—The 8240th Army Unit Rabbit II guerrilla warfare team infiltrates North Korea.

April 07

1966 (South Vietnam)—Operation Jackstay ends with sixty-nine VC either killed or captured and a number of VC supply bases and other facilities destroyed.

1967 (USA)—

The President of the United States takes pleasure in presenting the Silver Star Medal to

HERBERT MERTON RUTH
SENIOR CHIEF ENGINEMAN
UNITED STATES NAVY

for service as set forth in the following:

CITATION

For conspicuous gallantry and intrepidity in action while serving as a Squad leader and assistant Platoon Commander with SEAL Team ONE Detachment GOLF from February to June 1967. Senior Chief Petty Officer RUTH demonstrated constant determination and alertness during the course of reconnaissance patrols, demolitions raids, and ambushes in the demanding and hostile environment of the Rung Sat Tidal Swamp, Republic of Vietnam. Senior Chief Petty Officer RUTH led 15 patrols in the Rung Sat and participated in more than 15 others as an assistant patrol leader. On 7 April 1967 the SEAL LCM was ambushed by a company-sized Viet Cong force on the Vam Sat river. Fourteen of the 20 SEALs aboard were casualties, three were killed. Senior Chief Petty Officer RUTH was manning a 60mm mortar at the time of the attack. Although an enemy airburst killed the man next to him and caused a severe flash burn across Senior Chief Petty Officer RUTH's face, he continued to return fire in an effort to suppress the Viet Cong attack. His determination to remain at his battle station undoubtedly saved the lives of many others on the boat. After clearing the ambush area, Senior Chief Petty Officer RUTH, unmind-

ful of his own injuries, administered aid to his seriously wounded shipmates until they were MEDEVACED. His courage, leadership, and devotion to duty were in keeping with the highest traditions of the United States Naval Service.

For the President
John J. Hyland
Admiral, U.S. Navy
Commander in Chief U.S. Pacific Fleet

★ ★ ★ ★ ★

April 08

1945 (Pacific)—Off Okinawa, the men of UDT Twelve and the crew of the USS *Bates* (APD 47) conduct screening operations for the invasion fleet. Twenty-one survivors of a U.S. destroyer hit by a Japanese kamikaze are picked up and given medical aid by the UDT operators and crew of the *Bates*.

1968 (South Vietnam)—LDNN Class III from Vung Tau captures five suspected VC during a training exercise and turns them over to authorities. The training for the LDNNs is set up and run by U.S. Navy SEAL advisors. It is a hard and long course, but back in the United States, none of the trainees have the opportunity to capture enemy troops while going through maneuvers. By the end of April, there are only thirty-eight trainees still in the ranks of LDNN Class III.

April 09

1945 (Pacific)—Japanese shore batteries open fire on the U.S. fleet off Tsugen Shima near Okinawa. The USS *Hopping* (APD 51), with UDT Seven aboard, is struck by armor-piercing projectiles. One of the shells penetrates into the ship and detonates in the troop's quarters where the UDT men live. Nine UDT Seven personnel are injured by the blast, with one of the men soon dying from his wounds. The *Hopping* and UDT Seven leave the area the next day for the Ulithi Islands.

1970 (USA)—Many of the individuals who receive high medals for valor think of themselves as reacting to circumstances and doing their jobs. They consider what they do is not much more, or even less, than what their fellow SEALs and UDT operators have done in similar circumstances. At the very least, these men often consider themselves to just be holding the award in trust for their teammates who made a much greater sacrifice and never returned home. Chief Gunner's Mate Barry W. Enoch is one of those men who considers himself a trustee of the Navy Cross. The following is his award citation:

> *For extraordinary heroism on 9 April 1970 in connection with operations against enemy forces in the Republic of Vietnam. While serving with a detachment of SEAL Team ONE, Chief Petty Officer Enoch was the senior advisor and radioman/grenadier to a combined United States Vietnamese SEAL combat patrol against the Viet Cong infrastructure leaders in Long Phu District, Ba Xuyen Province. After insertion and patrolling to the target area, Chief Petty Officer Enoch observed six armed Viet Cong attempting to evade. Rushing forward and exposing himself to hostile fire, he succeeded in accounting for three enemy casualties. The SEALs then came under intense B-40 rocket and automatic weapon fire. Realizing that his small force was surrounded, Chief Petty Officer Enoch deployed his men in a defensive perimeter, and although under intense fire, continually shifted position to more effectively employ his weapon, relocate his men, and survey the enemy's weapons and tactics. Although his radio was damaged by enemy fire, Chief Petty Officer Enoch directed air strikes on the shortest route between his position and the river, and then led the patrol*

through the enemy encirclement before the latter could close the gap caused by the air strikes. By his heroic and decisive efforts in the face of almost overwhelming odds, Chief Petty Officer Enoch was directly responsible for the safe extraction of the patrol members and upheld the highest traditions of the United States Naval Service.

1987 (USA)—The Special Forces is established as a branch of the U.S. Army; a crossed arrow insignia is adopted as the official branch insignia.

April 10

1952 (USA)—The U.S. Army Psychological Warfare Center is established at Fort Bragg, North Carolina.

1972 (USA)—Thomas R. Norris earns the Congressional Medal of Honor for his actions in Vietnam. The presidential citation from Gerald Ford reads as follows:

For conspicuous gallantry and intrepidity in action at the risk of his life above and beyond the call of duty while serving as a SEAL Advisor with the Strategic Technical Directorate Assistance Team, headquarters, U.S. Military Assistance Command, Vietnam. During the period 10 to 13 April 1972, Lieutenant Norris completed an unprecedented ground rescue of two downed pilots deep within heavily controlled enemy territory in Quang Tri Province. Lieutenant Norris, on the night of 10 April, led a five-man patrol through 2,000 meters of heavily controlled enemy territory, located one of the downed pilots at daybreak, and returned to the Forward Operating Base (FOB). On 11 April, after a devastating mortar and rocket attack on the small FOB, Lieutenant Norris led a three-man team on two unsuccessful rescue attempts for the second pilot. On the afternoon of the 12th, a Forward Air Controller located the pilot and notified Lieutenant Norris. Dressed in fishermen disguises and using a sampan, Lieutenant Norris and one Vietnamese traveled throughout that night and found the injured pilot at dawn. Covering the pilot with bamboo and vegetation, they began the return journey, successfully evading a North Vietnamese patrol. Approaching the FOB, they came under heavy machine gun fire. Lieutenant Norris called in an air strike which provided suppression fire and a smoke screen, allowing the rescue party to reach the FOB. By his outstanding display of decisive leadership, undaunted courage, and selfless dedication in the face of extreme danger, Lieutenant Norris enhanced the finest traditions of the United States Naval Service.

★ ★ ★ ★ ★

April 11

Lieutenant Thomas R. Norris, SEAL Medal of Honor recipient. U.S. Navy

April 12

1969 (South Vietnam)—Working as part of a search-and-destroy operation on the Duong Keo River, a column of Swift boats (Patrol Craft, Fast [PCF]) comes under heavy attack from a VC ambush. As the column of boats slips through the kill zone, the VC gunners are able to concentrate their fire on fewer targets. The last Swift boat in the column, PCF 43, comes under the heaviest small arms and rocket fire. Disabled, the boat is turned into the bank of the river and beached rather than allowed to sink.

All crewmen and passengers man whatever weapons they can and fight back the VC. On board are members of UDT Thirteen and they fight the enemy as well as anyone can. The VC are held at bay for forty-five minutes of intense fighting. At one point, the fighting is so close that hand grenades are used effectively since the range is down to twenty meters. When the VC finally withdraw from the destroyed Swift boat, Chief Hospital Corpsman Robert Worthington of UDT Thirteen is killed, apparently by a B-40 rocket explosion.

April 13

1972 (South Vietnam)—Only once during the Vietnam War did a South Vietnamese receive the U.S. Navy Cross, this nation's second highest naval award for bravery and valor. The recipient is Nguyen Van Kiet, a South Vietnamese LDNN who trained with the U.S. Navy SEALs. Only two men—Lieutenant Thomas Norris and Kiet—are sent on an operation to recover a downed U.S. airman well behind enemy lines. Lieutenant Norris will later be the recipient of the Congressional Medal of Honor for his part in the operations, while Kiet received the Navy Cross. His citation reads as follows:

> *For extraordinary heroism while serving with friendly forces engaged in armed conflict against the North Vietnamese and Viet Cong, communist aggressors in the Republic of Vietnam. On 13 April 1972, Petty Officer Kiet participated in an unprecedented recovery operation for a downed United States aviator behind enemy lines in Quang Tri Province, Republic of Vietnam. He courageously volunteered to accompany a United States SEAL Advisor in an extremely*

hazardous attempt to reach the aviator, who was physically unable to move forward toward friendly positions. Using a sampan and traveling throughout the night, they silently made their way deep into enemy territory, past numerous enemy positions, locating the pilot at dawn. Once, after being spotted by a North Vietnamese patrol, he calmly continued to keep the enemy confused as the small party successfully evaded the patrol. Later, they were suddenly taken under heavy machine gun fire. Thinking first of the pilot, he quickly pulled the sampan to safety behind a bank and camouflaged it while air strikes were called in on the enemy position. Due to Petty Officer Kiet's coolness under extremely dangerous conditions and his outstanding courage and professionalism, an American aviator was recovered after an eleven-day ordeal behind enemy lines. His self-discipline, personal courage, and dynamic fighting spirit were an inspiration to all; thereby reflecting great credit upon himself and the Naval Service.

1987 (USA)—President Ronald Reagan approves the formation of the U.S. Special Operations Command (SOCOM).

April 14

1942 (South Asia)—OSS Detachment 101 is activated for service in the India-China-Burma theater.

1988 (Persian Gulf)—While on active patrol to maintain freedom of navigation and allow shipping to safely travel in the Persian Gulf, the guided missile frigate USS *Samuel B. Roberts* (FFG 58) spots three Iranian mines floating in the water about sixty-five miles east of Bahrain. While attempting to back away from the mines, the *Roberts* strikes a fourth mine, which detonates. The huge blast from the 253 pounds of high explosive tears a thirty-by-twenty-three-foot hole in the port side of the ship's hull below the engine room, causing extensive fires and flooding. Ten sailors are injured in the explosion. Immediate massive damage and fire control by the ship's crew keep the vessel afloat.

April 15

1943 (England)—The specialized training program to attack specific targets for the NCDUs and additional units gets underway at Appledore, England. The NCDUs have been assigned to Gap Assault Teams (GATs) for their upcoming operations in the invasion of Europe. The units have been broken up into three groups, with the first two groups being designated as "Force C" and the third as "Force U." Each group is made up of eleven GATs. Each individual GAT has thirteen men: a five-man NCDU, five army engineers, and three seamen sent from a pool of men in Scotland. In addition, each group has a unit of twenty-six army troops who will operate in support of the main group in clearing the beach during the invasion operation.

Much of the training of the new GATs is to get the men to operate effectively together and to learn to use the demolition techniques that had been developed specifically for the European invasion. The Hagensen pack, a two-pound charge of Composition Two (C-2) plastic explosive, is made up of the charge held in a cloth bag with a length of detonating cord buried in the explosive to detonate the charge. A length of the detonating cord lead runs from one end of the charge for attaching it to a main trunk line. A length of cord is attached to the charge with a flat metal hook on one end. The cord is used to secure the Hagensen pack to the target obstacle. It was such a convenient and useful explosive charge that it has remained in the inventory of Naval Special Warfare with few changes other than as an update of the explosive filler.

1960 (USA)—The Twentieth Special Forces Group is activated.

April 16

1945 (China)—The OSS First Chinese Commando begins training.

1987 (USA)—The USSOCOM is activated at McDill Air Force Base in Tampa, Florida. SOCOM will be commanded by a four-star flag or general officer who will direct all of the special operations forces in the U.S. military united under the single SOCOM command umbrella. Close to fifty thousand enlisted men and officers from the army, navy, and air force special operations units work together as a joint special operations force.

April 17

1945 (Pacific)—UDT Four is asked by the beachmaster in command of the invasion beach to blast improvements into the Blue T-1 Beaches on Ie Shima. Heavy Japanese sniper fire from the trees and brush of the island prevent the UDT operators from completing the demolition operation.

1961 (Cuba)—The attempted overthrow of the Communist government of Cuba takes place when over 1,300 Cuban exiles land on Cuba's southern coast at the Bay of Pigs. Combat swimmers trained by American UDT operators move in to shore at 0200 hours to begin the invasion. By 0300, two battalions of exiles from the Brigada Asalto 2506 have landed on shore. A third battalion lands nearby. Over 20,000 Cuban troops surround the invaders, capturing over a thousand of them. The invasion is a complete failure, due in no small part to the lack of active air support coming from the U.S. military during the invasion. This lack of support is by the direct instructions of President John F. Kennedy.

April 18

1945 (Pacific)—Operators from UDT Four conduct a demolition operation to improve the landing capabilities of the Red T-3 Beach on Ie Shima near Okinawa. In addition, a channel is blasted and marked with buoys on the left flank of Blue T-3 Beach on the same island. During the Blue T-3 operation, the men of the UDT only run into light sniper fire from the Japanese troops in the jungle.

1983 (Lebanon)—A terrorist suicide truck bomb is directed against the U.S. embassy in Beruit by agents of Hizbollah ("Party of God"), a radical Shiite terrorist group formed in Lebanon the year before. At 1300 hours local time, a van loaded with high explosives drives past the marine guard at the embassy gate and smashes into the building before exploding. The huge blast destroys the main portion of the embassy building, killing 63 people and injuring more than 100.

1988 (Persian Gulf)—Operation Praying Mantis is initiated. It is a calculated response to Iranian minelaying in the Persian Gulf, which resulted in damage to the ship USS *Samuel B. Roberts* (FFG 58) less than a week earlier. At 0755 hours local time, the U.S. Navy commander on site issues a warning, in both English and Farsi, for the Iranian crew to abandon the Sassan oil platform. Twenty-nine Iranians in two tugboats leave it as well as other platforms. Then, five minutes after the warning is issued, the navy ships open fire. A handful of Iranians return fire from the platform with their ZU-23mm antiaircraft cannon. The Iranian gun position is quickly silenced. A landing party aboard the platform goes after the remaining Irainan crew and evacuates it. Antiaircraft guns, ammunition, communications equipment, and RPG rounds are found on the platform. After the search, the platform is destroyed with explosives.

At 0815 hours, roughly the same procedure is conducted by another group of American ships at the oil platform Sirri. A number of Iranian warships and gunboats rampage through the Persian Gulf waters in retaliation for Operation Praying Mantis. By the end of the day, half of the operational ships of the Iranian navy have been either destroyed or put out of commission.

April 19

1945 (Pacific)—As requested by the beachmaster, the men of UDT Four return to the waters off Blue T-1 Beach on Ie Shima to blast the channel. The Japanese sniper fire comes from the jungle and has lessened considerably from what it had been a few days earlier; the UDT swimmers are successful in blasting the required channel through the reef.

1991 (Iraq)—A number of SEAL and other naval forces participate in Operation Provide Comfort. Food and relief materials are to be carried into the Kurdish refugee camps in the mountain areas of Iraq during the operation. Marine units conduct security for a number of Kurdish refugee and relocation camps along the Turkish border with Iraq. The SEAL detachment assigned to Provide Comfort, which consists of two SEAL platoons, conducts long-range reconnaissance efforts into Iraq. This will increase the security of the Kurdish camps. The SEALs also maintain their active search-and-rescue mission for downed Coalition pilots that they had conducted so successfully during Operation Desert Storm only a few months before.

2002 (USA)—SEAL Team Ten of Naval Special Warfare Group Two is commissioned in Little Creek, Virginia.

April 20

The symbol of the Special Operations Command, surrounded by symbols of the unit commands that make it up. At the 10 o'clock position is the patch of the Army Rangers, at the 2 o'clock position is the U.S. Navy Special Warfare Command shield, at the 4 o'clock position is the Joint Special Operations Command shield, and at the 7 o'clock position is the shield of the Air Force Special Operations Command. U.S. SOCOM PAO

April 21

1968 (South Vietnam)—SEAL Team Two's Eighth Platoon conducts a patrol and canal ambush. The patrol is inserted shortly after dusk and patrols to find a canal with a hut nearby. The SEALs secure it and establish an ambush over the canal in front of the hut. At 2245 hours, two Vietnamese fishermen in a sampan are observed in the canal passing in front of the hut. The fishermen have a lamp illuminating the water and make a very obvious target of themselves. The SEALs simply let the men continue on with their work in safety. At 0200 hours, the SEALs call in their extraction PBR and leave the area, considering that there has been negative contact with the enemy. The VC forces in the Mekong Delta region have taken a severe beating during their abortive Tet offensive and a number of SEAL missions are coming up dry with no contact with the enemy.

April 22

1970s (USA)—The Convair Model 14, a swimmer delivery vehicle, has been accepted by the navy as the Mark VII Mod 2 SEAL Delivery Vehicle (SDV). It begins combat use in 1969. The Mark VII is a large, heavy, fiberglass-hulled wet-type vehicle that can carry a crew of two and two additional passengers or equipment for an extended ride underwater. Because the boat is of the wet type, the interior is flooded with water when in use. This requires the crew and passengers to wear breathing equipment while underwater in the SDV.

Operational testing and evaluations by the UDTs and the SEALs result in a number of changes in the boat's design. These modifications result in the Mark VII Mod 6 SDV being made available in the very early 1970s. The SDV is soon known as the "Six boat" by the men of the UDTs and SEAL teams who operate it.

The Six boat is eighteen feet, six inches long, has a beam of thirty-five inches, and a draft of fifty-seven inches. The weight of the boat is over 2,200 pounds and includes six silver-zinc batteries that drive the 1.83 horsepower motor. The single five-bladed propeller can push the Six boat through the water for eight hours at four knots. Such a ride is long, cold, dark, and uncomfortable for the passengers who have nothing to do but wait in the dark. The situation is little better for the pilot (driver) and navigator. They have work to do during the trip, but the lack of physical movement prevents the men from being able to warm themselves up very easily.

April 23

1967 (South Vietnam)—Fire Team Five of SEAL Team One's Detachment Golf conducts a daylight reconnaissance patrol on the far southern tip of the Rung Sat Special Zone, almost on the shore of the South China Sea in Gia Dinh Province. The area is mostly mangrove swamps but in spite of the swamp location is partially dry. As the SEALs patrol, they find little in the way of fresh indications that the VC have been using the area. A single small base camp is found, consisting of one large and three small bunkers. But the camp appears to have been unused for a month or more and no enemy forces are encountered.

1972 (South Vietnam)—The evolution of the gunship concept first proven in Vietnam by the AC-47, a minigun-armed C-47 cargo plane, reached its zenith during the Vietnam War in the form of the AC-130 gunship. Converted from the very successful C-130 Hercules cargo plane, the AC-130 carried an incredible load of firepower. Two 20mm M61 Vulcan cannons, each capable of firing up to 6,000 rounds per minute, were located in the forward section of the aircraft. Behind the Vulcans were two 7.62mm miniguns, also capable of firing at rates of up to 6,000 rounds per minute. Toward the rear of the AC-130 is a 40mm Bofors M1A1 cannon and, for a very heavy punch, the 105mm M2A1 howitzer—the largest gun carried on a modern aircraft. These awesome aircraft had the call sign "Spectre."

As a forward element of the South Vietnamese military sighted a column of thirty North Vietnamese tanks and vehicles approaching, a Pave Aegis AC-130E gunship was called in. Positively identifying ten tanks and additional enemy vehicles, the Spectre gunship opened fire with its 105mm cannon, destroying one tank and damaging four more.

1980 (Iran)—Operation Eagle Claw, the military action to rescue U.S. hostages held in Teheran begins. Men from the U.S. Army Special Forces Operational Detachment Delta (Delta Force) move to rescue the fifty-two American hostages who have been held for almost half a year.

April 24

1980 (Iran)—During Operation Eagle Claw, the mission to free U.S. hostages held in Teheran, five Special Forces troopers are killed at Desert One Base.

April 25

1968 (South Vietnam)—During a twelve-hour ambush operation, SEAL Team One's Bravo Platoon Squad One runs into an unusual situation with the VC. The squad has been inserted by Mike boat into an area where the primary terrain feature is nipa palm. Once the SEALs establish their ambush site, they settle in and later observe fire about seventy-five meters south of their position. Following the gunfire, the SEALs hear the VC trying to imitate them on the radio: the VC are trying to convince the Mike boat that the SEALs want an emergency extraction, which would quickly lead to a VC ambush. The trick doesn't work, however, and the SEALs extract from the area soon afterward. The lesson learned from the mission is to be sure to change radio frequencies often and to use call signs that are used only by the SEALs.

1980 (Iran)—C-130 aircraft and Navy RH-53D helicopters arrive at Desert One, the covert refueling base in the Iranian desert. It has been set up as forward support for Operation Eagle Claw, the rescue of American hostages held in Teheran. A sandstorm puts several helicopters out of commission and the officer in charge is forced to abort the mission—too few operational helicopters are left to complete the mission. During the takeoff of the American assets from Desert One, a helicopter collides with a tanker aircraft, causing a huge fire; it kills five airmen and three soldiers. The mission becomes a disaster as four helicopters are left behind. The American rescue unit withdraws from the area.

April 26

1971 (USA)—SEAL Team One receives the second of three Presidential Unit Citations; it is awarded for its actions in Vietnam. The citation reads:

> By virtue of the authority vested in me as President of the United States and as Commander-in-Chief of the Armed Forces of the United States, I have today awarded
>
> ### THE PRESIDENTIAL UNIT CITATION (NAVY)
> ### FOR EXTRAORDINARY HEROISM TO
> ### SEAL TEAM ONE
>
> *For extraordinary heroism and outstanding performance of duty from 22 January 1968 to 20 May 1969 in connection with counterinsurgency operations against enemy forces in the Republic of Vietnam. Operating under the most trying and rigorous of warfare environments, invariably within enemy territory and virtually without communication or support from other allied forces, the various small detachments of SEAL Team ONE consistently demonstrated outstanding courage, teamwork, and resourcefulness in carrying out over 350 extremely hazardous combat missions, including combat area sweeps, demolition raids, search and seizures, and interdiction of lines of communications and supply routes. These actions resulted in the infliction of heavy casualties upon enemy forces, the severance of enemy lines of communications, the capture or destruction of large quantities of ammunitions and supplies, the collection of vitally important intelligence data, and the destruction of numerous enemy sampans, junks, and fortifications. The significant record of accomplishment achieved by SEAL Team ONE attests to the bravery, professionalism, esprit de corps, and dedication of the individual officers and men of this unique combat unit. Their exemplary and inspiring performance of duty contributed substantially to the overall United States effort in the Republic of Vietnam, reflected great credit upon themselves, and was in keeping with the highest traditions of the United States Naval Service.*
>
> Richard Nixon

April 27

1966 (South Vietnam)—Detachment Delta of UDT Eleven conducts a reconnaissance of the Phu Loc area in Thua Thien Province, twenty miles north of Danang. The Phu Loc district and the city of Phu Loc are located near a huge protected bay that connects directly with the South China Sea. The recon by the UDT operators is in support of Operation Osage, which consists of the insertion of marine amphibious units intended to hit the VC by surprise and in areas that they have previously thought are unapproachable. The actions of the operation do not catch much in the way of enemy forces, as such; the results of OSAGE are considered very disappointing by the higher command. The technique of amphibious landings along the shores of South Vietnam are continued through several more series of operations.

April 28

1969—The Navy Seawolves eventually become one of the most decorated units in naval aviation history. A large number of Airman's Medals are given according to the regulations and point system that have been written primarily for aircraft carrier pilots who just didn't fly as many sorties as the Seawolves did. This results in a large number of the Airman's Medal being awarded to Seawolves due to the point system. It is not unusual to have men return from a tour of duty with the Seawolves in Vietnam with two award certificates for Airman's Medals: one for the awarding of the decoration and the other for the second through twentieth or more awards for the same decoration. More than 16,000 Airman's Medals alone are awarded to the Seawolves. But the incredible actions of the pilots and crews of the Seawolves also earn much higher awards as the following citation for the U.S. Navy Cross reads for Petty Officer Lloyd T. Williams Jr.:

CITATION

For extraordinary heroism on 28 April 1969 while serving as a crew chief and door gunner with Helicopter Attack (Light) Squadron Three, Detachment Three, during a strike mission against enemy sampans in the Republic of Vietnam.

When the wing aircraft was struck by ground fire and crashed, and his own aircraft was also struck and forced to land, Petty Officer Williams calmly directed the preparations for forced landing while continuing to return the enemy fire. After his aircraft had landed and the crew had abandoned it, he advanced toward the enemy under heavy fire and established a defensive position on the path leading to the enemy positions. Observing a crewmember from the crashed wing aircraft moving in the midst of the wreckage, Petty Officer Williams exposed himself to the blistering fire and ran across an open field to rescue the casualty. After carrying the severely injured man across the open field to an area near the defensive perimeter, Petty Officer Williams returned to the wreckage in an attempt to find others from its crew. Obliged to suppress enemy fire in order to conduct his search, he persisted in his rescue attempts, despite the heat from the fire and the dangers of exploding ammunition, until his ammunition was exhausted. Petty Officer Williams then ran to the defensive perimeter to report that the enemy had started using mortars, and proceeded to assist a casualty aboard a rescue helicopter before boarding the craft himself to render first aid to the other wounded. Petty Officer Williams' determined efforts, his indomitable courage under fire, and his inspiring devotion to duty were in keeping with the highest traditions of the United States Naval Service.

April 29

1968 (Vietnam)—As a new weapon, first used by the SEALs in 1967, the Stoner has had some teething problems. These problems have resulted in a number of improvements suggested by the SEALs who use it operationally in the very harsh environment of the Vietnamese wetlands. Some improvements are the result of use and observation, others come at a very high cost.

In 1968, Mike Platoon of SEAL Team One's Detachment Golf is inserted to conduct an operation in Kien Hoa Province. Boatswain's Mate First Class Walter Pope is armed with a Stoner light machine gun loaded with a 150-round belt carried in an aluminum ammunition drum underneath the weapon. The drum is a popular item among a number of SEALs as it fully protects the belt of ammunition, covering it completely from the carry point underneath the weapon to where it feeds into the receiver. When the Stoner is recommended for further purchase in May 1967, the order for thirty-six Stoner 63A models is held up until the aluminum ammunition drum becomes available.

The Stoner fires from the open-bolt position, meaning that the bolt of the weapon is pulled back and held in place by the sear until the trigger is pulled. When it goes forward, it strips a round from the ammunition belt and chambers and fires it.

Pope stacks his Stoner up against the side of the boat his squad is traveling in as he sits down next to it. Some vibration of the boat causes the weapon to fall over and the retaining pin at the rear of the receiver mechanism falls out. With the receiver pivoting away from the trigger mechanism, the sear is separated from the bolt, slipping forward, and the gun starts firing. Without the sear being in place to stop the bolt, the gun just keeps firing. The aluminum drum, which keeps the belt covered, can't be grabbed and broken to stop the gun.

As the gun falls and starts firing, Boatswain's Mate Third Class Frank Toms is laying on the deck nearby. Toms is immediately struck with six to ten bullets from the runaway gun. He is severely wounded but he will respond to the quick treatment from his teammates and will eventually recover. Pope is not so lucky as he sacrifices himself to save his teammates.

Grabbing up the runaway gun, Pope pulls it into his chest to try to stop the gun or at least control it. He takes an estimated forty rounds from the weapon and is killed instantly. His actions prevent the gun from injuring or killing any of his teammates in the insertion boat.

Further acquisition of the Stoner is suspended by the navy until a new locking pin is developed and available for all the weapons in the SEALs' inventory. The cost of the lesson is high and Toms, among others, feel that Pope deserves a decoration for his actions.

April 30

1945 (Italy)—Just two days before a cease-fire is declared in Italy, Colonel William Darby is mortally wounded during a German artillery attack. He had organized the First, Third, and Fourth U.S. Army Ranger Battalions and was the commanding officer of the 6615th Ranger Regiment that was composed of the three Ranger battalions.

1962 (Caribbean)—Sharing the Caribbean island of Hispaniola with Haiti is the Dominican Republic. In 1965, a revolution of rebel factions in the military of the Dominican Republic overthrows the Ried Cabral government in a military coup. Unable to complete their seizure of control, the rebels cause a power vacuum in the country, raising fears in the United States of a possible Communist takeover of the country by forces from nearby Cuba.

In 1965, a small detachment of five enlisted SEALs under the command of Lieutenant Georg Doran boards the USS *La Salle* (LPD 3) for deployment to the Dominican Republic. Very soon after their arrival on the island country, two SEALs, Doran and Jack Rowell, are called away to conduct a covert mission elsewhere on the island. The two SEALs dress in civilian clothes and are assigned a U.S. Army Special Forces sergeant as interpreters. The three men then conduct a on-site examination of caves surrounding Samona Bay. No rebel arms caches are found and the worst thing actually faced by the SEALs is a recalcitrant boat engine that causes them to spend a very long night in rebel territory.

1975 (South Vietnam)—At 1015 hours local time, South Vietnamese president Duong Van Minh, who has only been holding the post for two days, declares that he is ready to transfer power to the North Vietnamese–backed Provisional Revolutionary government. By noon, Communist forces enter Saigon.

MAY

A UDT operator stands watch over a small stream in South Vietnam. While their teammate stands guard, the rest of the UDT detachment are preparing to demolish a Viet Cong bunker with explosives. U.S. Navy

May 01

1944 (England)—Special Forces Headquarters, G3 SHAEF, is established in the United Kingdom.

1961 (USA)—The Sixteenth, Nineteenth, and Twenty-first Special Forces Groups are activated.

1983 (USA)—All UDTs are officially decommissioned. Due to a major reorganization of Naval Special Warfare, the manpower from the prior UDTs is absorbed directly into new SEAL teams. The mission of the UDTs, beach and hydrographic reconnaissance and obstacle clearing, becomes one of the official missions of the SEAL teams in addition to their land operations. The change increases the flexibility and simplifies manning. Respectively, UDTs Eleven and Twenty become SEAL Teams Five and Four. UDTs Twelve and Twenty-two become SEAL Delivery Vehicle (SDV) Teams One and Two.

   The new SDV teams concentrate their efforts and training to develop and supply a long-range underwater transportation system for the SEAL teams. The SDVs are wet-type (filled with water and require individual breathing systems) submersible vehicles. All members of the SDV teams are fully qualified SEALs who receive extensive training in piloting, navigating, and supporting both the SDVs as well as the later Dry Deck Shelters (DDS), which can be attached to the deck of a modified nuclear submarine to give it amphibious, clandestine transportation capability.

May 02

1944 (England)—Jedburgh teams leave the United Kingdom for North Africa.

1964 (South Vietnam)—At 0515 hours local time, VC combat swimmer/sappers mine the USS *Card* (AKV 40), a World War II–era Bogue-class aircraft ferry. The *Card* has delivered a load of combat aircraft and helicopters at the Saigon waterfront. The mines blast a twenty-eight-foot hole in the starboard side of the hull of the ship, flooding the engine room but causing no casualties. The *Card* settles to the bottom of Saigon in forty-eight feet of water. A group of LDNN swimmers examine the hull and determine the type, size, and location of the mines used by the VC to attack the *Card*. The VC sappers apparently approached to within striking distance of the *Card* by traveling through the Saigon sewers. The *Card* is refloated and towed to the Philippines by May 20.

1972 (North Vietnam)—At exactly noon local time, two SR-71s over Hanoi break the sound barrier, one exactly ten seconds after the other. The huge, black reconnaissance planes fly recon operations over North Vietnam on a regular basis, operating out of their base on Okinawa. The nearly spacecraft-like SR-71 flies at over 2,000 miles per hour at an altitude of 80,000 feet. For this very unusual mission, the SR-71s are traveling at 75,000 feet, well out of the range of North Vietnamese interceptor aircraft or missiles, and do not break Mach 1 until they are over Hanoi at exactly the right time. The sonic booms heard below are signals to a group of American POWs that their smuggled messages have been received and understood. A rescue operation to pick up the escaped prisoners will be set up as Operation Thunderhead, one of the most ambitious operations of the Vietnam War.

May 03

1969 (South Vietnam)—One of the regular weapons of the VC is the booby trap. The fiendish devices can be designed to either kill or maim. The military axiom that it takes more soldiers to care for a wounded comrade than a dead one is not lost on the VC. Dud U.S. munitions are fuzed with contact, pressure, pull, or other firing devices and placed where they have the best chance of being fired by an unwary individual. The VC have subtle signs, such as bent branches, piles of pebbles, and so on, that they place in an area indicating where the booby trap is located and what type of device it is.

The SEALs learn what many of these signals and signs are, but sometimes they are missed. On January 14, 1969, Signalman First Class David Wilson from SEAL Team One's Charlie Platoon is killed by a booby trap that is later determined to have been a dud 105mm Howitzer round.

But booby traps can also be nonexplosive, and very simple as well. The simplest and most common booby trap in Vietnam is the punji pit. This is a simple hole in the ground that is covered by a light thatched frame that breaks easily when someone steps on it. At the bottom of the pit are punji stakes, sharpened slivers of bamboo; the sliced material of the bamboo gives the stake a razor edge. To increase the effectiveness of the punji stakes, they are often covered with some kind of biological material that will quickly cause a wound to fester and become infected in the jungle environment. Punji pits and stakes are fast and cheap to make and are found all over South Vietnam.

May 04

1943 (USA)—The OSS Operational Group Branch is established by Special Order 21.

1967 (South Vietnam)—Working at the far southern end of the Rung Sat Special Zone, within a very short distance of the South China Sea, Fire Team Six of SEAL Team One's Detachment Golf is inserted by helicopter. It will conduct a reconnaissance patrol, listening post, and demolition raid. The SEAL squad slips into dry farmland, well above sea level. Searching the area, the SEALs find thirteen fresh water wells, a single line of punji stakes, and a number of bunkers. An armed, but unplanted, U.S.-manufactured land mine is found inside one of the bunkers. The mine has probably been dug up and moved by a VC sapper.

The bunkers appear to the SEALs to have been made by U.S. forces. There is no contact with the enemy on the operation and, since the local farmers use the fresh water wells, they are left intact by the SEALs. Extraction is made by helicopter the following morning at 1000 hours.

1972 (North Vietnam)—In a repeat of their mission two days earlier, two SR-71s over Hanoi break the sound barrier at exactly noon and ten seconds past noon. The two loud sonic booms are a signal to American POWs held at the Hanoi Hilton prison camp, fourteen miles below the speeding aircraft. The POWs now have four to six weeks to break out of the prison and make their way down the Red River in North Vietnam. On the banks of the Gulf of Tonkin, the forces of Operation Thunderhead watch for the POWs' signal to pick them up and relieve them from captivity.

May 05

1951 (Korea)—The Eighth Army G3 guerrilla section becomes the 8086th Army Unit.

1980 (England)—The Twenty-second SAS B Squadron conducts Operation Nimrod, an assault against the terrorist-held Iranian embassy at 16 Princes Gate in the Knightsbridge area of London. This is the first major counterterrorist action to be widely seen by the public as a large number of news services and camera operators witness the action as the SAS troopers blast their way into the beseiged building. The embassy and hostages have been held for six days by six terrorists from the Democratic Movement for the Liberation of Arabistan.

May 06

1943 (USA)—A careful examination of the beaches of Europe, along with an analysis of expected German fortifications, causes the creation of a new unit trained specifically to deal with beach obstacles and demolitions. Admiral Ernest J. King, the chief of naval operations, signs and issues a two-part directive intended to address the obstacle clearance problems. The first part of the directive is written to allow for the necessary manpower to address the problem. The target and mission, the opening of a European front, are still very highly classified and no direct language regarding it is used.

The second part of the directive calls for two missions to be fulfilled. The first is to develop the necessary skills, techniques, and materials to conduct demolition operations and obstacle clearance. The second is for the training of permanent "Navy Demolition Units" for the removal of underwater obstacles.

1969 (South Vietnam)—Australian Warrant Officer Second Class Raymond S. Simpson, who is attached to the Fifth Special Forces Group, performs actions that later result in his receiving the Victoria Cross posthumously.

May 07

1954 (Southeast Asia)—The French are defeated in Indochina with the surrender of the garrison at Dien Bien Phu after a long siege by the Vietminh forces. Within a few months, the Geneva Accords are signed by both sides of the conflict, separating the country at the seventeenth parallel and establishing a demilitarized zone to act as a buffer between what is now North and South Vietnam. A referendum in 1956 approves the formation of the Republic of South Vietnam with Ngo Dinh Diem as its president. Within a year of taking office, Diem refuses to accept an election among the people intended to reunify the country. The Communist leadership in North Vietnam still expects to reunify the country, especially after a patient war of guerrilla factions in the South eventually causes the collapse of its government.

1958 (USA)—Converted during its construction as an attack submarine to one of two in a new class of missile launching boats, the USS *Grayback* (SSG 574) is commissioned. The conversion of the attack submarine design adds fifty feet to the length of the *Grayback* and its sister ship, the USS *Growler* (SSG 577). But the most noticeable part of the conversion to the missile submarine is the addition of two large sealed hangars on the upper part of the bow. The hangers are accessible from inside the submarine and the large cavities—eleven feet in diameter and seventy feet long—are to hold the Regulus II missile.

To fire a missile, the *Grayback* will surface, its hangars will be opened, and the Regulus II missile inside will be removed on a trolley and prepared for launch. The modifications to its original design make the *Grayback* the largest conventionally powered diesel-electric submarine in the world. And it has the unique capability to lay quietly on the bottom for as long as its batteries will last, still able to run the necessary machinery.

The Regulus II is a winged missile and can be armed with a nuclear warhead, making the *Grayback* the first nuclear missile boat in the U.S. Navy. After nine active deterrent missile cruises aboard the *Grayback*, the Regulus II is removed from the active U.S. nuclear arsenal as being too large, inaccurate, and undependable. The new Polaris missile launching submarine is becoming available in 1960 and quickly replaces the *Grayback*'s nuclear deterrent role.

1989 (Panama)—Democratic elections are held. General Manuel Noriega over-turns the results of the election and prepares to declare himself "President for Life."

May 08

1943 (USA)—Within a short time of the directive—issued from the Chief of Naval Operations office for the creation of Navy Demolition Units—an officer is chosen to create the training school for the new organization. Lieutenant Com-mander Draper Kauffman is married less than a week when he receives the orders to report to the Pentagon. Kauffman sets up the Navy Bomb and Mine Disposal School at the Washington Navy Yard. He has extensive experience in explosive ordinance disposal (EOD), having volunteered for operations with an EOD unit in England during the German bombing campaign there. After Pearl Harbor, Kauffman received the first of his two Navy Crosses for rendering safe a Japanese 500-pound bomb for examination.

Kauffman first looks for officer volunteers for his new training organiza-tion and units at the Bomb and Mine Disposal School. The most explosive-experience enlisted men are to be found among the ranks of the former powder men, hard-rock miners, and construction engineers of the Seabees. For a training center, Kauffman chooses the relatively obscure and hard to approach area of Fort Pierce, Florida, and the Amphibious Training Base there. The Scouts and Raiders who are already conducting training at Fort Pierce are able to help Kauffman and his staff start up what will eventually become the hardest course of training in the U.S. Navy. The Naval Combat Demolition Unit School and the NCDUs it creates are the direct ancestors of today's SEAL teams. And over time, the course of training at Fort Pierce will become known as Basic Underwater Demolition/SEAL (BUD/S) Training.

1945 (Europe)—Victory in Europe (VE) Day. After more than five long years of war, Nazi Germany is defeated. The thousand-year Reich lies in ashes, along with what is left of its leader Adolf Hitler. The unconditional surrender of Ger-many is signed on May 7 and all hostile operations end at 2301 hours May 8. The battle for the Pacific and the defeat of the Japanese empire are still to come.

May 09

1969 (USA)—After a long refit, the diesel-electric submarine USS *Grayback* (LPSS 574) is recommissioned and is sent to join the Seventh Fleet in the Pacific. Converted into an amphibious transport submarine, the *Grayback* has the capability to support up to sixty-seven UDT or SEAL operators (sixty enlisted and seven officers). The two large bow hangars on the *Grayback*, originally intended for the transport of the Regulus II missile, are accessible and operable from inside the submarine while it is submerged. Inside the cavernous hangars can be up to eight inflatable rubber boats or four SDVs. Once on site in the west Pacific, the *Grayback* relieves the USS *Tunny* (APSS 282) in its operations to support the UDT detachments operating from the Philippines and off Vietnam.

May 10

1967 (USA)—One of the items desired by the SEALs in Vietnam is a suppressed pistol. They don't necessarily want this for taking out enemy sentries or for conducting assassinations; instead, the suppressed pistol is used for the quiet elimination of village dogs and geese who act as a primitive and very effective alarm system. Beginning in 1966, the Navy Surface Ordnance Center in White Oak, Maryland, begins the development of a suppressed pistol, eventually to be mounted on the Smith and Wesson Model 39 9mm automatic pistol that is already in SEAL hands. By the end of 1967, what becomes available to the SEALs is the Mark 22 Mod 0 Pistol and the Mark 3 Mod 0 noise suppressor.

A disposable cylinder containing flexible plastic wipes is inserted into the Mark 3 suppressor. With the suppressor mounted in place on the threaded, extended barrel of the Mark 22 pistol, the Mark 23 Mod 0 suppressed pistol is made. A pair of slide locks on either side of the pistol hold the slide forward when the weapon is fired. The plastic wipes in the suppressor allow the bullet to pass but slow the escaping propellant gases, which will make the sound of the gunshot if they simply escape into the air.

The quiet pistol is issued with a kit containing sealing and maintenance materials, a suppressor insert, and sixteen rounds of special heavy-bullet subsonic ammunition. With the special ammunition, there isn't even a sonic "crack" from the bullet passing through the air. The weapon is nicknamed the "Hush-Puppy" for its ostensible use to silence guard dogs. Though it was popular with the SEALs and remained in use well into the 1980s, there never were enough of them so that one was available for every operation.

May 11

1961 (Vietnam)—President John F. Kennedy approves the sending of 400 additional Special Forces personnel to Vietnam.

May 12

1968 (South Vietnam)—While leading a unit of fifty-three men from his PRU on a mission in Vinh Binh Province, the SEAL advisor, Storekeeper Second Class Ronald Zillgitt, is killed as his unit comes under attack. The PRU is trying to counterattack a large group of VC that has overrun the hamlet Giang Lon. The PRU comes under heavy enemy fire shortly after being inserted by helicopter near the hamlet. The unit is pinned down in a rice paddy by heavy fire and is in great danger of being overrun. Zillgitt directs his men in the defense and leads two counterattacks against the surrounding VC. It is during the second counterattack that Zillgitt is wounded and killed. The PRU continues aggressive action against the surrounding enemy and eventually drives the VC away. Not, however, before killing seventeen VC. It is leadership by SEALs such as Zillgitt that helps make the PRUs an effective force to eliminate the VC infrastructure in the province.

May 13

1969 (South Vietnam)—Sometimes even the SEALs can be rained out of a game by the weather in South Vietnam.

1969 (South Vietnam)—And sometimes it's just a matter of luck.

BARNDANCE # __8 - 19__   SEAL TEAM __2__ ; DET. __ALFA__ ; __8th__ PLT.

DATE(S): __13 May 1969,__   OTHER UNITS: __MST 2, LDNN,__

MSG REF(S): _____

NAMES OF PERS: __LTjg Schutzman, Tuure, Matthews, Finley, Evancoe, Porter, Shoulders__
__McMahon__

MISSION TASK: __Ambush__

INTEL/INFO SOURCE(S): __Agent__

INSERTION: TIME: __1300__   METHOD: __WATER TAXI__   AMS COORD: _____

EXTRACTION: TIME: __1800__   METHOD: __LCM__   AMS COORD: _____

TERRAIN: __Banana groves/ Fields__
WEATHER: __Fair/ heavy rain__   TIDE/SURF: __high__   MOON: _____

BRIEF MISSION NARRATIVE: __Patrolled 300 M. South, 100 M. West and set trail ambush__
__heavy rains came over area at 1710, broke ambush at 1740 and patrolled to river__
__for extraction.__

FRIENDLY PERS/MATERIAL CASUALTIES: __NONE__

ENEMY PERS/MATERIAL CASUALTIES: __NONE__

REMARKS (SIGNIFICANT EVENTS, OPEVAL RESULTS, ETC.): __Rain was so dense, had to pop__
__mk 13 night flare for rendezvous/ extraction.__

RECOMMENDATIONS/LESSONS LEARNED:: _____

BD COPY DIST: _____

(FORM REV. 4/69)   BARNDANCE # __8 - 19__

BARNDANCE # 8 - 20   SEAL TEAM __2__ ; DET. __ALFA__ ; __8th__ PLT.

DATE(S): 13 May 69   OTHER UNITS: LDNN

MSG REF(S): _____

NAMES OF PERS: Thuan , Tu _____

MISSION TASK: APPREHENDED KNOWN VC

INTEL/INFO SOURCE(S): __AGENT__

INSERTION: TIME: o800   METHOD: _____ AMS COORD: _____

EXTRACTION: TIME: 0830   METHOD: _____ AMS COORD: _____

TERRAIN: city of My Tho

WEATHER: clear   TIDE/SURF: _____ MOON: _____

BRIEF MISSION NARRATIVE: 2 LDNN in coffee shop recognized VC as he passed, apprehended and turned over to authorities.

FRIENDLY PERS/MATERIAL CASUALTIES: None

ENEMY PERS/MATERIAL CASUALTIES: None

REMARKS (SIGNIFICANT EVENTS, OPEVAL RESULTS, ETC.): one VC captured and turned over to QC

RECOMMENDATIONS/LESSONS LEARNED:

BD COPY DIST: _____

(FORM REV. 4/69)   BARNDANCE # 8 - 20

May 14

1943 (USA)—The OSS Operational Group A is activated.

1968 (South Vietnam)—Eighth Platoon of SEAL Team Two's Detachment Alfa is conducting a large number of successful operations throughout its tour in Vietnam. After setting up an ambush on a suspected VC infiltration route from Cambodia, Eighth Platoon almost runs out of luck. Instead of engaging a small VC force by ambush, the SEALs find themselves facing an eighty-two-man force that is well trained and well armed. Taking cover in a graveyard, the SEALs move from tombstone to tombstone as the Communist force tries to overrun their position. The SEALs beat back the enemy each time it makes a run at the graveyard over the course of four hours. Just as ammunition is beginning to run low, the Seawolf helicopter gunships called in by the SEALs arrive on the scene.

   The remaining enemy forces are driven back across the Cambodian border as the Seawolves add their own fire and artillery support is brought to bear. A large percentage of the enemy forces are killed or wounded, with twenty-four enemy known dead and forty more wounded.

May 15

1964 (South Vietnam)—Project Leaping Lena is established to provide forces that can conduct long-range reconnissance missions well behind enemy lines in Southeast Asia. The six-man units that conduct these missions are called Long-Range Reconnaissance Patrols (LRRPs).

1968 (South Vietnam)—An insertion goes badly for SEAL Team One's Mike Platoon of Detachment Golf during a night operation. The mission is on patrol to a suspected VC cadre. The moon is bright and the SEALs begin to insert with no enemy forces in sight. A sudden explosion at the bow of the boat throws everyone aboard out of place. The small landing craft being used as the insertion platform is immediately extracted and returned to the APL boat that has transported the SEALs and their support forces to the location. Petty Officer First Class Nonnie Patrick is killed and seven more SEALs and one Vietnamese are injured. The cause of the explosion is determined by Intelligence to have been a rifle grenade or a large hand-thrown grenade. The SEALs themselves, however, believe they might have struck a mine or other type of booby trap.

May 16

1964 (South Vietnam)—Detachment B-52, Fifth Special Forces Group, nicknamed Project Delta, is activated.

1965 (Carribean)—As the rebel fighting in the Dominican Republic heats up, an additional detachment of three SEAL officers and ten enlisted men from SEAL Team Two are flown to the island. This gives SEAL Team Two three operational platoons in the republic during the crisis.

Armed with the new AR-15 rifle, the SEALs see firsthand the destructive power of what will soon be known as the M16A1 rifle. There are a number of fire fights between the SEALs and the rebels who are trying to control the city of Santo Domingo.

1968 (South Vietnam)—A squad from SEAL Team Two's Eighth Platoon, Detachment Alfa, leads a PRU into a heavy engagement with enemy forces that have been conducting 82mm mortar attacks against the city of Chau Doc. A heavy force of helicopter gunships, including Seawolves and Army Cobras, has been assigned to the operations, as well as a number of PBRs, artillery support, and a unit of the ARVN police. As the SEALs and PRU patrol the area, they receive B-40 rocket and 82mm mortar fire throughout the day. In return, they direct Cobra and Seawolf air strikes against targets.

The VC expends an estimated 200 rounds of combined B-40 and 82mm mortar rounds during the engagement. Enemy small arms fire comes from a pagoda and its surrounding area as the SEALs continue to fight. During a sweep of the area the following day by ARVN units, forty B-40 rounds are found as well as thirty-two rounds of 82mm mortar ammunition, several SKS rifles, and thirty-six enemy dead.

May 17

1944 (Burma)—The OSS Detachment 101 guerrillas and the 5307th Composite Unit (Merrill's Marauders) capture Myitkyina Airfield in Burma.

1987 (Persian Gulf)—An Iraqi Mirage F1 fighter jet reportedly mistakes the USS *Stark* (FFG 37) in the Persian Gulf as an Iranian craft. The Iraqi Mirage launches two French-made Exocet antiship missiles at the *Stark*. The missiles strike the ship, causing heavy damage and casualties. Thirty-seven Americans are killed in the attack. The Iraqis admit responsibility for the attack but reiterate that the missile launch was made in error.

May 18

1969 (South Vietnam)—A number of SEAL casualties in Vietnam are not due to direct enemy action. At the MACV compound in Rach Gia in Kien Giang Province, two SEALs from Charlie Platoon, SEAL Team One, attempt to remove an explosive charge from a Chicom 82mm high-explosive mortar round when the shell detonates. The blast from an approximately three-quarter-pound charge of TNT in the iron body sends fragmentation ripping throughout the area. Aviation Electronics Technician First Class Kenneth Van Hoy, Machinist's Mate Second Class Lowell Meyer, and Quartermaster Second Class Ronald Pace are killed outright in the blast. Hospital Corpsman Lin Mahner dies a week later from wounds received during the incident.

May 19

1952 (USA)—The Headquarters Company, Tenth Special Forces Group, is constituted.

1968 (South Vietnam)—While leading his PRU on an operation in Kien Giang Province, Chief Electrician's Mate Gordon Brown of SEAL Team One is killed by a booby trap. The PRU patrol has come across a wooden box that is being examined by Brown when it detonates. Brown is killed in the blast and six members of his PRU are seriously wounded. The box could have been a booby trap set to explode when someone approached it, or it could have been a command-detonated mine that was set off while the PRUs were under observation.

May 20

1945 (Europe)—The seven-man NORSO II (OSS) group accepts the surrender of several battalions of German troops in Norway.

1968 (South Vietnam)—A Letter of Commendation is issued from the Office of the Special Assistant, United States Embassy, Can Tho. It is for Engineman First Class Billy Davis and his actions as a PRU advisor. The letter gives a detailed look into the actions of a PRU and the results it achieves over a six-month period from August 1967 to February 1968. The results as mentioned in the letter include:

a. A total of 139 major operations were conducted. Of these, seventy-four were covert intelligence operations and sixty-five were covert military operations.

b. A total of 56 VC were captured, 104 VC were killed in action, and 61 VC were wounded in action.

c. A total of 26 weapons, 30 rounds of 75mm recoilless rifle ammunition, 12 mines, and nearly 5,000 rounds of small arms ammunition were captured.

d. The above results were achieved at a cost of only five PRU personnel killed and six PRU personnel wounded in action.

e. Also seized were numerous VC documents of great value to the intelligence community.

The letter also notes how Davis dealt with a corrupt Vietnamese PRU chief, firing him shortly after the SEAL arrived, and then considerably improved the PRU program in Ba Xuyen Province. In the letter's words, Davis had "refashioned [the PRU] into the cutting edge of the assault on the VC infrastructure." The letter goes on to say that the SEAL advisor prior to Davis had been an outstanding man and that it had not been thought that he could have been replaced by an even better man.

May 21

1946 (USA)—During World War II, of the approximately 3,500 men of the UDTs and NCDUs, 148 men are wounded and 83 are killed. Thirty-four UDTs are commissioned by the end of the war, and a number of others continue to undergo training. Thirty UDTs are gathered in southern California and decommissioned at the end of the war. Five postwar UDTs are commissioned and manned by the remaining UDT personnel, the first of these being UDT One on May 21, 1946. Three UDTs will be stationed at Coronado, California, to operate with the Pacific Fleet, while the two other UDTs go to the smaller Atlantic Fleet and are stationed at Little Creek, Virginia. Odd-numbered teams will be on the West Coast and even-numbered teams on the East Coast—a situation that continues to remain in effect.

1979 (USA)—Colonel Arthur "Bull" Simons dies. He was the commander of the Special Forces ground force during Operation Kingpin, the raid on the Son Tay prison camp in North Vietnam on November 21, 1970.

1963 (Turkey)—Lieutenant (j.g.) William Painter is one of the first officers of Mobile Training Team (MTT) 1-63 to arrive in Turkey. MTT 1-63 is one of the first MTTs to come out of SEAL Team Two and be deployed to help the Turkish military set up their own UDT training program. Other Team Two MTTs had been sent to Greece and South Vietnam.

During the training, Turkish students are given seven weeks of scuba training at Istanbul and Chubukla. The Turkish students take classes in buoyant ascents. This is when the accident involving Mr. Painter takes place. He puts on a scuba rig, dives down once, and surfaces, asking about a decompression time for a given depth. Diving a second time, Painter never surfaces again. Extensive searches of the water and shoreline are conducted for several days but his body is never recovered. He is the first SEAL loss ever of SEAL Team Two.

May 22

1970 (South Vietnam)—SEAL Team Two's Fifth Platoon conducts a search of an area only about eight miles southeast of Saigon. The SEALs are trying to locate a VC base camp according to information they have received from a local agent. After their insertion at 1250 hours, they search the area and find a number of fresh VC footprints as well as four home-made hand grenades. When the SEALs question the Vietnamese civilians in the area, they are told that a five-man VC squad has left the area only a few hours earlier. The SEALs continue to search the area for an additional hour or so and then call in their extraction boat and return to their base at Nha Be.

1990 (USA)—At Hurlburt Field, Florida, the Twenty-third Air Force is designated as the Air Force Special Operations Command. All of the air force special operations units are put under the command of the new organization, which is now the air force component of the SOCOM.

May 23

1967 (Vietnam)—One of the weapons the SEALs use to great effect during many of their operations in Vietnam and elsewhere is the M18A1 Claymore mine. The rectangular Claymore is a directional weapon, much like a gigantic shotgun, that has to be aimed in the direction that the operator wants the main effect to be going. The main effect of firing a Claymore is the launching of some 700 steel balls, in a 60 degree arc, that move at the velocity of a rifle bullet. Though they lose velocity much more quickly than a rifle bullet, the steel shot of a Claymore can shred a target within 50 meters of its firing point and remain dangerous for another 200 meters.

The curved plastic body of the Claymore has a sight cast into the top of the mine. Two sets of folding legs on the bottom of the mine allow it to be easily embedded into the ground and aimed. Inside the body of the mine are 1.5 pounds of C-4 plastic explosive. An entire firing kit, including the mine, firing device, electric wire, blasting cap, and instructions, are issued in a cloth bandoleer.

May 24

1994 (Haiti)—As part of the multinational force conducting Operation Support Democracy, the first two 170-foot-long Cyclone-class patrol craft to become operational depart the United States for Guantanamo Bay, Cuba. From there, they go on to the waters off Haiti, where they are ordered to join Joint Task Force 120 to help enforce the economic embargo against that country.

May 25

1961 (USA)—President John F. Kennedy promotes the Freedom Doctrine, which prompts the U.S. military to promote counterinsurgency units and operations.

1964 (USA)—The submarine USS *Grayback* (SSG 574) is decommissioned for the first time. Sent up to the Mare Island shipyards in late 1967, it undergoes an extensive refit to convert it into an amphibious transport and launching platform for combat swimmer and SDV operations. It will be recommissioned in 1969.

1968 (South China Sea)—When a CH-46 helicopter crashes into the water off the stern of the USS *Valley Forge* (CV 45), operators from UDT Twelve's Detachment Foxtrot are immediately available for recovery operations. Working from its assigned ship, the USS *Thomaston* (LSD 28), the UDT detachment saves the fourteen men who are aboard the helicopter; all the men are saved without serious injury to any of them.

1984 (El Salvador)—Lieutenant Commander Albert A. Schaufelberger III is assassinated as he sits in his armored Ford Maverick, supplied by the U.S. embassy. Faulty air conditioning has caused him to roll down the window of his vehicle when he goes to pick up a female acquaintance. Several terrorists from the Farabundo Marti National Liberation Front dart from a Volkswagen microbus parked nearby and one fires four rounds from a .22 Magnum into the SEAL officer. The terrorists escape in their vehicle and none are ever captured
   As a U.S. Navy SEAL, Schaufelberger was serving as the senior naval representative at the U.S. Military Group, El Salvador.

May 26

1942 (USA)—Having operated as the U.S. liaison with the British general staff, Major General Lucian K. Truscott drafts a proposal to create an American military unit along the lines of the British commandos. His proposal is accepted by the U.S. War Department and results in the formation of the First U.S. Army Ranger Battalion, named after the pre–Revolutionary War organization, Rodger's Rangers.

1969 (South Vietnam)—A squad from SEAL Team Two's Sixth Platoon, Detachment Alfa, conducts a daylight canal ambush on the bank of the Rach Soi Canal north of the Song Dong Tranh River in Bien Hoa Province. The area is in the northernmost portion of the Rung Sat Special Zone. After preparing the ambush site, including setting out Claymore mines, the SEALs wait almost seven hours until they hear voices coming from the darkness on their left flank. Detonating two Claymore mines in the direction of the voices, the SEALs see an individual running and another crawling away. They take the two men under fire. The bodies cannot be found due to the heavy undergrowth in the area. It is the 104th mission Sixth Platoon has conducted since arriving in Vietnam six months earlier.

May 27

1943 (USA)—As the fourth training class gets underway at the joint service Scout and Raider training school in Fort Pierce, Florida, an army group reports for a four-week scouting and raiding course. The group is made up of men from the Twenty-eighth Division Reconnaissance Group. During their training, the army troops and navy Scouts learn a great deal about amphibious operations and working with each other's services. The Twenty-eighth Division group completes its training and leaves Fort Pierce on May 27.

1943 (USA)—Detachment 101 departs for India.

1972 (South China Sea)—The USS *Grayback* (LPSS 574) leaves Subic Bay in the Philippines bound for the waters of the Gulf of Tonkin off North Vietnam. Aboard the submarine are the fourteen-man detachment from UDT Thirteen and Alfa Platoon from SEAL Team One led by Lieutenant Melvin S. Dry. The men will be conducting a major part of Operation Thunderhead, the recovery of escaped American POWs held near Hanoi in North Vietnam.

The prisoners are to have escaped already as part of Operation Diamond. The escapees are to have made their way down the Red River to its mouth where they will signal any watchers to recover them. The SEALs and UDT men aboard the *Grayback* intend to be the people who see that signal. Using the Mark VII Mod 6 SDVs carried in the bow hangers of the *Grayback*, the UDT operators will move a number of SEALs to an observation point on an island offshore of the river mouth of which the POWs are expected to come out. The mission will be dangerous, difficult, cold, wet, and uncomfortable. And recovering American POWs is the very best thing anyone aboard the *Grayback* can think of doing.

1994 (Cuba)—The USS *Cyclone* (PC 1) and the USS *Tempest* (PC 2) arrive at Guantánamo Bay to join with Joint Task Force 120.

May 28

1965 (Caribbean)—The large SEAL Team Two detachment that has been conducting operations in the Dominican Republic returns to Little Creek, Virginia, having suffered no casualties. Order is established and the fight for control of the city of Santo Domingo and the Dominican Republic subsides.

May 29

1952 (USA)—The U.S. Army Psychological Warfare Center is activated at Fort Bragg, North Carolina.

1965 (South Vietnam)—UDT Twelve's Detachment Alfa receives a commendation for a series of clandestine surveys it conducted along the South Vietnamese coast. The clandestine and overt hydrographic recons were conducted between December 1, 1964 and May 29, 1965. A number of marine amphibious assaults along the shores of South Vietnam have been successfully conducted because of the efforts of Detachment Alfa.

May 30

1944 (USA)—Seabees from Camp Peary, Virginia, volunteer for duty conducting "hazardous demolition work in a classified unit." The men who volunteer find themselves at Fort Pierce, Florida, and go through the Naval Combat Demolition Unit School as Classes 5 and 5A during March and April 1944. One officer and five men train as NCDUs, with the officer going through exactly the same mud, water, and work as his men. The six-man size of an NCDU has been determined during training as the maximum number of men that can work from a standard rubber boat while still leaving room for explosives and equipment.

Graduating and shipping out, the men arrive at the Naval Combat Underwater Demolition Training and Experimental Base on Maui in Hawaii on April 9. Once in Hawaii, the men go through even more extensive demolition and reconnaissance work, this time spending a great deal of time swimming. On May 30, UDTs Six and Seven are commissioned. They very quickly leave in the company of UDT Five for Operation Forager, the invasion of Saipan, Guam, and Tinian in the Marianas Islands.

1994 (Haiti)—The USS *Cyclone* (PC 1) and the USS *Tempest* (PC 2) arrive off Haiti. During their first patrol, the *Cyclone* encounters a Bahamian-flagged sailing vessel trying to slip through the embargo on a smuggling run. The *Cyclone* finally stops the smaller boat by launching flares as a warning and putting a Rigid Hull, Inflatable Boat (RIB) into the water with a detachment of SEALs on board. At first light, three SEALs and a group of six Canadian sailors from the HMCS *Terra Nova* (0029) conduct a board-and-search operation on the smugglers' boat. Embargoed goods are found on board and the seized boat is towed by the *Cyclone* to Guantánamo Bay.

May 31

1944 (England)—The final operational plans for the GATs are submitted. From the United Kingdom, one GAT will be assigned to one Landing Craft, Tank (Armored) (LCT[A]). The team will be made up of thirteen men, one officer, and twenty-six additional army personnel in reserve. Each LCT(A) has fifty-two men and three medium tanks on board in addition to the crews. The tanks and additional men will land and assist the demolition units by giving fire support and removing any obstacles that are not taken care of during the initial assault. The men of the GATs have spent the last several weeks in Salcombe making the 10,000 Hagensen pack demolition charges they will use for the invasion. The officers and men of the GATs have yet to receive a full briefing on just what their exact mission will be and where and when they will conduct it.

JUNE

Rodger Three by Robert Benny. A painting of Scout and Raider personnel slipping their rubber boat through a swamp during training in the Florida Everglades. NAVY HISTORICAL CENTER COLLECTION

June 01

1944 (England)—Force "U," made up of the Group Three GATs, obtains the use of LCVPs for its part in the D day landings. The three groups of GATs are assigned as additional loads on the LCTs and LCT(A)s that will take them to the French coast. Plans for moving the men and the tremendous amount of explosives that will go with them are now going into effect. On June 1, Force "U" is scheduled to attack Utah Beach and it leaves Salcombe for the marshaling area and its transport boats.

June 02

1944 (USA)—The men of UDT Eight complete their training at the Naval Combat Demolition Unit School at Fort Pierce, Florida, and depart by train for San Francisco and points west. They will continue their UDT training in Maui, Hawaii. From the time they leave Fort Pierce, eighteen months will pass before they permanently return to the United States at Coronado, California, on November 12, 1945. During these months, the men of UDT Eight will travel more than 70,000 miles in a straight line by ship, not counting the zigzag turns the ships will make at irregular intervals to avoid Japanese submarines. They will stop at the Hawaiian, Marshalls, Solomons, Palaus, Admiralty, Philippines, Ryukyus, and several other Pacific islands during their travels, either for training, rest, or to conduct recons and demolition swims. Before returning to the States after the end of the war, UDT Eight continues on to conduct recons in Korea and on the Shangtung Peninsula of China.

1944 (USA)—In March, Class 6A undergoes training at the Naval Combat Demolition Unit School at Fort Pierce, Florida. When the officers and men complete their training, they divide into UDTs Eight, Nine, and Ten and are sent off to Maui, Hawaii, for further training. At the Maui base, UDT Ten is joined by twenty-one men and five officers from the OSS. This group already has undergone extensive training as part of the OSS Maritime unit. It knows a great deal about underwater swimming and further advanced explosive techniques. As part of the UDTs, the OSS men freely exchange their training with their team-mates. One significant item that comes from the men of the OSS is the proper technique for swimming with fins on, something that hadn't been commonly done by the UDTs up to that point.

June 03

1944 (England)—The remaining two groups of GATs in Salcombe, assigned to attack Omaha Beach, leave for Portsmouth for embarkation aboard their transportation boats.

1951 (Korea)—Operators from UDT Three assist in a covert landing of a guerrilla force on Song-Do Island, a piece of land less than a mile from the Korean mainland. The landing force travels aboard the USS *Begor* (APD 127), leaving Pusan after dark on June 2. The men from UDT Three operate the landing craft used to transport the guerrilla force of 235 Korean natives and their equipment to Song-Do.

Beginning at 0200 hours, UDT swimmer scouts conduct a beach examination of Song-Do to locate a suitable landing site for the guerrilla force. After some searching, a suitable site is found and the landing is completed by 0445 hours. The operation is the first operational landing of guerrillas from Task Force Kirkland, which is part of the U.S. Eighth Army's G-3 Miscellaneous Group.

June 04

1944 (Italy)—The First Special Service Force seizes bridges over the Tiber River near Rome.

1944 (Pacific)—With UDT Three aboard, the USS *Dent* (APD 9) leaves the Solomon Islands for Roi-Namur in the Marshall Islands. UDT Three is one of the five original UDTs organized in March 1944 at Maui using selection from the men who made up UDTs One and Two. Three officers and twenty-two men from UDT One and Two give UDT Three a cadre of combat-experienced veterans of the Marshall invasion. A breakdown on the *Dent* forces UDT Three to transfer its men, equipment, and tons of explosives to the USS *Dickerson* (APD 21) for further transportation. UDT Three will act as a reserve unit for the upcoming invasion of Saipan.

1972 (North Vietnam)—After having moved undetected underneath the bulk of the U.S. Seventh Fleet, the submarine USS *Grayback* (LPSS 574) arrives in the Gulf of Tonkin off the coast of North Vietnam. During the long transit, the officers and men of the UDT and SEAL detachments aboard the *Grayback* receive their briefings on their part in the upcoming Operation Thunderhead. The mission is so secret that even aboard the sealed submarine, the briefings are kept compartmentalized. Men are given the information that they need to know to do their jobs, and nothing more.

The *Grayback* will launch its Mark VII Mod 6 SDVs off the coast of North Vietnam. The single Six boat going in on the operation will transport two SEALs to a small island off the coast where they will set up an extended observation post. The plan is for the SEALs to be prepared to stay at their observation post for up to twenty-two days, switching crews every forty-eight hours with the SEALs on the *Grayback* by means of its SDVs.

A huge number of navy assets are watching the coast of North Vietnam already. They have been conducting surveillance since May 29 and this will continue until June 19, unless orders come otherwise. The SEALs at their observation post in enemy territory stand the best chance of spotting the escaped American POWs for which the entire operation has been staged. At 0200 hours, the *Grayback* launches the Six boat for the first of many times throughout this operation.

June 05

1944 (English Channel)—Officers of the Omaha Beach force are gathered up from the LCT(A)s that will transport their GATs and transferred to the flagship USS *Ancon* (AGC 4). This is their first and only briefing of the upcoming invasion. The plans that have been practiced for weeks involve the men of the GATs blowing cleared channels through the multiple rows of obstacles on the Normandy coast.

At Omaha Beach, the sixteen GATs are intended to each blow a 50-yard-wide gap through the obstacles, with each gap being spaced 200 yards from the next.

As troops and support come ashore through the gaps, the GATs will move over and blow further gaps, extending and widening the cleared area until the entire beach is open. The NCDU men of the GATs are to blast the obstacles in the water while the army engineers are to attack the obstacles above the waterline and up to the high water mark on the beach. As the obstacles in a gap are charged and ready to blow, a purple smoke signal will be fired to show that the two-minute fuse has been ignited.

To support the GATs while they conduct their part of the operation, thirty-two special dual-drive (DD; amphibious) medium tanks will go ashore, exiting from the LCT(A)s 500 yards from the beach, and cover the demolition men with their cannon and machine guns. Sixteen DD tanks are assigned to each half of Omaha Beach.

1972 (North Vietnam)—The SDV operations from the submarine USS *Grayback* (LPSS 574) prove extremely difficult to conduct for Operation Thunderhead. Very heavy currents in the area drain the batteries of the SDV much faster than has been planned. The first SDV has to be abandoned and the UDT and SEAL operators are picked up by a search and rescue helicopter from the USS *Long Beach* (CGN 9). Due to a technical difficulty in communications, the current problems are not known aboard the *Grayback* until after it has launched a second SDV the next day. The first group of SEALs and UDT operators are returned to the *Grayback* by helicopter. To maintain secrecy, they jump from the helicopter into the water near the submarine after detecting a signal from its raised periscope.

A night free-jump into the water from a moving helicopter is difficult at best. Combined errors and a strong desire to see the mission through have the SEALs and UDT men jumping from the helicopter at far too great an altitude and speed. Lieutenant Melvin S. Dry breaks his neck on impact with the water or on floating material in the water and is instantly killed. He is the last SEAL loss of the Vietnam War. But Operation Thunderhead is so highly classified that his family is not told the truth about how he died for years. Instead, they are informed that Dry has been killed in a training accident. Operation Thunderhead does not recover any escaped POWs. The POWs' escape attempt is canceled from inside their prison and there is no way for them to get word to the outside world in time.

June 06

1944 (France)—At dawn, Operation Neptune, the amphibious portion of the Operation Overlord D day landings, begins with the largest naval armada in history arriving off the coast of France. The goal of the Allied forces is to land on the beaches of Normandy. Of the five beaches selected for landing by the Allies (code-named Sword, Gold, Juno, Omaha, and Utah) the U.S. targets will be Omaha and Utah beaches. The plan is for a first wave of infantry and armored support to provide coverage for the NCDUs, as the naval component of the GATs, that will clear the beach obstacles in order to provide access for the main landing force. The NCDUs use 10,000 Hagensen pack explosive charges that they have hand-fabricated for weeks before in order to destroy obstacles that the Germans have erected to prevent any enemy landings on the beaches. Destruction of these obstacles opens channels for the main landing force.

The landing at Utah Beach goes relatively well with the NCDUs being able to clear the obstacles quickly. This is in large part due to the fact that they have landed nearly one and a half miles southeast of their originally planned site. The first-wave landing also goes as planned with twenty-eight tanks providing some protection for the NCDUs while they execute their mission. The Germans have not anticipated landings on these beaches, so they are relatively unfortified. Lighter enemy fire, fewer blockades and mines, smaller waves, and a slower tide enables the NCDUs to open and mark eight channels for the main landing force within thirty minutes, with a total of fourteen channels marked before the tide turns. NCDU casualties at Utah Beach are about 30 percent, with six men killed and eleven wounded.

There are severe problems with the Omaha Beach operation, however. The amphibious phase of the landings does not go as planned due to several factors. A major one of these is erroneous weather reports. Unexpectedly turbulent seas cause problems with the transfer of personnel to landing craft. Armored support doesn't get to Omaha Beach because the DD tanks either sink soon after they're launched or are quickly destroyed by the Germans when they come into range. This prevents the armor from providing the protection much needed by the NCDUs in order to accomplish their objectives.

Also, the German fortifications have been increased, which causes greater resistance than anticipated and air support is ineffective in disrupting the

German response because the ground targets are too far inland to provide coverage for the NCDUs. German defense of these beaches include mined blockades, in addition to trenches, gun emplacements, rifle pits, howitzers, mortars, and flamethrowers.

In spite of these adverse conditions, the NCDUs proceed with their mission. On the first day of the invasion at Normandy, 1,000 U.S. troops are killed. The NCDUs have greater than 50 percent casualties at Omaha Beach, with thirty-one of their team members killed and sixty wounded.

1944 (France)—At Ponte Du Hoc, the Second Ranger Battalion (Rudder's Rangers) climbs the cliffs overlooking the beaches with the use of fire ladders and rocket-launched grappling hooks. The target of the Rangers is the reported battery of six German 155mm guns that could devastate the U.S. forces landing on Omaha Beach. In thirty minutes, the Rangers scale the cliffs and find the gun emplacements empty.

June 07

1952 (USA)—Under the command of Aaron Bank, a veteran of the OSS during World War II, the Tenth Special Forces Group is activated.

1967 (South Vietnam)—While conducting a patrol and demolition operation, a squad from Fourth Platoon, SEAL Team Two's Detachment Alfa, comes under heavy enemy fire. The SEALs have been moving along the south shore of Cu Lao Tan Dinh Island in the Bassac River, blasting enemy fortifications as they find them. The SEALs destroy five bunkers and a number of hooches.

The area the patrol is moving through is believed to be an enemy rest and relaxation (R&R) location. Interrogating the locals, the SEALs find a large number of hogs, ducks, and chickens and large supplies of food in the area, all of which support the R&R idea. One Vietnamese woman speaks of there being twenty VC staying in the area only a few days earlier. Also, large punji pits are spotted by the SEALs in locations marked by Vietnamese "Keep Out" signs.

While on point, the patrol leader spots an armed VC and opens fire. Killing the VC prematurely triggers an ambush set up by the twelve to fifteen VC to trap the SEALs. The VC ambush opens fire from the patrol's right flank, striking the patrol leader with a single round in the left wrist. Quickly responding to their situation, the SEALs move back along their line of march, leapfrogging and covering one another. Once they reach a defensive position near the river bank, the SEALs consolidate and lay down a heavy base of fire against the approaching VC forces. At least three VC are killed before the SEALs are able to extract.

The patrol's heavy demolition work is later determined to be the cause of the VC ambush.

June 08

1945 (Pacific)—UDT Nineteen moves into the camp on Guam built by the men of UDT Eight. UDT Nineteen will eventually arrive in Oceanside, California. There, the team will join with a large number of other UDTs to train and equip themselves for cold water work. The planned invasion of Japan will be in very cold water and will utilize thousands of UDT swimmers.

1945 (Borneo)—UDT Eleven conducts a reconnaissance of Labuan Island in Brunei Bay. Although the mission receives very little opposition from the enemy, the UDT men are mistaken for Japanese by U.S. bombers supporting the operations on Borneo. The bombers drop a load of high explosives on the UDT men in the water below. Six men suffer internal injuries from the concussions of the bombs. After a long search, C. F. Masren is declared missing in action and his body is never recovered.

Up until the incident with the bombers, the most hazardous part of the operation for UDT Eleven had been the transport to the target area. For twenty miles, the men moved through a floating minefield before they reached their objective. A large number of floating mines were sighted, one of the men said they looked like apples floating in a bucket.

June 09

1943 (USA)—The OSS Maritime Unit is established.

1944 (Pacific)—UDT Four has a variety of misadventures as it moves out to take part in Operation Forager, the invasion of Saipan, Guam, and Tinian in the Marianas. This is the first combat operation for the new UDT and it leaves aboard the USS *Talbot* (APD 7) from Eniwetok in the Marshall Islands. Before UDT Four leaves, the *Talbot* collides with the USS *Pennsylvania* (BB 30). The damaged *Talbot* returns to Eniwetok for repairs.

1965 (Vietnam)—The Battle of Dong Xoai takes place. Special Forces First Lieutenant Charles Q. Williams performs the actions that result in his being awarded the Congressional Medal of Honor.

June 10

1944 (France)—Jedburghs Ammonia, Frederick, and George are infiltrated into France.

1968 (South Vietnam)—The trail and canal ambush patrol takes place near Ap Cay Quit on the northern bank of the Song Cai Be River in Dinh Tuong Province. The Moon is in its last half and the weather is clear, making visibility during the night operation comparatively easy. The area the SEALs patrol is full of deserted hooches with a large number of bunkers scattered about. Only one VC is encountered and eliminated by the SEALs. Searching the bunkers and area results in a number of VC flags being found as well as Communist propaganda pamphlets on the Paris peace talks. The SEALs extract without incident shortly before 0700 hours.

June 11

1942 (USA)—The Coordinator of Information (COI) is redesignated the Office of Strategic Services (OSS).

1946 (USA)—UDTs Two and Four arrive at Little Creek, Virginia, as a permanent change of station. They will continue to operate as UDTs, but now they will work directly in support of the Atlantic Fleet. The two UDTs are made up by the remaining personnel from the wartime UDTs.

June 12

1964 (North Vietnam)—The number and tempo of operations in support of Oplan 34A pick up. The first successful LDNN-run sabotage mission takes place when a storage facility is attacked and destroyed.

1992 (USA)—The OSS Memorial is dedicated at the CIA headquarters in Langley, Virginia.

June 13

1942 (USA)—The OSS is established by military order; control of the OSS is passed from the president to the Joint Chiefs of Staff.

1943 (France)—The first OSS agent is infiltrated.

1944 (Pacific)—UDT Six is assigned to standby duty for Operation Forager, the invasion of Saipan, Guam, and Tinian in the Marianas.

June 14

1944 (Pacific)—The damaged USS *Talbot* (APD 7) with UDT Four aboard finally leaves the Marshall Islands. Fast steaming by the APD catches them up with the invasion force near Saipan.

1944 (Pacific)—For landings the next day by the marines of the Second Division, UDT Five is assigned to recon the Red 2 and 3 and Green 1 and 2 beaches on the west coast of Saipan.

All the UDT operators are dressed in what could be called minimum equipment. Each man has swim fins, swim shoes, swim trunks, four three-by-ten-inch Plexiglas slates, two grease pencils, a waterproof first aid packet, knife, life belt, dive mask, gloves, and knee pads. Leading UDT Five is Lieutenant Commander Draper Kauffman, who has moved to the UDTs in the Pacific from the Naval Combat Demolition Unit School at Fort Pierce, Florida.

A number of men from UDT Five are casualties off Saipan with several men being killed by enemy fire and six more receiving internal injuries from the concussion of Japanese mortar rounds detonating in the water around them as the Japanese shell UDT swimmers in the water.

1944 (Pacific)—Recons of Guam are conducted. UDT Three conducts two daylight and one nighttime recon operation.

1993 (Adriatic Sea)—Joint Special Operations Task Force Two (JSOTF Two) is established in February of this year in part to assist in Operation Maritime Guard. General mission assignments of JSOTF Two include combat search and rescue, fire support, air drops, and visit board, search, and seizure actions to enforce the UN blockade of former Yugoslavian waters. This is the last day of Operation Maritime Guard.

June 15

1944 (Pacific)—Operation Forager, the invasion of the Marianas, begins. The Second and Fourth Marine Divisions land on the west coast of Saipan at 0830 local time.

1989 (USA)—The First Special Warfare Training Battalion is redesignated the First Special Warfare Training Group.

1993 (Adriatic Sea)—Operation Sharp Guard begins. Much like Operation Maritime Guard, this new operation conducts security patrols to protect the former Yugoslavian waters.

June 16

1944 (Pacific)—The beachmaster of Blue Beach requests UDT Seven to blast a 100-foot channel though an offshore reef to allow the landing of supplies and materials. The earlier recons conducted by UDT Seven showed that the waters off the reef are too shallow to allow the types of ships to come in and use the beach as desired by the beachmaster. Regardless, the UDT prepares for a nighttime demolition operation.

The blasting of the channel ends in failure for a number of reasons. In spite of properly placing the charges on the coral, the UDT men find that the coral around the Mariana Islands is particularly dense and mixed with sand, turning it into a kind of natural concrete that doesn't blast well. In addition, during the night charges that are exposed to the action of the seawater and waves increase the chance of duds and lower the power of the shot. As the marines keep moving on shore, battling the Japanese sometimes only 200 yards from the blast site, the explosions have to be constantly postponed. The UDTs are still learning practical operational techniques and will just keep getting better, even after their failures.

1966 (South Vietnam)—Operation Deckhouse I is initiated as men from UDT Eleven conduct recons along the South Vietnamese coast of beaches at the Song Cua and Song Cai Rivers. The UDT is operating in a clandestine manner from the USS *Cook* (APD 130).

June 17

1968 (South Vietnam)—In an area of flat rice paddies, a SEAL unit sets up a twenty-four-hour ambush site. The terrain allows it to be inserted and extracted by truck. In spite of a lot of contact with friendly Vietnamese in the area, the intelligence the SEALs have of the area isn't good enough for them to run into a target. They truck out the next morning.

June 18

1944 (Pacific)—Conducting a demolition operation off of the invasion beaches at Saipan, UDT Seven places explosives to blast a ramp through coral to allow LSTs to come in to shore and land their cargoes. The ramp cut through the coral is usable, though rough and somewhat irregular in its contours.

1951 (Korea)—Army Special Mission Unit Baker, Eighth Army, conducts the Spitfire guerrilla warfare mission in North Korea.

1967 (South Vietnam)—SEAL Team Two's Fourth Platoon splits into two squads and conducts two separate operations on the same day: Bravo Squad plans an early morning snatch operation to capture a prisoner and Alfa Squad goes out on a late morning capture operation in Kien Hoa Province. For intelligence purposes, both operations are trying to capture the same type of high-quality prisoners: VC communications liaison personnel. Such people will know many more individuals and locations of VC assets than just a regular VC guerrilla. The capture of VC infrastructure targets is already a high priority for the SEALs.

Bravo Squad begins its operation at 0100 hours, using a Mike boat as transportation with a Boston Whaler and an outboard motor for insertion. The mission is aborted when it's determined that the VC have detected the SEALs and are setting up an ambush. The later report states that the SEALs spotted three VC on the shore. Since the Johnson motors on their boat were too loud, the mission was compromised.

Alfa Squad has better luck later that morning. Inserting at about 1030 hours, the SEALs encounter the VC communications liaison squad that they had been expecting. In the operation, the SEALs kill three VC, wound three more, and capture four. In addition, the SEALs capture a Mauser rifle, sixty rounds of ammunition, and two grenades and destroy a two-ton rice cache. Their final opinion is that the area should be thoroughly worked for enemy personnel and emplacements.

1996 (Adriatic Sea)— Operation Sharp Guard, the prevention of unauthorized ships from entering formerly Yugoslavian waters, ends.

June 19

1942 (England)—The first U.S. Army Ranger Battalion is officially activated and begins training at the Bristish Commando depot at Achnacarry, Scotland. The unit is named "Darby's Rangers" after its commander, Major William O. Darby.

1952 (USA)—The Tenth Special Forces Group is activated under the command of Colonel Aaron Banks. Although the unit will eventually have 2,300 personnel, its total strength on its first day of existence is all of ten men: Colonel Banks, eight enlisted men, and a single warrant officer.

1952 (USA)—The first Special Forces Founders Day celebration is held.

1967 (South Vietnam)—SEAL Team One personnel from Detachment Golf are inserted for an overnight ambush at the Rach Ngay Canal near the shore of the Soirap River in the northern part of the Rung Sat Special Zone. The terrain is flat with poor cover for the SEALs. Even though the cloudy weather helps block the light from the three-quarter moon, the men still feel very exposed. Waiting in chest-deep water, the SEALs spend an uncomfortable night without encountering any enemy forces. They leave considering the stream to be good for the VC, but bad for a SEAL ambush.

1987 (USA)—Army General Order 35 establishes the Special Forces as a separate branch of the U.S. Army.

June 20

1967 (South Vietnam)—SEALs are great operators. Their objective is to accomplish the mission, and they will go to great lengths and sacrifices to do so. What they aren't good at is maintaining detailed records. In the Barndance card for June 20, 1967, Fourth Platoon of SEAL Team Two states little more than the mission objective, to ambush VC waterborne traffic, that the terrain was mangrove canals, and that they encountered four VC. The results were four VC killed in action and two sampans destroyed. Nothing else is considered important enough to write down after the operation.

June 21

1945 (Borneo)—UDT Eighteen learns that the team will be taking part in the invasion at Balikpapan in southeast Borneo. The orders and operations plan are published to the team. They then receive their prereconnaissance data, all of three aerial photographs of their target area. Aboard its transport, the USS *Schmitt* (APD 79), the team leaves its anchorage at Moratai and heads for Balikpapan.

1968 (South Vietnam)—Searching for a reported VC jungle workshop arms factory, Mike Platoon of SEAL Team One's Detachment Golf encounters a number of VC while out on a seven-hour-long operation. In spite of not locating the factory, Mike Platoon considers the operation at least a partial success as it can account for nine VC killed.

June 22

1968 (South Vietnam)—The third LDNN replacement class of South Vietnamese SEALs graduates two officers and thirty-eight enlisted men.

June 23

1970 (South Vietnam)—A heavy loss is taken by SEAL Team One when five SEALs, two from Golf Platoon and three from Echo Platoon, are lost as the U.S. Army helicopter they are riding in crashes near Can Tho. The cause is not determined. The helicopter is enroute to Can Tho from the Seafloat base. The movement is a simple administrative one and no combat is expected. The helicopter and the remains of those on board are recovered. The SEALs lost are Fireman Toby Thomas, Machinist's Mate Second Class Richard Solano, Signalman Third Class John Durlin, Seaman Radioman John Donnelly, and Boatswain's Mate Third Class James Gore.

1993 (Caribbean)—The UN places an economic embargo against most shipping to Haiti. The UN is trying to put pressure on the Haitian army after they overthrew democratically elected President Jean-Bertrand Aristide, who was elected almost two years before. The embargo increases the desperation of the Haitian people who leave their island in droves. The Haitian refugees mostly travel in unsafe boats to the United States, which is over 1,000 miles away.

June 24

1944 (USA)—A second draft of NCDUs leave Fort Pierce, Florida, bound for further training at Salerno, Italy. The eight NCDUs, forty-eight officers and enlisted men, leave Norfolk in a slow convoy of 110 ships and 16 escort vessels for the long trip across the Atlantic and into the Mediterranean. They will join up with the twenty-two NCDUs already undergoing training at Salerno. A number of the NCDUs going in on Operation Dragoon, the invasion of southern France, are veterans of the Normandy landings on Utah Beach.

June 25

1945 (Borneo)—One light cruiser and two destroyers provide heavy fire support for the men of UDT Eighteen as they move in to the beaches at Balikpapan. In spite of heavy smoke in the area due to oil fires, the movement to the beach goes smoothly and is well organized. B-24 bombers from the Thirteenth Bomber Command provide high-level bombing support on targets inland from the beaches, while B-25 bombers from the same outfit run low-level strafing and bombing runs. This support is considered effective and accurate by the men of the UDT as no bombs are dropped in the water around them.

At 0800 hours, the men of UDT Eighteen go on to the beach and work an area conducting reconnaissance next to one being worked by their brother operators in UDT Eleven. The men are picked up by 0900 hours without having taken any casualties. It is determined that they will go on a demolition swim the next day. The balance of the day is spent in preparing charges and equipment for the demolition swim.

1950 (Korea)—Initiating the first armed conflict between the Communist and the Western world, North Korean forces cross the thirty-eighth parallel and enter South Korea at 0400 hours. Orders from President Harry S. Truman to General Douglas MacArthur, the U.S. commander in the Far East, to fully support the democratic government of South Korea keeps the country from falling.

The North Korean People's Army (NKPA) quickly captures Seoul, the capital of South Korea, and it continues its movement toward the end of the peninsula. In a mistake that is never to be repeated, the Soviet delegates to the UN Security Council walk out in response to a minor argument with the American delegation. They are not present to veto the Security Council's resolution to back the government of South Korea and drive the NKPA invasion forces back across the thirty-eighth parallel. The Korean War has begun.

June 26

1945 (Borneo)—At 0730 hours, UDT Eighteen leaves the USS *Schmitt* (APD 74) to go in for a demolition swim against the obstacles off the beach at Manggar Ketjil. A large number of obstacles have been found and the entire UDT goes in on the demolition swim, with each boat filled with high explosives and UDT swimmers. A heavy shore bombardment is conducted by navy ships, cutting back at 0810 hours to allow the UDT swimmers to approach the beach.

The mission is a huge one. The swimmers have 110 minutes to complete their operation, and it looks like they will need every minute. Each swimmer goes in towing 100 pounds of explosives in floating haversacks. Two-pound charges are used to demolish the posts that have been found blocking the beach. One charge is placed at the base of the post and the second up at the top. Placing the second charge causes many of the swimmers to expose themselves above the water since the posts extend three feet out of the water. The Japanese mortar fire that could have badly harassed the UDT swimmers is kept down by high-level bombing of the target area, only 400 yards inland from the beach.

By 1005 hours, all charges are placed and the swimmers retire from the area. The ten-minute-delay fuses are pulled by the fastest swimmers in the unit who immediately leave the area for pickup. At 1020 hours, a massive blast lifts the water over 700 yards of beach and the way is clear for the incoming landing forces, who will never come.

Earlier recons by UDTs Eleven and Eighteen have determined that the beaches at Manggar are not suitable for an amphibious landing by the forces available. The demolition swim, however, is completed to deceive the Japanese into thinking that the landings will take place there. The mission is a deception operation.

June 27

1945 (Borneo)—The morning of Fox 4 (four days before the planned landings on Fox day), UDTs Eleven and Eighteen conduct a reconnaissance of the beaches at the Klandasan Beach area off Balikpapan. The weather conditions are poor with waves and general visibility cutting off the view of the beaches from the fleet. At 0545 hours, UDTs Eleven and Eighteen go in for their reconnaissance, the boats having to pass though an area that is heavily laced with mines.

The heavy sea makes working in the water very difficult, but the men of the UDTs complete their reconnaissance and return to their ships. The issue of a brandy ration to the nearly exhausted men reportedly serves to "stimulate and reenergate" them.

June 28

1945 (Pacific)—Almost two weeks after the invasion of Saipan, UDT Five experiments with the best way to eliminate a problem it has run in to during its operations: Japanese boat mines. The hemispherical, flat-bottomed mines weigh over 100 pounds and contain almost 50 pounds of a high-explosive filler. On top of the mines are two lead horns that each hold a glass vial of acid. When the horns are bent or dented, something that takes a force of at least 250 pounds, the acid vile breaks, pouring its contents down to the plates of a battery, which detonates the filler.

The best method UDT Five finds to blow up the mines is to tie a half-pound block of TNT to one of the horns. The charge has to be placed so that it is in contact with both the horn and the body of the mine. This technique is used by the UDTs until the Mark 1 Destructor is developed. The Mark 1 Destructor is a simple chemical fuse with a large detonator attached. After clipping the Mark 1 to the horn of a mine, it is detonated, the blast cap dents the horn, which breaks the vial of acid within, which detonates the filler.

1945 (Borneo)—UDTs Eleven and Eighteen continue their operations off Balik-papan with a demolition swim the morning of Fox 3. Visibility is still poor, which works both for and against the UDTs. Close-in bombing runs are delayed in arriving and when they do, the bombers move in at a very low altitude. The Japanese gunners on shore also don't see very well, which works out for the UDTs as the Japanese are firing heavily into the swimming area.

To blast the obstacles out of the way, UDT Eighteen is using the Mark 127 demolition charge. The charges are limited in availability so the men of UDT Eighteen have reserved them for the Klandasan beaches, the "hotter" operation since the invasion forces will actually be landing there. The Mark 127 charges are a canvas haversack apron that slips over an operator's head. The haversack has two pockets, one at the front and the other on the back, each of which holds ten Mark 20 demolition charges. The Mark 20 charge is the official navy-adopted version of the Hagensen pack. Each charge holds two pounds of plastic explosive and can be quickly tied to a target. By 1030 hours, the swimmers from UDT Eighteen complete their demolition swim and are back on their boats returning to the USS *Schmitt* (APD 74).

UDT Eleven conducts its demolition swim with some incidents. One of the UDT officers has a fragment of an exploding shell dent the steel helmet he is wearing. A nearby operator is burned by the hot fragment when it lands on his leg, but otherwise no real damage is sustained. When the UDT swimmers complete charging the obstacles on 900 yards of beach front, they pull the ten-minute-delay fuse igniters and return to their boats. But two minutes later, a Japanese shell lands among the charges and detonates the shot prematurely. If that shell had landed just a few minutes earlier, it would have caught most of UDT Eleven in the blast.

June 29

1945 (Pacific)—Lieutenant Commander Draper Kauffman, the commanding officer of UDT Five, conducts an aerial survey of the beaches at Tinian for Vice Admiral Richmond Kelly Turner. Further information will have to be gathered by the UDTs during normal beach recon swims later on.

1968 (South Vietnam)—Mike Platoon of SEAL Team One's Detachment Golf goes out on a late morning snatch operation to capture a VC tax collector who has been reported as being in the area of Cho Lach in northern Vinh Long Province. The SEALs insert at 1030 hours from a civilian junk to blend in with the surrounding area and will extract by the same method. The point of insertion is on the east bank of the Kinh Sang Canal, just about four kilometers southeast of Cho Lach. The canal is considered navigable and was last dredged, to a depth of thirteen feet, in the mid-1930s. The weather is overcast and rainy.

Along with the tax collector, the SEALs run into his four-man retinue and a platoon-sized force of VC bodyguards and escorts. Anticipating a show of force by the VC, the SEALs have their own backup, the Seawolves of Helicopter Attack (Light) (Hal) 3, Detachment 6. In addition, the SEALs have brought a number of troops from the Cho Lach Provincial Force. The results of the fire fight are three VC killed in action, two detained, eight cargo carriers killed, two hooches destroyed, and ten hooches and two sampans damaged.

1990 (USA)—The Third Special Forces Group (Airborne) is reactivated to cover Special Forces operations in the North Atlantic Treaty Organization's European Command's African region.

June 30

1964 (North Vietnam)—A major OPlan 34A operation by the LDNNs and Nasty-class boats demonstrates both the advantages and dangers of the missions. On the North Vietnamese coast near the mouth of the Kien River, a party of South Vietnamese launches rubber boats from the Nasty-class boats Fast Patrol Craft (PTF) 5 and PTF 6. In spite of being spotted by North Vietnamese fishermen who quickly raise the alarm during its insertion, the raiding force continues toward the target: a reservoir pump house.

After first sending in a pair of swimmer scouts, the balance of the raiding force lands and sets up a security perimeter on the beach. Leaving behind a five-man security force, the balance of the team moves inland toward its target. At 0215 hours, the raiders illuminate their target with parachute flare rounds from a 60mm mortar. With the target plainly in sight, it is destroyed with eighteen rounds of 57mm M18 recoilless rifle rounds.

As the raiders attack their target, a North Vietnamese security force sets up a perimeter to secure the beach landing site. The five-man security force left behind by the raiders comes under heavy fire from the surrounding North Vietnamese. The two Nasty-class boats offshore come in and attack the North Vietnamese with 20mm and 40mm cannon fire from their shipboard weapons.

Even though the North Vietnamese eventually break their encircling attack of the security force, the raiding force inland still has to make its way back to shore and safety. The battle gets down to hand-to-hand combat until the raiders make a breakthrough to the beach location. PTF 5 picks up all of the raiding party except for two men who are lost and presumed dead. In addition, two M18 57mm recoilless rifles are left behind by the raiders. Regardless, twenty-two of the enemy are reported to have been killed in the engagement, along with the destruction of the target.

JULY

A Mark VI landing craft converted into a medium SEAL support craft (MSSC) for operations in Vietnam. Lining the sides of the craft are fifty-caliber machine guns behind armored shields to protect the gunners. The heavy fire support of this "Six" boat comes from the 57mm M18A1 recoilless rifle on the overhead at the rear of the boat. U.S. NAVY

July 01

1944 (Pacific)—The first letter from D. M. Logsdon, the commanding officer of UDT Six, is written to the team:

UNDERWATER DEMOLITION TEAM NO. 6

1 July 1944

From: The Commanding Officer

To: The Officers and men of U.D.T. No. 6

Subject: Forager Operation—Performance of Team Personnel

1. Inasmuch as the end of the subject operation is near enough to permit a preliminary review of its performance, I wish to take this opportunity to thank the officers and men of U.D.T. No. 6 for the manner in which they have performed their duties.

2. In every military operation it falls to the lot of certain units to be held in reserve. The selection of the reserve units is seldom based on any conception of inferiority in those units, but rather on the military necessity that forces must be held ready for use whenever and wherever they may be needed. The task of adequately preparing for such a varied assignment requires a greater degree of application than is required of those performing definitely assigned duties. Furthermore, the inactivity and uncertainty necessarily arising from the reserve status imposes a severe strain on the morale and efficiency of any organization. You have borne that strain very well.

3. You have grumbled and occasionally felt left out; you have thought that the parts played by all the teams in general and by this team in particular have no military value; and you have often said to yourselves that you want to get into an outfit that

sees real service. To all of these complaints there are very obvious answers. The first is that it's a fighting man's privilege to grumble and gripe; his officers are always wrong, his outfit is "no good," and he's in the wrong branch of the service. If he doesn't feel that way at times he's ready for the doctors. The second is that if the work of the teams were of no military value the Commander in Chief of the Pacific area would very quickly disband the teams; and the commanders of these large task forces would hardly waste so much of the force's naval strength in supporting the work of the teams if that work did not markedly further the successful performance of the operation. And the third answer is that if you want to get a better view of what the service thinks of your work, talk to the men in other parts of the task force.

4.   In spite of the difficulties under which you have worked you have done a good job on everything that this team has been directed to do. You have shown courage, skill and obedience in the face of the enemy. You have proved what I felt from the outset—that ours is the best team in the outfit. Let's keep it so.

5.   This war is not yet over. There is still much unfinished business before us. In many respects our ability to do our work can be improved. It is hoped that certain changes can be made in our organization and equipment, but we must recommend those changes to the proper authorities. You are the ones who can best discover how we can improve our team. If you have any suggestions, I would like for you to discuss them with me so that proper action can be taken on them.

6. There are greater operations ahead of us; operations that before too many months will put an end to Tojo's fantastic dreams of empire and will permit us all to return to our homes and loved ones in a victorious America. I sincerely hope that it will be my privilege to be your Commanding Officer in those operations.

D. M. LOGSDON

1945 (Borneo)—The invasion of Balikpapan begins. UDT guides from UDTs Eleven and Eighteen help pilot the first wave of landing craft in to the cleared beaches.

1962 (Vietnam)—The First Special Forces Group assumes the Civilian Irregular Defense Force advisory mission in Vietnam.

1968 (USA)—With the West Coast UDTs having the Southeast Asia commitment that includes Vietnam and Thailand, the constantly increasing workload threatens to overwhelm the West Coast teams. SEAL Team One is also draining manpower from the West Coast Naval Special Warfare pool to meet its commitments to Vietnam and elsewhere. To lighten the workload of the UDTs, UDT Thirteen is commissioned to join the ranks of UDT Eleven and Twelve at Coronado, California. The UDT Thirteen command is considered a recommissioning by some as another team by that name had served well during World War II.

July 02

1970

BARNDANCE# 5-77   SEAL TEAM___2___DET_A_PLT_5th___

DATE(S): 2 July 1970   OTHER UNITS: MST-2 DET D, SWAMP FOX
                                            COBRA GUNSHIPS
MSG REF(S):_____

NAMES OF PERS: ~~RICHARDSON~~ ASHTON BM1, DAVIS, BM1, HOOD ABH2, MULBY SGT(AUS)
PIERSON, GMG3, QM2 BLACKISTON

MISSION TASK: Recon Patrol

INTELL/INFO SOURCE(S)___No Intell

INSERTION: TIME: 0500 1st insertion   METHOD: MSSC   AHS COORD: XS341398
                   0900 2nd insertion   MSSC   XS337397
EXTRACTION: TIME: 0845 1st extraction METHOD: MSSC   AHS COORD: XS341398
                   0935 2nd extraction   MSSC   XS337397

TERRAIN:___Banana and coconut groves and thick jungle
WEATHER: clear   TIDE: HIGH LOW   MOON NONE

BRIEF MISSION NARRATIVE   Departed Dong Tam 0430 and inserted XS341398. Patrolled
150 mtrs and set G/P until daylight. Patrolled west along canal approx 100 mtrs. Stopped
2 SanPans and took 3 detainees. Patrolled north and East back to extraction point and
extracted. Reinserted at 0900 approx XS337392 to check Sanpan and warning shots. Patrolled
south up canal approx 50 mtrs., found footprints leading south. Followed same south approx
200 mtrs. Heard voices, spotted and took under fire approx 25 VC with weapons. Called
for air support and extracted.

RESULTS OF ENEMY ENCOUNTERED: 6 KIA (BC) 2 KIA (PROB)

FRIENDLY CASUALTIES: None

REMARKS (SIGNIFICANT EVENTS, OPEVAL RESULTS, ETC.): None

RECOMMENDATIONS/LESSONS LEARNED: None

BD COPY DIST:

FORM REV. 8/68   BARNDANCE # 5-77

174

July 03

1965 (South Vietnam)—UDT Twelve's Detachment Bravo receives a commendation for the series of clandestine and overt hydrographic recon surveys it has conducted between May 21 and July 3, 1965, along the South Vietnamese coast.

1992 (Yugoslavia)—Operation Provide Promise begins. In it, U.S. forces airlift supplies for groups of civilian populations that are trapped in the war-torn areas of Bosnia-Herzegovinia as humanitarian assistance.

July 04

1945 (Borneo)—In an unusual Fourth of July celebration, the light cruisers USS *Nashville* (CL 43) and USS *Phoenix* (CL 46), in addition to five American destroyers, fire a twenty-one-gun salute into enemy positions near Balikpapan. Later reports state that the salute destroyed an enemy ammunition magazine, adding to the effectiveness of the celebration.

1967 (South Vietnam)—On an ambitious snatch operation in the Second Corps area in the central region of South Vietnam, SEALs from Juliette and Kilo Platoons of SEAL Team One's Detachment Golf secure several members of the VC infrastructure. It is accomplished near the border of the Hai Long and Hoa Da districts of Binh Thuan Province. The actual target location is near the shore of the South China Sea, about twenty miles northeast of the city of Phan Thiet in an area known as the Le Hong Phong Secret Zone.

With units from the U.S. Army's Second Battalion, Seventh Cavalry, First Air Calvary as well as from the USS *Brush* (DD 745), a Sumner-class destroyer, and the U.S. Coast Guard *Point White* (WPB 82308), an eighty-two-foot patrol boat supplying naval gunfire support, the SEALs insert on a classic "over-the-beach" SEAL raid, which they launch from the *Brush*. The SEALs move in to the secret zone in small boats, sending out swimmer scouts to the landing area before the balance of the force is brought in. During the twenty-one-hour-long operation, the SEALs quietly move in to the area where their intelligence says there will be a meeting of several members of the local VC infrastructure. After a long patrol and wait, followed by a quick chase, the SEALs capture two VC cell leaders and a female VC woman's organization leader. A number of important documents regarding VC political actions are also taken. During the chase of the VC, a fourth VC was killed.

1976 (Uganda, Africa)—Israeli Sayaret Matkal Unit 269 conducts Operation Thunderball, rescuing more than 100 hostages held by Popular Front for the Liberation of Palestine–Special Operations Group terrorists who hijacked Air France Flight 139 and landed at Entebbe Airport.

July 05

1942 (USA)—The First Special Service Force, a combined unit of U.S. and Canadian forces, is established. Trained to operate in cold and mountainous terrain, the unit does not go on to its originally planned operations in Norway. Instead, it is later sent to Italy where it is soon nicknamed the "Devil's Brigade" by the Germans.

1968 (South Vietnam)—SEAL Team Two's Third Platoon's Alpha Squad conducts a patrol and ambush operation utilizing a unique insertion technique developed by the SEALs in Vietnam. For the operation, the SEAL squad conducts an underway insertion from a PBR. As the patrol boat passes the insertion point, the SEALs roll off the back of the boat, slipping into the water with very little splashing, as the PBR continues on its way. With no change in the sound of the boat's motor or speed, there is no reason for any local VC to get particularly suspicious of a PBR passing by—at least not until they meet up with a group of SEALs in the darkness.

The "underway" goes well enough, but the SEALs end up conducting their insertion right in front of a Vietnamese hooch. With the group badly compromised, the SEALs call in their extraction boat and cancel the balance of the operation.

July 06

1945 (Pacific)—UDT Seventeen receives a pleasant set of orders: it's being moved from its present location in Guam and will return to Pearl Harbor aboard the USS *Bull* (APD 78). Pearl Harbor means fresh food and more comfortable living conditions, among other amenities.

1964 (South Vietnam)—Captain Roger Hugh Charles Donlon, the commanding officer of Special Forces Team A-726, performs the actions that later cause him to be awarded the Congressional Medal of Honor, the first awarded since the Korean War more than ten years earlier. The citation reads:

> *For conspicuous gallantry and intrepidity at the risk of his life above and beyond the call of duty while defending a U.S. military installation against a fierce attack by hostile forces. Capt. Donlon was serving as the commanding officer of the U.S. Army Special Forces Detachment A726 at Camp Nam Dong when a reinforced Viet Cong battalion suddenly launched a full scale, predawn attack on the camp. During the violent battle that ensued, lasting 5 hours and resulting in heavy casualties on both sides, Capt. Donlon directed the defense operations in the midst of an enemy barrage of mortar shells, falling grenades, and extremely heavy gunfire. Upon the initial onslaught, he swiftly marshaled his forces and ordered the removal of the needed ammunition from a blazing building. He then dashed through a hail of small arms and exploding hand grenades to abort a breach of the main gate. In route to this position he detected an enemy demolition team of 3 in the proximity of the main gate and quickly annihilated them. Although exposed to the intense grenade attack, he then succeeded in reaching a 60mm mortar position despite sustaining a severe stomach wound as he was within 5 yards of the gun pit. When he discovered that most of the men in this gun pit were also wounded, he completely disregarded his own injury, directed their withdrawal to a location 30 meters away, and again risked his life by remaining behind and covering the movement with the utmost effectiveness. Noticing that his team sergeant was unable to evacuate the gun pit he crawled*

toward him and, while dragging the fallen soldier out of the gun pit, an enemy mortar exploded and inflicted a wound in Capt. Donlon's left shoulder. Although suffering from multiple wounds, he carried the abandoned 60mm mortar weapon to a new location 30 meters away where he found 3 wounded defenders. After administering first aid and encouragement to these men, he left the weapon with them, headed toward another position, and retrieved a 57mm recoilless rifle. Then with great courage and coolness under fire, he returned to the abandoned gun pit, evacuated ammunition for the 2 weapons, and while crawling and dragging the urgently needed ammunition, received a third wound on his leg by an enemy hand grenade. Despite his critical physical condition, he again crawled 175 meters to an 81mm mortar position and directed firing operations which protected the seriously threatened east sector of the camp. He then moved to an eastern 60mm mortar position and upon determining that the vicious enemy assault had weakened, crawled back to the gun pit with the 60mm mortar, set it up for defensive operations, and turned it over to 2 defenders with minor wounds. Without hesitation, he left this sheltered position, and moved from position to position around the beleaguered perimeter while hurling hand grenades at the enemy and inspiring his men to superhuman effort. As he bravely continued to move around the perimeter, a mortar shell exploded, wounding him in the face and body. As the long awaited daylight brought defeat to the enemy forces and their retreat back to the jungle leaving behind 54 of their dead, many weapons, and grenades, Capt. Donlon immediately reorganized his defenses and administered first aid to the wounded. His dynamic leadership, fortitude, and valiant efforts inspired not only the American personnel but the friendly Vietnamese defenders as well and resulted in the successful defense of the camp. Capt. Donlon's extraordinary heroism, at the risk of his life above and beyond the call of duty are in the highest traditions of the U.S. Army and reflect great credit upon himself and the Armed Forces of his country.

★ ★ ★ ★ ★

1969 (South Vietnam)—Planning from information developed by a SEAL agent in their own intelligence gathering network, a small group from SEAL Team Two's Eighth Platoon, Detachment Alfa, goes out on an early morning ambush operation. The SEALs insert by boat onto the north bank of the Mekong River just a short distance east of where it flows into the Song My Tho River. After patrolling north 100 meters, the SEALs set up a trail ambush. Almost two hours after the insertion, warning shots are heard in the distance. The SEALs immediately break their ambush and patrol to a nearby hooch where they question the occupants. The SEALs learn that the VC are immediately north of their position. The unit patrols back to the trail when one VC is seen walking down from the north. The SEALs take the VC under fire. As another male is taken under fire, the SEALs note four more VC further up the trail. The result: one VC is known to be killed and a second wounded. A single Russian-manufactured AK-47 is captured.

July 07

1942 (Europe)—The term "Jedburgh" is first applied to uniformed personnel dropped behind enemy lines.

1944 (Pacific)—In preparation for the invasion of Tinian, UDT Five receives expected orders to conduct a joint night reconnaissance of landing beaches White 1 and 2 on Tinian. The joint operation will be conducted by the men of UDT Five and a detachment from the marine reconnaissance battalion. The UDT operators will recon the approaches to the beaches and the beaches themselves, looking for obstacles and mines as well as making notes of the offshore waters and beach conditions. The marines will go in from the beaches and try to find exits from them into the jungles and the hinterland beyond. The mission is to be conducted on day J-14 (July 10), fourteen days before the invasion.

1945 (USA)—UDT Sixteen arrives at San Francisco, California, aboard the USS *Attala* (APA 137). The men are granted a thirty-day leave before they are to report to Oceanside, California, for cold water training. The training is part of the preparations for the invasion of the main islands of Japan.

July 08

1944 (Pacific)—Three battleships under the command of Admiral Walden L. Ainsworth shell targets on Guam a number of times. The smashing of Guam with the huge main-gun shells of the battleships is part of the preinvasion bombardment of the island.

1966 (North Vietnam)—Radio Hanoi announces that several U.S. pilots shot down over North Vietnam have been captured and are being paraded through the streets of Hanoi. North Vietnam, acting as if it is not bound by the Geneva Conventions, consistently treats U.S. POWs severely, considering them to be criminals.

1969 (South Vietnam)—The new policy of "Vietnamization" of the war, the turning over of ground and other combats to the South Vietnamese forces, results in 814 men being sent back to the United States from the U.S. Army's Ninth Infantry Division. They are the first U.S. troop withdrawals guided by the new policy.

July 09

1942 (USA)—The First Special Service Forces activated at Fort W. H. Harrison, Montana.

1944 (Pacific)—To conduct a specialized clandestine recon of several Japanese-held islands in the Palau group, the Balao-class submarine USS *Burrfish* (SS 312) sets out with a group of UDT operators on board. The two officers and six enlisted men are volunteers from UDT Ten. Several of the men are from the OSS Maritime Unit, who came from the Naval Combat Underwater Demolition Training and Experimental Base at Maui. The recon operations are conducted in the waters off Peleliu and the Yap Islands, with the men launching from the deck of the submarine in rubber boats. After the recon is complete, they will be recovered the same way.

The *Burrfish* arrives off Peleliu having been delayed by a mechanical failure. One of the UDT operators is able to swim along the outside of the submarine's hull and skillfully help with the repairs. The launching of the rubber boats and recon of Peleliu complete on schedule and the first submarine-launched UDT reconnaissance finishes. The *Burrfish* continues on to the Yap Islands. Meeting with the submarine USS *Balao* (SS 205) while at sea, the *Burrfish* turns over the charts, data, and photographs it has taken during its two-week-long recon of Peleliu. The *Balao* heads back for Pearl Harbor while the *Burrfish* continues on its mission.

At Yap, the situation turns serious for the submarine and the UDT Ten detachment. Launching the rubber boats in rough seas, several of the UDT operators still manage to land on the island. As dawn approaches, no signal comes from the island and the *Burrfish* finally has to get underway or risk detection from the Japanese. Ignoring the very real danger of detection, the *Burrfish* continues to cruise along the reefs of Yap, maintaining a constant watch through the periscope for any signal from the island. With the possibility increasing that the Japanese know the submarine is there and the weather continuing to worsen, the *Burrfish* finally leaves Yap waters.

Documents taken from the Japanese later indicate that the UDT men were taken prisoner on the island. While undergoing interrogation at the hands of the Japanese, the men repeatedly gave the cover story that they had been told. They do not survive the war.

Chief Howard Roeder, John MacMahon, and Robert Black were the only men of Naval Special Warfare ever taken prisoner. All the UDT men who conducted the *Burrfish* reconnaissance received the Silver Star. It was awarded to Roeder, MacMahon, and Black posthumously. The UDT does not conduct another submarine-launched reconnaissance during World War II.

July 10

1943 (Mediterranean)—Operation Husky, the Allied invasion of Sicily, takes place. The combined operation will put U.S. and British forces on Sicily at five different points. The U.S. Seventh Army under Lieutenant General George S. Patton will land with seven divisions on beaches at Licata, Gela, and Scoglitti.

To establish a Naval Demolition Unit for the Sicily operation, a group of volunteers consisting of six officers and twelve enlisted men from the Seabee training base in Little Creek, Virginia, are assembled as Naval Demolition Unit One.

The men are experienced with explosives and are given additional training in military demolition and obstacle clearance. The men are very competent with demolition but very inexperienced with the navy.

Divided into three groups and assigned one group to a beach, the men are issued a lavish amount of equipment and explosives. With all of their knowledge and explosives, the men of the three groups are not engaged in active operations during the invasion. The single target a group is assigned is to blast clear rubble blocking the streets of Scoglitti. Returning to the United States, many of the men go to the Naval Combat Demolition Unit School at Fort Pierce, Florida, with some taking the position of instructors.

1944 (Pacific)—UDT Five conducts a night reconnaissance of the waters off White Beaches 1 and 2 on Tinian. The night sky is clear and bright, making visibility at the outbreak of the operation relatively easy. Four officers, including Lieutenant Commander Draper Kauffman, and eight enlisted men from UDT Five conduct the actual recon.

The two rubber boats, each with a six-man crew, go out to their starting position off the White Beaches as a light fog comes in, limiting visibility. The reconnaissance continues, even though the UDT cannot tell if it is on the right beach or not. As it turns out, only one of the correct landing beaches, White 1, is examined. A second reconnaissance is called for the next night and, without calling attention to themselves by the Japanese work party on the beach, the operators of the UDT complete their recon of the correct beaches at Tinian and the information is sent on to higher command.

July 11

1941 (USA)—The Office of Coordinator of Information (COI) is initiated by presidential order to assemble and study intelligence information for the U.S. government. Directed by General William Donovan, within a year the mission of the COI is absorbed into a new organization: the Office of Strategic Services (OSS). The OSS not only analyzes information, it also goes out and actively gathers it and conducts covert operations against enemy forces. To conduct these operations, the OSS develops a number of unconventional forces. One of these forces is the Maritime Unit, the first unconventional underwater combat and sabotage unit in the United States.

BARNDANCE # __8 - 66__   SEAL TEAM __2__ ; DET. __A__ ; __8th__ PLT.

DATE(S): __11 JULY 69__   OTHER UNITS: __3 PRU ADVISORS, 40 PRU'S__
MSG REF(S): _____   __114th AVN CO.__
_____   __SEAWOLF__
_____   __CAPT. KIRKPACTRICK__

NAMES OF PERS: __LTjg SCHUTZMAN, TUUBE, PACHELCK, FINLEY, HEIDREAUX, EVANSON,__
__PORTER, MCMAHON__
_____
_____

MISSION TASK: __POW RELEASE__
_____

INTEL/INFO SOURCE(S): __COMBINED 525 MI__

INSERTION: TIME: __0955__   METHOD: __Slick__   AMS COORD: __xr762897/ 7729__

EXTRACTION: TIME: __1045__   METHOD: __Slick__   AMS COORD: __xr768908__

TERRAIN: __Fields/ Nipa Swamp__
WEATHER: __overcast__   TIDE: __N / A__   MOON: __N / A__

BRIEF MISSION NARRATIVE: __Inserted 3 and 2 elements, all elements swep toward center__
__mass, southern 2 elements encountered booby traps, tripwire and foot mine. Northern__
__elements questioned inhabitants of area who said a large number of VG passed into the__
__Nipa Swamps within the hour. Inhabitants also mentioned "LARGE MEN BEING PUSHED".__
_____
_____

RESULTS OF ENEMY ENCOUNTERED: __5 Bunkers, 5 Sampans destroyed.__
_____

FRIENDLY CASUALTIES: __NONE__
_____

REMARKS (SIGNIFICANT EVENTS, OPEVAL RESULTS, ETC.): __NONE__
_____
_____
_____
_____

RECOMMENDATIONS/LESSONS LEARNED: __NONE__
_____
_____
_____

BD COPY DIST: _____

(FORM REV. 8/68)   BARNDANCE # __8 - 66__

July 12

1945 (USA)—OSS Detachment 101 is disbanded and awarded the Presidential Distinguished Unit Citation.

```
BARNDANCE#  5-84                    SEAL TEAM   2        DET   A   PLT 5th

DATE(S):  12 July 1970          OTHER UNITS:    MST -2 Det D

MSG REF(S):

NAMES OF PERS:  LT JUKOSKI, DMC CRESCINI, BM1 DAVIS, BM1 ASHTON, STG2 GLASSCOCK,
BM2 WATERS, HM1 LASHOMB, QM2 BARON, GMG3 PIERSON


MISSION TASK:  Recovery of 1 82MM and 60 MM Mortar Tubes


INTELL/INFO SOURCE(S) 525 MIG AND MSS MYTHO

INSERTION:    TIME:    120445 H        METHOD:  MSSC      AHS COORD: XS330422

EXTRACTION:   TIME:    120815         METHOD:  MSSC      AHS COORD: XS330422

TERRAIN:  Bannana Groves and Rice Fields
WEATHER:  Clear              TIDE:  low to high       MOON __

BRIEF MISSION NARRATIVE  Inserted and with guide leading the way, patrolled 700 mtrs
to bannana grove containing mortars and guard force.  Grove was deserted and showed signs
of no recent activity.  Guide was unable to find xxxxx cache.


RESULTS OF ENEMY ENCOUNTERED:  NA


FRIENDLY CASUALTIES:          na


REMARKS (SIGNIFICANT EVENTS, OPEVAL RESULTS, ETC.):  NA




RECOMMENDATIONS/LESSONS LEARNED:  XX Guide was using what I believe to be third
hand intell which proved not to be very current.



BD COPY DIST:

FORM REV. 8/68                      BARNDANCE #  5-84
```

July 13

1942 (India)—OSS Detachment 101 arrives.

1965 (North Vietnam)—Special Forces Sergeant First Class Isaac Comacho escapes from VC captivity.

1967 (South Vietnam)—With both SEAL teams sending platoons into Vietnam for direct-action operations, the SEALs are becoming well known for their skills in the jungle—not for their typing.

> Thursday 13 July 67   Revellie was held and all hands had breakfast after which they proceded to the quansit area to get ready for operation. The platoon left the base at 0315hrs by Mike boat for an inserotion point in the Hoa Binh sub sector on the MyTho river, Tong Hoa island. The platoon led by Mr. Boitnott inserted by stab at 0530hrs and proceeded on patrol through the area for approx. 4hr The patrol picked up 3 men who didn't have I.D. cards which were extracted with the patrol by stab and taken to the Mike boat. The three captives were taken to Hoa Binh for interrogatio Results, All three were V.C. one being a Hamlett Chief. The patrol then proceeded by Mike Boat to the base at MyTho arriving approx 1030 hrs. After which cleaning weapons and equipment R&R was granted. Another operation was schedual for later that night byt was called off due to some information concerning the operation not being quite thourgh enough.

July 14

1944 (Pacific)—UDT Three conducts a daylight reconnaissance of 2,000 yards of beach at Asan on Guam. A second recon run that same day occurs at Agana Beach. The Agana Beach operation is conducted as a diversion to confuse the enemy as to just which beach might be the landing target. In what is later considered to be a response to a bet between the teams, the men of UDT Three place a sign on Agat Beach to prove that they had been there well before the marines. The sign reads: "Welcome U.S. Marines by Seabee Demolition 7.14.44 U.D.T. 3."

That evening, another recon is conducted of all four landing beaches at Asan. One of the rubber boats used by UDT Three operators is taken under machine gun fire from the jungle above the beach and three men are lost.

July 15

1941 (Washington, D.C.)—The formation of the COI Office is announced.

1943 (Mediterranean)—All OSS forces in the western Mediterranean combine to form the 2677th Regiment (Provisional) in Algiers.

1964 (North Vietnam)—A Nasty boat, the Norwegian-designed eighty-foot Fast Patrol Craft (PTF)—a new version of the World War II patrol torpedo boats—conducts an operation in support of Oplan 34A during the night against a security post at Cape Ron. Things go wrong during the attack, however, and two men are killed before the mission is aborted. It is the first Oplan 34A maritime operation to fail in three months.

July 16

1944 (Pacific)—UDT Four arrives off Guam for what is its first combat operation. The reconnaissance is delayed until the next morning.

1966 (South Vietnam)—Operation Deckhouse II runs from July 16 to 18. It is a series of amphibious landings intended to keep the VC from gathering in large groups along coastal areas. In spite of rapid actions by UDT Eleven to support the landings by elements of the Third Marine Amphibious Force, the VC consistently refuse to stand and fight, blending in with the local population rather than fight a conventional battle of fire and maneuver.

1968 (South Vietnam)—A SEAL ambush only six miles east of Saigon eliminates two VC. No intelligence material is recovered due to the quick sinking of the VC boat and the depth of the water. The next day, however, divers recover a number of assault rifles and more than 400 rounds of ammunition from the site.

July 17

1944 (Pacific)—Starting in the midafternoon, two platoons from UDT Four conduct a preassault reconnaissance of Yellow Beach 2 on Guam. The recon involves a hydrographic survey of the offshore waters from the three-fathom line (18 feet) to the high water mark.

A number of coral-filled palm log cribs, boxes made from palm tree trunks, are found, as well as barbed wire fences. The decision is made to return that evening to conduct a demolition swim and to mark the extremities of the beach with buoys. At 2110 hours, the platoons leave the USS *Talbot* (APD 7) for the mission. As they place demolitions, the operators of UDT Four can hear conversations and other sounds coming from the Japanese troops on shore. These same Japanese will be surprised when the obstacle clearing charges go off early the next morning.

1957 (Pacific)—The Fourteenth Special Forces Operations Detachment (Okinawa) and the 8231st Army Special Operations Detachment (Korea) join together to form the First Special Forces Group (Airborne).

July 18

1944 (Pacific)—A recon of White Beach indicates that a demolition swim has to be made to clear obstacles and blast channels through the reef. This will allow landing craft to reach the beach. As swimmers from UDT Four conduct their demolition operation, they are covered by a number of fire support ships, including a destroyer, cruiser, and battleship, along with half a dozen gunboats.

The beach area is closely examined for mines by UDT Four, which takes advantage of its time close to the shore to post a sign. When the marines land on Guam later that day, they are greeted not only by Japanese fire, but also by a piece of plywood reading: "Welcome Marines AGAT USO Two Blocks Courtesy UDT 4."

Although UDT Three has placed an earlier sign, the one from UDT Four receives the most publicity. The story of the sign quickly spreads through the fleet and the Marine Corps. There has long been a standing statement by the marines that they are always the first to land on an enemy beach. With the placement of the sign, there is no question of who is on the beaches first.

1988 (Iran)—Iran accepts the UN cease-fire offer, ending the eight-year war between Iran and Iraq.

July 19

1945 (USA)—UDT Thirty is formally commissioned at Fort Pierce, Florida, after completion of its training at the Naval Combat Demolition Unit School. The men are granted a ten-day leave before they are shipped out to Oceanside, California, to begin cold water training. UDT Thirty is one of the last of the wartime UDTs to be formally commissioned.

1968 (South Vietnam)—The graduation class of LDNN Replacement Class III completes its advanced training at Vung Tau. The LDNNs go out on a large ambush mission as their first official operation. The nighttime ambush is set up thirty miles southeast of Saigon. During the night, a sequence of actions results in the LDNNs ambushing five different groups of sampans traveling the river. During the ambushes, at least six sampans are destroyed, fifteen VC killed, and another two VC captured.

July 20

1942 (USA)—The First Special Service Force has its first formation in Helena, Montana.

1968 (South Vietnam)—Juliette Platoon of SEAL Team One's Detachment Golf sets up a canal ambush. It is designed to eliminate or capture a VC tax collector who is reported to be in the area extorting money or materials from the locals to support the VC operations. The SEALs insert by a Boston Whaler in the north part of the Chau Thanh district in Ving Long Province. The area is a tidal flat, with long stretches of mud, tall grass, and tree lines. To help give them the range to take out the tax collector, the SEALs have a bolt-action 7.62mm sniper rifle, something they rarely carry for the short-range combat operations so common in Vietnam. In addition, they have arranged for Seawolf helicopter support from HAL 3, Detachment 3.

The SEALs spot their quarry, the tax collector accompanied by three guards, about 500 meters from the ambush site. The range is too great for the SEALs and the tax collector doesn't stay in the open long enough for them to get a shot at him. Even though the SEALs can see sampans being called in to the river bank to be taxed and forced to pay what was effectively a toll at the barrel of a gun, the collector stays in the brush out of sight. The SEALs call in a helicopter strike on the area after first light. Well guarded by an unknown number of VC, there are many bunkers scattered about the area. The SEALs don't move in to examine the area around the air strike.

July 21

1944 (Pacific)—For the United States, the most important of the Mariana Islands is Guam. Before the war, it had been a U.S. possession for more than forty years. The invasion was originally planned to take place on June 18, but was delayed for a number of reasons. With the typhoon season due to break in July, the invasion finally goes forward. Thousands of rounds of naval gunfire pour into the island, including over 6,000 rounds of 14- and 16-inch shells from the battleships and more than 16,000 rounds of 5-inch shells from the other ships of the fleet.

W day, the invasion of Guam, is set for 0600 hours. Later on, Rear Admiral Richard Conolly states that the landings could not have gone forward without the clearance and reconnaissance operations conducted by the men of UDTs Three, Four, and Six.

1983 (USA)—The U.S. Army Institute for Military Assistance is renamed the U.S. Army John F. Kennedy Special Warfare Center and School.

July 22

1968 (South Vietnam)—Alpha Squad from Third Platoon of SEAL Team Two's Detachment Alpha conducts a patrol and ambush north of the Rung Sat Special Zone. The SEALs insert by PBR at 2030 hours and set up an ambush next to a waterway in open terrain. During the night, a single sampan with two VC occupants comes into the SEAL's kill zone. The results of the operation include two VC killed and no injuries on the part of the SEALs. They extract at 0400 hours the same way they had come in.

This sudden violence in the darkness has given the SEALs a terrifying name among the VC. They call the camouflage-painted apparitions that come out of the dark the "Men with Green Faces."

July 23

1944 (Pacific)—The main operation conducted by UDT Seven at Tinian is a diversionary reconnaissance off Red, Green, and Blue beaches. The beaches cover an area 2,500 yards long near Sunharin Town. Three boats launch seven UDT swimmers each along the outer barrier reef of the target beaches, while a fourth boat remains in reserve. The heavy support fire that drives the enemy under cover proves its worth as a total of only three rounds of sniper fire are noticed by the UDT swimmers. In spite of it being a diversionary operation to help confuse the enemy, the UDT swimmers conduct a complete reconnaissance of the reef, though they do not go any closer to the island than the inner reef edge facing the beach. The UDT swimmers are recovered after forty-five minutes of swimming.

1952 (Korea)—Off the coast of Korea, men from UDT Five, operating from the USS *Diachenko* (APD 123), conduct the first mission in support of Operation Fish. To effectively disrupt North Korean fishing operations, the men of the UDT are ordered to destroy any fishing nets they locate. Starting on July 23 and ending August 1, the *Diachenko* and its UDT Five detachment destroy two large nets with twenty buoys and anchors, damage or destroy five sampans, kill or wound an unknown number of enemy personnel, and capture five North Korean prisoners. In addition to the specific targets of Operation Fish, the UDT men also damage a number of buildings and installations on shore.

July 24

1944 (Pacific)—The third stage of Operation Forager, the invasion of Tinian, begins with H hour being 0717, in which the first wave moves in to the beaches. Heavy Japanese resistance is met with even heavier naval firepower. Mines destroy only a few tracked landing vehicles when they run up the beach. By the end of the J day, 15,614 U.S. Marines, soldiers, and navy personnel are on the beaches at a cost of 15 lives and about 200 wounded.

1957 (Pacific)—The First Special Forces Group (Airborne) is activated in Okinawa.

1971 (USA)—Eleven officers and seventeen enlisted men of SEAL Team Two attend the launching ceremonies of the Knox-class frigate USS *John C. Brewton* (FF 1086) in New Orleans. The ship is named after Lieutenant (j.g.) John C. Brewton, a SEAL who had been killed in Vietnam the year before. Admiral Elmo Zumwalt, the chief of naval operations, presides over the ceremony and the reception for the SEALs. Admiral Zumwalt is an enthusiastic SEAL supporter.

July 25

1959 (Laos)—Special Forces teams begin arriving.

1968 (South Vietnam)—On the night of July 25–26, west of Vinh Long Province, Juliette Platoon begins a body snatch on a reported VC cadre member. The SEALs are inserted by boat and move into an area of rice paddies. The overcast skies dump wind-driven rain, giving the SEALs additional cover in the darkness. Locating their target hooch, the SEALs grab the single VC they find. Later, they are told that he was a village-level VC regular.

July 26

A group of NCDU (naval combat demolition unit) operators in France shortly after the D day landings at Normandy. Though their normal arms consist of large haversacks of explosives and a sheath knife, several of these NCDU men have secured M1 Thompson submachine guns. The wide gray band on their helmets helped identify these men as Navy personnel in the confusion of the landing forces. National Archives

July 27

1953 (Korea)—A long-awaited cease-fire is signed between the North Koreans and the UN forces. The Korean War is over, though not officially ended. Nevertheless, an armistice has been declared, one that both the North and South Koreans, along with the UN forces, will follow for the next fifty years.

During the Korean War, the UDTs conducted new types of operations such as going behind enemy lines and up on dry land to conduct demolition raids and recon operations. Working in smaller units than during World War II, the UDTs also assisted in sixty-one assault landings. UDT One alone accounted for 125 reconnaissance missions, 12 demolition raids, and several special operations missions. UDTs Three and Five had also conducted operations in Korea, undergoing a rotation system that put the UDT operators incountry for six months, not including the one month of travel time it took to either come from or go to the United States.

July 28

1945 (USA)—A B-25 bomber strikes the Seventy-eighth floor of the Empire State Building in New York City. The ten-ton U.S. Army Air Corps plane is traveling at about 200 miles an hour in heavy fog when it strikes the north side of the building, 913 feet above the ground. The crew aboard the B-25 is killed by the impact. The high-octane fuel of the bomber, which splashed across the floor of the building during the impact, ignites. Eleven people are killed, many of them while at their desks, and dozens more are injured. The Empire State Building remains standing, while the B-25 sticks half in and half out of the structure. Three months later, the building reopens for business.

July 29

1945 (Pacific)—While returning to the United States, after delivering the first atomic bomb to the U.S. air base on Tinian, the cruiser USS *Indianapolis* (CA 35) is sunk by a Japanese submarine, the I-58. Even though the Japanese are very close to being defeated, the waters of the Pacific remain very dangerous. Because of the extremely secret nature of its mission, combined with other errors, the *Indianapolis* is not noticed as missing for three days. It is several days more before the 316 survivors of the ship's crew are located and rescued.

July 30

1966 (South Vietnam)—Regular North Vietnamese Army (NVA) troops are spotted crossing the demilitarized zone (DMZ) separating North and South Vietnam. For the first time during the war, U.S. aircraft bomb targets in the DMZ, striking at the NVA troop concentrations there.

July 31

1964 (North Vietnam)—Nasty boats PTF 3 and PTF 6 arrive at Hon Me Island at 0020 hours to attack the North Vietnamese Navy facilities there. Two additional Nasty boats, PTF 2 and PTF 5, attack targets at Hon Nieu. In spite of the knowledge that the North Vietnamese probably know they're coming, the South Vietnamese crews of PTFs 3 and 6 move in for the attack. Their mission is to place demolition charges on land targets as the Nasty boats provide gunfire support.

Approaching the target area, a single North Vietnamese patrol boat is spotted. At that moment, the enemy opens up with the Soviet/Communist equivalent of .30 and .50 caliber machine guns against the boats. The incoming fire wounds four crewmen aboard PTF 6.

Landing on the island is out of the question now, so the South Vietnamese commander orders a bombardment of the targets with the boats' guns. Using illumination rounds to help see the targets already visible in the moonlight, the PTFs fire high-explosive shells in to the targets with 20mm and 40mm mounted cannon as well as 57mm rounds from shoulder-fired M18 recoilless rifles. The fire from the boats destroys several buildings and a gun emplacement. The PTFs leave the area at 0048 hours.

North Vietnamese Swatow motor gunboats give chase to the PTFs. The North Vietnamese commander of the Swatow motor gunboat T-142 later admits that he was unable to close the distance with the Nasty boats, who had been completely unaware of the chase.

1994 (USA)—The administration of President Bill Clinton receives approval from the UN Security Council to conduct a multinational-force military invasion of Haiti. The object of the invasion is to reinstate the democratically elected president of the country Jean-Bertrand Aristide, who has been overthrown by an army coup. Fifteen thousand multinational troops, the bulk of them being from the United States, conduct Operation Uphold Democracy. The two-part operation will first land invasion forces to restore public order and reinstate Aristide. Afterward, 6,000 UN troops will keep the peace and help train a Haitian police force to continue maintaining order.

AUGUST

Nine Soviet Mark M-08/39 moored contact mines sit lined up along the deck of the Iranian minelayer *Iran Ajr*. The *Ajr* was caught in the act of laying mines in international shipping lanes of the Persian Gulf during the Iran-Iraq war. U.S. NAVY

August 01

1944 (Italy)—The OSS 2677th Special Reconnaissance Battalion is formed in Caserta.

1944 (Pacific)—The second letter from D. M. Logsdon, the commanding officer of UDT Six, is written to the team:

UNDERWATER DEMOLITION TEAM NO. 6

1 August 1944

From: The Commanding Officer

To: The Officers and men of U.D.T. No. 6

Subject: Commendation

1. This team has now completed its part in the Saipan-Tinian-Guam operation. As you know, this operation has consisted of three distinct but interrelated phases. Although military operations of two of these phases are still underway there is no room for doubt that their outcome will be a complete victory for the American forces. When this operation is concluded a tremendously important link will have been forged in the United States' chain that is being inexorably wound around the Japanese Empire.

2. The part that you have played in the progress of that operation should have cleared your minds of any thoughts that Naval Combat Demolition can serve no useful purpose in furthering our ultimate victory. The organization of which you are a part was born out of the blood and misery of Tarawa. Without your work and that of the personnel of the other teams that have participated in this operation many more of our forces would have died on the beaches of Saipan, Guam, and Tinian than died in trying to land at Tarawa. If that work had not been done many would also have been needlessly slaughtered because of the inability to get vital equipment ashore when and where it was needed.

3.   A high ranking Marine Officer has stated that without the work done by these teams the attempted landings at Guam would have been disastrous failures. In consideration for the bravery which you have shown and of the skillful manner in which you have done your work, the commander of the Southern Attack Force has recommended that each officer and man of the teams participating in the Guam operation be awarded the Bronze Star. Such recognition of the work performed by each man in an organization is a very rare thing.

4.   In the forenoon of 27 July 1944 this team was ordered to blast ramps for tank landing craft over an area of at least 700 feet on the reef off Dadi Beach on the southwest coast of Guam. This work was required to be completed before 1400 the following day. A predemolition reconnaissance of the reef indicated a very irregular reef front with numerous fissures and a large number of coral heads. Lieutenant (jg) Y. F. Carr was directed to take two platoons and make a test loading of about 200 feet of the reef. This work was begun at 1400 and the charge was fired about 1800. About nine tons of tetrytol were used in this charge. A hurried check the next morning showed that the test shot had produced an excellent ramp with a clear approach. At about 0730 on 28 July 1944 Lieut. (jg) Carr resumed operations with the entire team, less certain personnel left aboard the Clemson to handle explosives. By 1230 an additional 550 feet of reef and offlying heads had been loaded with about twenty-nine tons of tetrytol. This shot was fired at 1245. Due to the departure of the Clemson from the area that afternoon is was impossible to test the ramp that was blasted, but it was probably as good as that of the previous day. It is believed that this is a record for U.D.T. reef loading and blasting and has been reported as such to the base of Maui.

5. While this work was going on Lieutenant (jg) F. M. Methvin organized a detail of U.D.T. No. 6, aided by personnel generously furnished by the Clemson, and transferred all unexpended U.D.T. explosives from the ship to the beach as well as loading all boats returning for tetrytol. A total of twenty-two tons of various types of explosives were removed from storage space and sent to the beach and seventeen tons of tetrytol were sent out over the reef.

6. As a result of the excellent job of organizing done by Lieutenants (jg) Methvin and Carr and by the other officers of the team and the careful and diligent work done by the men of U.D.T. No. 6 the team accomplished what seemed an impossible task.

7. My heartiest congratulations on a tough job well done.

D. M. LOGSDON

August 02

1964 (North Vietnam)—The North Vietnamese Navy units close to the DMZ are on a high-alert status due to the Nasty-boat raids against North Vietnamese facilities. Responding to the detection of a large surface ship in the waters of the Gulf of Tonkin, a trio of torpedo boats are launched. The ship is the Sumner-class destroyer USS *Maddox* (DD 731) on a routine electronic intelligence gathering mission off North Vietnam. The ship is in international waters at the time and conducts no aggressive mission.

The three naval craft, identified as P-4 torpedo boats that could be a legitimate threat to the *Maddox*, are detected by lookouts and radar aboard the destroyer shortly after 1230 hours. The naval craft move in to cover in a cove on Hon Me and go off the screen of the *Maddox*.

About 1500 hours that same day, surface radar aboard the *Maddox* detects the three targets moving from Hon Me out to sea at high speed on a course almost parallel to the destroyer. Within thirty minutes, after maneuvering and seeing that the contacts are setting up for an attack, the *Maddox* is put on general quarters. The three P-4 torpedo boats, the T-333, T-339, and T-336, conduct an attack run on the *Maddox*. Three torpedoes are launched against the destroyer in a matter of minutes, along with gunfire from at least one of the boat's 14.5 mm heavy machine guns. The torpedo boats are taken under fire from the *Maddox*'s three- and five-inch guns. In addition, U.S. aircraft of the VF-51 fighter squadron attack the torpedo boats. The action results in very minor damage to the *Maddox* and the sinking of T-339.

1990 (Kuwait)—At 0200 local time, Saddam Hussein orders 10,000 troops and tanks to move across Iraq's southeastern boarder into Kuwait. The sudden action takes most of the Western and the Arab world by surprise. The Iraqis move in strength and the small country is quickly overwhelmed, conquered, and occupied in less than half a day. Within a week of the invasion, Hussein declares that Kuwait no longer exists and the area is now the nineteenth province of Iraq.

1990 (USA)—The UN adopts Resolution 660 condemning the Iraqi invasion of Kuwait and demands that Iraqi forces withdraw from the country immediately.

August 03

1964 (North Vietnam)—The Nasty boat PTF 6 takes the security post near the mouth of the Ron River under fire at 2352 hours. Illuminating the area with star shells, the Nasty boat fires 20mm and 40mm cannon, as well as 57mm recoilless rifle shells into the target. Responding to the attack with small arms fire, the on-shore North Vietnamese fail to reach the PTF 6 and cause it any damage. Easily outrunning a North Vietnamese craft sent out to pursue it, PTF 6 returns to the Danang base without further incident.

Shortly before midnight, operating in concert with the shelling attack at the Ron River, Nasty boats PTF 1 and PTF 5 fire on the radar facility near Vinh Son with 40mm cannon and 57mm recoilless rifle shells. Both boats fire 770 rounds of high-explosive shells into their target and then withdraw back to their home base at Danang.

August 04

1964—The Sumner-class destroyer USS *Maddox* (DD 731), with the Sherman-class guided missile destroyer USS *Turner Joy* (DD 951) in escort, returns to continuing an electronic intelligence-gathering DeSoto patrol in the Gulf of Tonkin. Neither of the two ships are aware of the Oplan 34A attack by the Nasty boats from Danang the night before. The destroyers are operating, however, at a higher state of readiness due to the attack incident against the *Maddox* on August 2.

The evening of August 4 includes several detections of small craft moving toward the *Maddox* on attack vectors. Contacts in the water are taken under fire as a reported torpedo launch is detected in the combat information center. Sonar aboard the *Maddox* reports torpedo sounds in the water shortly afterward. Both ships respond to the attack with maneuvers; shortly thereafter, a torpedo wake passes the *Turner Joy* about 500 feet from the ship.

Further radar contacts are immediately taken under fire by the five-inch guns on the *Turner Joy*. Additional contacts over the next several hours result in fire and depth charges being put out by the destroyers. Over the length of the engagement, the two destroyers fire 249 five-inch shells, which include 24 rounds of star shells for illumination, and 123 three-inch rounds. Four or five depth charges, one of which failed to detonate, were also dropped. No real damage is taken by either destroyer during the engagement, which is later referred to as the Tonkin Gulf Incident.

1970 (USA)—SEAL Team Two receives the first of two Presidential Unit Citations for its actions in the Vietnam War. The citation reads:

> By virtue of the authority vested in me as President of the United States and as Commander in Chief of the Armed Forces of the United States, I have today awarded

> ### THE PRESIDENTIAL UNIT CITATION (NAVY)
> ### FOR EXTRAORDINARY HEROISM TO
> ### SEAL TEAM TWO

> *SEAL Team TWO distinguished itself by exceptionally meritorious and heroic service from 1 July 1967 through 30 June 1969 in the conduct of unconven-*

tional warfare against an armed enemy in the Republic of Vietnam. Although often required to conduct their operation in almost impenetrable terrain and in a violently hostile environment, this small, elite fighting unit nonetheless accounted for numerous enemy casualties and the capture of large numbers of troops, weapons, ammunition, and documents of significant intelligence value. The outstanding valor, professionalism and esprit de corps of SEAL Team TWO are illustrated by the following instances: On 13 March 1968, a seven-man SEAL squad engaged an enemy force numbering approximately thirty men. During the fierce fire fight, although five SEALS were wounded, heavy casualties were inflicted upon the enemy. Exposed to a withering hail of fire by the pursuing enemy, the SEALS withdrew through 1,000 meters of enemy-occupied territory to an extraction point, with the less seriously wounded carrying their stricken comrades to safety. On another occasion, a six-man SEAL squad carried out an offensive patrol deep into the enemy-infested Rung Sat Special Zone and accounted for six enemy casualties. On still another occasion, a SEAL squad penetrated 4,000 meters into a VC base camp and overcame two of the enemy, one in hand-to-hand combat, before withdrawing to an extraction point 2,000 meters away, eluding a twenty-man element of the enemy which swept within fifteen meters of their position while attempting to locate them. Engaging this larger force, the SEALS accounted for ten enemy casualties before they were extracted. The distinguished and heroic combat record achieved by the officers and men of SEAL Team TWO reflects the highest credit upon themselves and the United States Naval Service.

Richard Nixon

August 05

1950 (Korea)—As the North Korean People's Army moves across the seventeenth parallel and into South Korea, a single UDT detachment of one officer and ten enlisted men is assigned to Commander, Amphibious Group One to conduct training operations with the U.S. Army at Camp McGill in Japan. The detachment has been conducting beach surveys in support of amphibious exercises when hostilities break out in Korea. The officer in charge of the detachment, Lieutenant (j.g.) George Atcheson, suspends regular operations for the detachment and reports in. After meeting aboard the USS *Mount McKinley* (AGC 7), the detachment is ordered to Sasebo, Japan, where it will board the USS *Diachenko* (APD 123).

Proceeding to Korea on the morning of August 5, the *Diachenko* arrives in the waters near Yosu, Korea, where the UDT conducts a demolition operation against a railroad bridge and tunnel. The UDT operators have not conducted this type of dry-land operation before, though their demolition training easily accommodates attacking the target with explosives. The target is well behind enemy lines by this time and only two men from the UDT, Lieutenant Atcheson and Boatswain's Mate Warren Foley, go in on the operation as swimmer-scouts. Other members of the UDT holding the demolitions remain on the rubber boat and wait for the signal to come ashore.

The submachine guns that Atcheson suggested taking on the operation are too heavy to swim with without flotation aids, which have been forgotten. Dividing some hand grenades between them, as well as taking a knife and a .45 pistol, the two UDT operators go in to the target aboard a rubber boat after being transported to within range of the beach by a landing craft from the *Diachenko*.

A large embankment on the beach separates the two UDT operators from their target, which takes some time to clamber over. The arrival of a party of about ten North Korean soldiers prevents the UDT operators from being able to reach the target and then call in the rubber boat with their teammates aboard. In the confusing extraction, while under fire from the North Koreans, the UDT operators throw hand grenades and head back to the beach. An alert U.S. sailor almost shoots Atcheson as he comes over the beach seawall. Foley is injured by a North Korean bullet, though later stories will swear that he has been accidentally shot by Atcheson in the confusion. The UDT men withdraw from the beach, with Foley earning the distinction of being the first U.S. Navy casualty of the Korean War.

August 06

1945 (Japan)—The first atomic bomb in history is dropped on the city of Hiroshima. Code-named Little Boy, the nuclear weapon is 120 inches long, 28 inches wide, and weighs 9,000 pounds. Dropped from the B-29 *Enola Gay*, the bomb detonates as an air burst at approximately 1,900 feet above the city at 0815 hours local time. The explosive blast of Little Boy is estimated to range between twelve and fifteen kilotons—equivalent to 12,000 to 15,000 tons of exploding TNT—and immediately destroys 60 percent of the city and kills an estimated 80,000 people. The Little Boy bomb actually devastates less than that of other bombing attacks, such as the March fire bomb raids on Tokyo, but this is one aircraft dropping a single bomb. A further 40,000 or more Japanese die days, weeks, and even years later from the aftereffects of the nuclear explosion.

1990 (USA)—Adopting Resolution 661, the United Nations imposes trade sanctions on all materials moving to or from Iraq. The only exceptions to the sanctions are for medicines and foodstuffs that qualify as humanitarian assistance. No means for enforcement for the trade sanctions are included in the language of the resolution.

August 07

1942 (USA)—Over a period of years, the criteria for awarding the Navy Cross, as distinct from the Navy Distinguished Service Medal, has become blurred. On August 7, 1942, the distinction of the Navy Cross is finalized by the passage of Public Law 702. Now, the Navy Cross will specifically be awarded to

> any person while serving in any capacity with the Navy or Marine Corps who distinguishes himself with extraordinary heroism not justifying the award of the Medal of Honor—(1) while engaged in an action against an enemy of the United States; (2) while engaged in military operations involving conflict with an opposing foreign force; or (3) while serving with friendly foreign forces engaged in an armed conflict against an opposing armed force in which the United States is not a belligerent party. To warrant this distinctive decoration the act should involve the risk of life so extraordinary as to set the person apart from his contemporaries.

The result of this law, therefore, rates the Navy Cross as second only to the Congressional Medal of Honor as an award that can be bestowed by a grateful nation for heroism in combat.

1945 (USA)—UDT Thirty arrives at Oceanside, California. With the situation in the Pacific theater indicating an imminent Japanese surrender, UDT Thirty is assigned to Oceanside as a permanent duty station. The unit will remain at Oceanside until decommissioning orders come on October 20, 1945.

1965 (USA)—The Tonkin Gulf Resolution proposed by President Lyndon B. Johnson's administration, unanimously passes in the House of Representatives and overwhelmingly (at a vote of eighty-eight to two) in the Senate. The resolution allows the president, as commander in chief, to use the armed forces to defend the non-Communist nations of Southeast Asia.

Secured to the top of this wooden post is a German Tellermine 43. The angle of the post is such that landing craft coming in at high tide would probably strike the mine and explode it. If the craft came in at low tide to avoid the mines, the incoming troops would have to cross a longer stretch of beach, swept by enemy machine gun fire. U.S. NAVY

August 09

1945 (Japan)—The second atomic bomb ever used in warfare is dropped on the city of Nagasaki. The weapon is code-named Fat Man and is a more advanced plutonium-implosion type weapon than Little Boy. Fat Man is 144 inches long, 60 inches wide, and weighs 10,800 pounds. Dropped from the B-29 *Bock's Car*, Fat Man detonates as an air burst at approximately 1,650 feet above the city at 1102 hours local time. The explosive blast of Fat Man is carefully estimated to be twenty-two kilotons, plus or minus two kilotons, which is equivalent to 20,000 to 24,000 tons of exploding TNT. Because of the industrial nature of the Nagasaki target at ground zero, Fat Man is not as devastating to life as Little Boy at Hiroshima. However, an estimated 40,000 Japanese are immediately killed in the blast.

The American threat of a possible wave of such bomb attacks forces Japan to capitulate in the face of complete destruction. In fact, the only two nuclear weapons in the world have just been used and no more will be available for some time. The estimated horrific losses among both the Allied forces and the Japanese are calculated to be less with the bombings, however, than if a conventional invasion of the home islands of Japan were to take place. Japan surrenders within days.

1965 (USA)—Detachment Eight is activated as part of the U.S. Air Force. The new unit will conduct training and operations with the new FC-47 gunship. As the new unit begins to conduct operations, it is designated the Fourth Air Commando Squadron. The gunships are renamed as AC-47D aircraft and soon earn the nickname "Puff" for "Puff the Magic Dragon." Many Vietnamese who witness the long flickering red tongues of flame as tracers pour out of the side of the gunship to lick at the ground simply call them Dragons. The term causes the crews of the new gunships to develop the call sign "Spooky."

1990 (USA)—The United Nations adopts Resolution 662, declaring null and void the Iraqi annexation of Kuwait.

August 10

1944 (India)—The 5307th Composite Unit (Provisional) (Merrill's Marauders) is deactivated.

1990 (Saudi Arabia)—The 105-man Naval Special Warfare Task Group One arrives in Saudi Arabia from Naval Special Warfare Group One assets in Coronado, California.

August 11

1968 (South Vietnam)—SEAL Team Two's Detachment Alfa sets up a trail ambush on a suspected VC communications liaison route based on intelligence from defected VC. Inserting at 2030 hours just six miles downriver from My Tho, on the north bank of the Sog Tien Giang River in Dinh Tuong Province, the SEALs, armed with their usual small arms and Claymore mines, set up an ambush site. At 2345 hours, a group of about seventeen VC enter the ambush's kill zone. Among them are eight VC carrying arms. When it looks like the point man in the VC group is becoming suspicious of the area, the SEALs initiate their ambush and fire the Claymores. The devastating wave of fragmentation from the Claymores sweeps the kill zone of the ambush. Following the stunning explosions of the mines, the SEALs open up with small-arms fire.

In the aftermath of the ambush, five VC are known to be dead, and three more are suspected killed, although their bodies are not found. Two AK-47 rifles and six magazines are captured, along with a package of documents. Later agent reports state that these VC were the reconnaissance squad of the Cho Gao local force company. They were members of a sapper-communication liaison patrol just completing a reconnaissance of the Cho Gao Canal for the placement of a water mine.

August 12

1990 (Saudi Arabia)—SEALs arrive incountry.

August 13

1945 (USA)—With the impending Japanese surrender, UDT Twenty-seven at Oceanside, California, receives orders to join five other UDTs aboard the USS *Walter B. Cobb* (APD 106). Joining the U.S. fleet forces in Tokyo Bay, they will conduct operations in support of the formal surrender and Allied occupation of Japan.

August 14

1945 (Japan)—The Allied forces announce that Japan has accepted a complete and unconditional surrender. Victory in Japan (VJ) Day is declared throughout the United States, in spite of the fact that there has not yet been a formal surrender signed by Japanese emperor Hirohito. In a radio broadcast to the people of Japan, however, he states that they should "bear the unbearable." A last-minute coup attempt to prevent the broadcast by Japanese military officers who want to destroy the speech's recording is foiled.

The Japanese people, stunned by the news from their emperor, accept the situation. They have been kept completely unaware of the deteriorating military situation due to a constant control of the news by the government. The possibility of an Allied invasion has been successfully averted, saving millions of lives among the Japanese people.

1945 (USA)—At Oceanside, California, a number of UDTs are ordered to embark immediately for duties in Japan. The UDTs will clear the way for the landings of U.S. and Allied occupation forces. UDT Three embarks aboard the USS *Ira Jeffery* (APD 44). The modern high-speed converted destroyer escort is much more comfortable than the converted four-stack destroyers the UDT had been transported in earlier. Not only is the UDT traveling in greater comfort than it has previously, it no longer faces an active enemy shore and the very real possibility of death or injury.

1984 (USA)—The Navy Security Coordination Team OP-6D is established with offices in the E-Ring of the Pentagon. The three officers and eleven enlisted SEALs who make up the security team soon become known by a much simpler designation: Red Cell. The mission of the new unit is to test and evaluate security at U.S. Navy installations all over the world. Terrorist actions in Beruit and elsewhere show that the present navy security measures are insufficient to stop a terrorist attack. The Red Cell acts as official U.S. Navy terrorists when simulating attacks against navy facilities. Nevertheless, in spite of Red Cell holding seminars and instructional meetings, demonstrating the weaknesses in the security of an installation, and following up their operations with specific suggestions on how to eliminate these weaknesses, commanders of a target that has been "defeated" by Red Cell feel the situation is simply grandstanding at the commander's expense.

August 15

1943 (Pacific)—The First Special Service Force lands at Kiska in the Aleutians.

1944 (France)—The last NCDU operation in Europe, Operation Dragoon, the invasion of southern France, begins. During most of its planning stages, it has been known as Anvil. Following two months after the success of the D day landings in Normandy, Operation Dragoon lands Allied forces on the beaches between Toulon and Cannes. Thirty-two NCDUs, a number of which landed at Normandy, go in with the first wave. Enemy resistance is very light, especially when compared to the Normandy landings; the NCDUs complete their limited obstacle demolitions with little incident.

The day after the landings, the NCDUs conduct a demolition operation to remove a blocking wreck from the St. Tropez Harbor. When the demolition charges detonate at the wreck, the shock waves set off a number of explosive mines and ordnance all around the harbor waters. The blast is huge, sending water and rubble high into the air, where it rains back down on the locals and the Allies for some time.

August 16

1967 (South Vietnam)—Information from a VC defector indicates that a large number of VC, possibly 200 men or more, are located on the island of Cu Lao Dung near the mouth of the Bassac River in the Mekong Delta. The island, called Dung Island by most, has long been known as a VC haven. A squad from Second Platoon of SEAL Team Two's Detachment Alfa conducted an operation on Dung Island earlier in the year and located a number of VC there.

For this sweep of Dung Island, twenty SEALs combine forces with six South Vietnamese and are backed up by assets from the Navy Brown Water boats and the Seawolves. The unit begins its assault on Dung Island at 0900 hours and over the next five hours it fights several brief fire fights with scattered units of VC. Fourteen tons of rice are destroyed, along with fifty-three hooches and six sampans. Also, three VC are taken under fire and killed.

August 17

Underway in a South Vietnamese river, this side view of a Mark I STAB shows the 7.62mm M60 machine guns the boat was usually armed with. The engines of the twin outboard motors at the rear of the STAB are covered with armored cowlings. U.S. NAVY

This SEAL coxswain sits at the center control position of an early Mark I SEAL team support boat (STAB Mk I). A number of the lightweight, agile craft were modified from civilian Powercat Trimerans by the men of SEAL Team Two. Modifications included armoring sensitive areas of the boat and installing mounting positions for a variety of weapons. U.S. NAVY

August 19

1942 (Europe)—The first major Allied amphibious landing in the European theater takes place at Dieppe in northern France. British and Canadian Commandos, along with a much smaller unit of Free French and American forces, land on the pebble beach at Dieppe to destroy German gun positions and radio locations among other targets. The American detachment is made up of fifty men from the First U.S. Army Ranger Battalion.

The landings run into disaster due to planning errors, a lack of intelligence in the area and the obstacles that could be found there, and the stiffness of the German resistance. Of the nearly 6,000-man-strong force, 3,369 Canadians alone are lost. Losses on the Allied side include 106 aircraft, a navy destroyer, 30 tanks, and 33 landing craft. To prevent such losses and errors occurring again in the planned future of Allied amphibious operations of the war, new specialized units plan to meet the needs uncovered at Dieppe. One of these new organizations will be the NCDUs.

1966 (South Vietnam)—By August, some members of SEAL Team One, Detachment Golf, are finding it increasingly difficult to locate targets during their night ambush operations. Daylight operations allow a greater view of the area for reconnaissance purposes, but the SEALs prefer night operations as the darkness helps conceal them as well as the enemy.

During a daylight reconnaissance operation near the center of the Rung Sat Special Zone, Petty Officer Billy W. Machen operates as the point man of his SEAL squad. In this position, he moves ahead of the main body of the patrol, keeping in sight of the unit while searching out the best path to take, looking for trip wires and booby traps, as well as maintaining a careful watch for enemy activity.

While following a fresh set of tracks that lead the patrol to a group of bunkers and fighting positions, Machen spots a VC base camp with a number of bunkers and a watch tower. The overhead air support the SEALs have available to them up to this point has returned to base for refueling, so the SEALs are without support for the time being. It is now that Machen spots a number of VC waiting in ambush for his teammates.

Being in the kill zone of the ambush, Machen has no time to take cover or try to go back the way he came without triggering the ambush against his teammates. Falling to the ground, Machen opens fire against the VC while shouting a warning to his teammates.

The SEALs face heavy fire from the VC, but are able to pull back from the estimated fifteen- to twenty-man-strong enemy force. While fighting the ambushers, Machen is hit several times in the face and abdomen, but is still able to crawl back to his squad. He dies within moments of returning to his teammates.

Carrying his body, the SEALs fight out of the engagement, covering 500 meters of swampland in the process. They are able to extract intact, taking Machen's body with them. Machen is the first SEAL Team One loss in combat of the war.

1990 (Saudi Arabia)—The SEAL elements deployed to the Saudi Arabian–Kuwaiti border are the first U.S. combat forces to directly face Iraqi troops. The SEALs will act as a "tripwire" warning system, sounding the alarm if Iraqi forces should make a sudden run across the border into Saudi Arabia. Other aspects of the SEALs' mission include directing close air support if it becomes necessary and gathering intelligence on Iraqi movements and deployments inside occupied Kuwait. The listening and observation posts maintained by the SEALs are dangerously close to the border. If the Iraqis are to make a run for Saudi Arabia, the SEALs know that they will have little time to be recovered by their own support. In their positions, the SEALs make plans to make a break for it on their own once they have sounded the alarm that the Iraqis are "heading south."

August 20

1944 (Pacific)—The Sixth Ranger Battalion, "Mucci's Rangers," is activated on New Guinea. They are the only Ranger unit to see action in the Pacific campaign.

1968 (South Vietnam)—During an example of the confusion of war that even the SEALs are susceptible to, Warrant Officer Eugene Tinnin of SEAL Team One's Juliette Platoon is killed. Tinnin was an enlisted man in SEAL Team Two until receiving his commission as a warrant officer and transferring over to the West Coast and SEAL Team One.

The SEALs are going in on a night ambush operation on a moonless evening with overcast clouds and a light rain falling. Locating a pagoda, the SEAL unit splits into two elements, one taking ground near the pagoda in an ambush position, while the other continues to patrol, with Tinnin, and locates a second structure that had been reported in the area.

In the darkness, the SEALs of the second element accidentally circle back and enter the kill zone of the ambush set by the first element. The two SEAL groups are in radio contact with one another, but it is thought that there is a much greater distance between them than there actually is. Thinking a group of VC has entered their kill zone, the SEALs initiate their ambush.

Tinnin is killed in the first bursts of gunfire, four other SEALs are wounded along with one of the two LDNNs who had accompanied the SEALs. The incident is carefully investigated, but no fault can be found in the actions. The errors that were made, including the splitting of the SEAL elements and the unfamiliarity of the unit leader with the area, will not be allowed to happen again.

1988 (Persian Gulf)—The Iran-Iraq war is officially over. During Operation Earnest Will, the U.S. Navy escorts 249 ships in 127 convoys through the Persian Gulf over a fourteen-month period.

August 21

1942 (France) British Commandos, U.S. Rangers, and the Royal Air Force raid Dieppe.

1966 (South Vietnam)—An action in support of Operation Deckhouse III comes very close to causing a number of losses among the fourteen men of UDT Eleven's Detachment Charlie aboard the submarine USS *Perch* (APSS 313). The mission of the planned amphibious landing is to attack a VC stronghold north of Qui Nhon in the Tuy Phuoc district of Binh Dinh Province. On the night of August 20, the UDT operators slip onto shore in three rubber boats launched from the deck of the *Perch*. The UDT men conduct their recon without incident and return to the submarine.

The next night, August 21, the VC are alert and wait for the UDT operators. In the darkness, the VC can't locate the UDT they know are on shore. Conducting a reconnaissance by fire, the VC shoot into the surrounding area in hopes of discovering the team. The two-man swimmer scout group that had first come in to shore becomes separated from the main group and lost in the confusion. A search party from the *Perch* is launched to look for the UDT men.

While the search party is on shore, the original recon group, including the missing swimmer scouts, makes it back to the submarine, which has closed in to within 2,000 meters of shore. But the original search party is now missing. Another search with two UDTs and the UDT commander go onshore in another rubber boat to locate the original search party. Risking detection by the VC forces, the UDT officer ignites a signal flare while still offshore to help guide the search party back out to sea in the right location. Very quickly, the lost search party sees the signal, as do the VC. As the VC open fire, the *Perch* moves closer to shore and opens fire with its mounted weapons. Fifty-caliber machine gun fire and 40mm cannon shells tear into the beach, covering the extraction of all the UDT men in toward shore. All the men are recovered and the *Perch* moves back out to sea and submerges.

1970 (South Vietnam)—There is never a greater mission for the SEALs than the possible rescue of American POWs held by the VC. The SEALs are trained and equipped to put an operation together quickly and respond to intelligence on

BARNDANCE # 6-54   SEAL TEAM TWO; DET ALFA ;   6th   PLT.

DATE(S) 220855H-221145H   OTHER UNITS: SEE REVERSE SIDE

MSG REF (S) O 221700Z AUG 70

NAMES OF PERS PARTICIPATING LT. BOINK (PL), NELSON, LEWIS, SPRINKLE BLACKISTON, 2 KCS, I INTERPRETER, 974 COMPANY

MISSION TASK: LIBERATE 58 PRISONERS OF WAR

INTEL/INFO SOURCES: SECTOR S-2; ESCAPEE FROM POW CAMP

INSERTION: TIME: 220910H METHOD: SLICK   COORD: WQ 445931

EXTRACTION: TIME: 221130H METHOD: SLICK   COORD: WQ 433913

BRIEF MISSION NARRATIVE: ACTING ON INTEL SUPPLIED BY SECTOR S-2 THE FOLLOWING SEQUENCE WAS FOLLOWED IN TARGETING A FIFTY EIGHT MAN POW CAMP IN VIC WQ 440928. 220815H SIX ROYAL AUSTRALIAN B-57 BOMBERS BEGAN PLACING 750 LB BOMBS ALONG CANAL FROM WQ 420974 TO WQ435908 TO ESTABLISH BLOCKING FORCE BY FIRE TO S. OF CAMP. AT 220855H SEALS AND 974 RF CO. INSERTED ALONG NARROW BEACHLINE AND

RESULTS OF ENEMY ENCOUNTERED: 3 VC KIA (BC), OTHER CASUALTIES BY GUNSHIPS UNKNOWN. ONE CHICOM CARBINE CAPTURED. 28 POWS LIBERATED

FRIENDLY CASUALTIES: NEG

REMARKS (SIGNIFICANT EVENTS, OPEVAL RESULTS, ETC) PRELIMINARY READOUT INDICATES AMONG POWS WAS EX VC COMPANY CDR 1109 VC COMPANY, HIS PLATOON LEADER, SQUAD LEADER CAUGHT TRYING TO CHIEU HOI AND FOUR OTHERS VCI IM PRISONED FOR SAME REASON. OTHER POWS WERE MEMBERS OF OUTPOST WHICH WAS OVERRUN BY VC TWO YEARS AGO.

RECOMMENDATIONS/LESSONS LEARNED: THE COOPERATION AND PROFESSIONALISM SHOWN BY THE VARIOUS SERVICES ARE LIKE THINGS ONE READS IN STORY BOOKS. THE SIXTH PLATOON SENDS THANKS AND 28 LIBERATED SEND A GREAT DEAL MORE.

BD COPY DIST: COMNAVFORV, CTF 116.6, OIC DET ALFA, SEAL 2, SEAL 1

SIGNATURE OF PERSON MAKING OUT REPORT: LOUIS H. BOINK, LT, USNR

BARNDANCE # 6-54

prisoners that can expire in hours. The following is one of the more ambitious operations put together by a single SEAL platoon in a very short time.

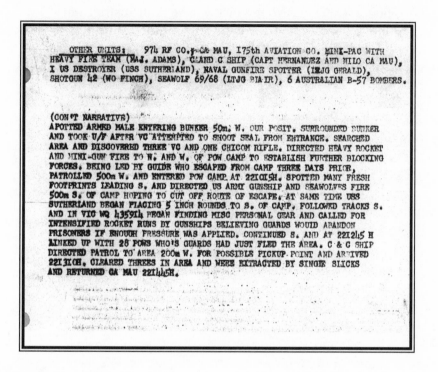

OTHER UNITS: 974 RF CO. CA MAU, 175th AVIATION CO. MINI-PAC WITH HEAVY FIRE TEAM (MAJ. ADAMS), C AND C SHIP (CAPT HERNANDEZ AND NILO CA MAU), I US DESTROYER (USS SUTHERLAND), NAVAL GUNFIRE SPOTTER (LTJG GERALD), SHOTGUN 42 (WO FINCH), SEAWOLF 69/68 (LTJG BLAIR), 6 AUSTRALIAN B-57 BOMBERS.

(CON'T NARRATIVE)
SPOTTED ARMED MALE ENTERING BUNKER 50m. W. OUR POSIT. SURROUNDED BUNKER AND TOOK U/F AFTER VC ATTEMPTED TO SHOOT SEAL FROM ENTRANCE. SEARCHED AREA AND DISCOVERED THREE VC AND ONE CHICOM RIFLE. DIRECTED HEAVY ROCKET AND MINI-GUN FIRE TO N. AND W. OF POW CAMP TO ESTABLISH FURTHER BLOCKING FORCES. BEING LED BY GUIDE WHO ESCAPED FROM CAMP THREE DAYS PRIOR, PATROLLED 500m W. AND ENTERED POW CAMP AT 221015H. SPOTTED MANY FRESH FOOTPRINTS LEADING S. AND DIRECTED US ARMY GUNSHIP AND SEAWOLVES FIRE 500m S. OF CAMP HOPING TO CUT OFF ROUTE OF ESCAPE. AT SAME TIME USS SUTHERLAND BEGAN PLACING 5 INCH ROUNDS TO S. OF CAMP. FOLLOWED TRACKS S. AND IN VIC WQ 435914 BEGAN FINDING MISC PERSONAL GEAR AND CALLED FOR INTENSIFIED ROCKET RUNS BY GUNSHIPS BELIEVING GUARDS WOULD ABANDON PRISONERS IF ENOUGH PRESSURE WAS APPLIED. CONTINUED S. AND AT 221245 H LINKED UP WITH 26 POWS WHO'S GUARDS HAD JUST FLED THE AREA. C & C SHIP DIRECTED PATROL TO AREA 200m W. FOR POSSIBLE PICKUP POINT AND ARRIVED 221310H. CLEARED THREES IN AREA AND WERE EXTRACTED BY SINGLE SLICKS AND RETURNED CA MAU 221445H.

August 23

1968 (South Vietnam)—While searching by helicopter for a suspected VC hospital complex in the jungle, Tenth Platoon of SEAL Team One's Detachment Alfa observes a large number of VC on the ground. A Seawolf air strike and

81mm mortar fire from the Mike boat in the river are called in on the target by the SEALs. As they continue on their mission, the SEALs insert by sampan near the Rach Ba Tu Canal on Cu Lao Loi Quan Island. The island is at the mouth of the My Tho (Song Tien Giang) River in the Hoi Binh district of Go Cong Province, just a short distance from the waters of the South China Sea.

At the patrol's second objective, a suspected VC hand grenade factory, the SEALs encounter another twenty-five VC. Calling in a second Seawolf strike on the area, the SEALs note heavy fire coming from the VC location. While waiting for extraction after patrolling to the north side of the island, the SEALs come under fire from a number of automatic weapons. They call in fire from the 81mm mortar and 7.62mm minigun aboard the Mike boat.

The operation results in thirty-six VC killed and another four known wounded. The mission destroys approximately forty structures. The SEALs destroy one large sampan and take in grenade molds and tools, six 81mm mortars, nine 60mm mortars, twenty-five 105mm cannon rounds, twenty-one grenades, and three kilograms of documents.

August 24

1944 (Pacific)—After their mission has been completed at Tinian, UDT Seven thinks that it might be heading home. Instead, UDT Seven is eventually transferred to the USS *Elmore* (AA 42) and transported to Turner City on Florida Island. The *Elmore* arrives at the island in the Solomons on August 24. The men of the UDT will recondition themselves for further operations in support of the campaign against the Palau Islands and Peleliu Island. The tropical climate, heat, and humidity on Florida Island, however, does not lend itself to strenuous physical activity.

August 25

1942 (USA)—Rear Admiral Henry K. Hewitt orders the formation of the Scout and Raider School in order to provide trained personnel to assist the Amphibious Force of the Atlantic Fleet in landing troops on enemy beaches.

Lieutenant Lloyd Peddicord is put in charge. Trained men from the school will take part in Operation Torch, the invasion of North Africa later in the year. Peddicord already has some experience with what it will take to train the men in amphibious scouting operations: the year before he was an army sergeant assisting in the design of the first seven-man inflatable rubber boat—soon to be a mainstay of the NCDUs and the UDTs, among others. The new school will be located at the new Naval Amphibious Base being built at Little Creek, Virginia.

1990 (International)—The means for enforcement of the trade sanctions against Iraq are put into effect. The UN's adopted Resolution 665 allows the use of limited naval force to ensure the compliance of the embargo of goods to Iraq. The resolution includes the right to stop shipping on the high seas and inspect cargoes. The SEALs become a close part of the UN's naval enforcement of the sanctions against Iraq as they begin performing visit, board, search, and seizure operations on Iraqi ships. SEALs quickly board a suspect ship by using small boats or fast roping down from hovering helicopters, in all kinds of weather and sea states. While under the careful overwatch of SEAL snipers in circling helicopters, the rest of the unit quickly secures and searches a ship for contraband cargo.

August 26

1942 (Europe)—The Joint Chiefs of Staff approves the OSS–Special Operations Executive agreement on combined operations in Europe.

1945 (USA)—The Ninety-sixth Civil Affairs Group is activated.

August 27

1942 (USA)—Secretary of War Henry Stimson authorizes the First Special Service Force to wear the Crossed Arrows insignia formerly worn by the Indian Scouts.

August 28

1942 (Pacific)—The Alaska Scouts infiltrate Adak Island in the Aleutians.

1945 (Japan)—UDTs Eighteen and Twenty-one arrive in Tokyo Bay to undertake recon operations prior to the arrival of the bulk of the Allied fleet. The formal surrender of Japan has not yet taken place, although the emperor has told the Japanese people not to resist the incoming Allied troops. The opinion of a number of the UDT operators is that even though the Japanese have given up, every man in the Japanese military may not know the war is over.

The first American occupation forces on Japanese soil are the five platoons from UDT Twenty-one who come in to recon landing sites for the incoming forces. Commander Edward Clayton, the commanding officer of UDT Twenty-one, is presented with the sword of the Japanese commander of a small fort on Futsusaki, a small peninsula at the mouth of Tokyo Bay. The act is the first formal surrender of Japanese soil and causes a stir among the higher command. Commander Clayton is ordered to relinquish the sword to the higher ups.

The one thing that can't be taken from UDT Twenty-one is its carrying out of a tradition that has developed among the UDTs, one that is strictly against directives. This tradition involves the placement of a large beach sign that reads: "USN Underwater Demolition Team-21 Welcomes the U.S. Marines to Japan."

During later missions, the UDT men check docks and beaches for mines, booby traps, and other obstacles. In the UDT searches of caves along the coast of Japan, they find thousands of explosive motorboats, midget submarines, and other weapons that would have been used against the incoming Allied forces by the local population had the Allies attacked. There is no question in the UDT operators' minds that the cost of taking the islands by force would have been horrendous. There are so many suicide boats and submarines that they are difficult to get rid of. Burning them is out of the question since there might be hidden explosive charges. So, the bulk of the weapons are taken out to sea and sunk.

August 29

During a demonstration, a pair of SEALs raise a Marine welcoming flag—a tribute to the actions of their UDT forefathers.
KEVIN DOCKERY

August 30

1968 (South Vietnam)—A pair of Vietnamese who have escaped from a VC POW camp are interrogated on the night of August 27. It is reported that the camp had held about thirty-five Vietnamese and eight American POWs. Orders go out immediately to stage a rescue operation of the suspected POW camp, and a PRU force led by a Navy SEAL is selected to conduct the mission.

Nine PRUs led by their SEAL advisor go to the location of the camp, where they find radios, cutting equipment, starlight scopes, and additional materials. Toward dawn, the SEAL and nine PRU men are spotted by the VC guard force. The small unit attacks against what turns out to be only four guards; regardless, sixty more PRUs arrive by helicopter and swarm over the camp. Forty-nine Vietnamese are freed, but no American POWs are found. The eight U.S. POWs at the camp were moved the next day after the original two Vietnamese escaped.

1993 (Somalia)—The Seventy-fifth Ranger Regiment, reinforced with operators from Special Forces Detachment Delta, arrive in Mogadishu.

August 31

1990 (Iraq)—The Fifth Special Forces Group teams arrive for Operation Desert Shield.

SEPTEMBER

While being covered by their teammates in the troop well of the landing craft, SEALs accompanied by explosive ordnance disposal personnel climb aboard the abandoned minelaying ship *Iran Ajr*. U.S. NAVY

September 01

1942 (USA)—The first training class for Scouts and Raiders begins at the new Amphibious Scout and Raider School (Joint) at NAB Little Creek, Virginia. Part of the first class is made up of forty sailors volunteering from the Boat Pool at the Solomons, Maryland navy facility. Ten chief specialists join with the navy personnel in the first class. The navy group is put under the command of Ensign John Bell and is broken up into ten Scout boat crews of one officer and four men each. The men train to scout enemy beaches and mark the proper locations to help guide the landing craft prior to a landing by Allied forces. This means that they have to land on an enemy-held beach prior to an invasion and hold their position without being discovered.

Within a short time, all of the Scout and Raider–trained personnel are assigned to the invasion forces for Operation Torch, the U.S. landing in North Africa, and the school at Little Creek is closed down.

1943 (France)—Operational Group Williams is infiltrated into enemy territory.

September 02

1945 (Japan)—The formal surrender of Japan takes place. The instrument of Japanese surrender is signed aboard the battleship USS *Missouri* (BB 63) in Tokyo Harbor. The Japanese foreign minister Mamoru Shigemitsu signs on behalf of Japan. General Douglas MacArthur accepts the surrender on the part of all the Allied forces, signing the formal document for the same. Admiral Chester W. Nimitz signs for the United States, and Admiral Bruce Fraser signs for Britain. The formal surrender has been delayed while MacArthur ensures that Generals Arthur Percival and Jonathan Wainright, who had been captured at the beginning of the war, are able to attend.

World War II is officially over. U.S. casualties alone are over 400,000 dead and almost 700,000 wounded. Of the nearly 3,500 UDTs and NCDUs, 148 are wounded and 83 are dead or declared missing.

September 03

1967 (South Vietnam)—Since the 1963 assassination of President Ngo Dinh Diem, South Vietnam has suffered through a series of unstable government leaders and internal power struggles. The election of President Nguyen Van Thieu ends these difficulties and allows a more concentrated effort against the VC and North Vietnamese Communists to go forward. In spite of his stated position for a free press, and his pointing out that his opposition during the election was allowed free speech, two opposition newspapers are closed on the same day that Thieu's victory is announced.

September 04

1945 (Japan)—UDT Twenty-seven arrives at Tokyo Bay aboard the USS *Walter B. Cobb* (APD 106), along with five other UDTs on their own transports. In spite of rushing to arrive in Japan, UDT Twenty-seven is never used. After several weeks of inactivity, the *Cobb* and UDT Twenty-seven return to the United States.

1945 (Japan)—UDT Twenty aboard the USS *Cook* (APD 130) and UDT Twenty-five aboard the USS *Knudson* (APD 101) arrive at the Yokosuka Naval Base. Both transport ships are anchored off the Japanese naval base and the commanding officers of the UDTs both receive the disappointing news that local operations clearing beaches and conducting recons have been assigned to UDTs Eighteen and Twenty-one. With no assigned duties, the two UDTs are able to release their men for liberty and they go ashore to see Yokosuka and Yokohama.

UDT Twenty-five receives orders to head back to the United States by way of Guam. UDT Twenty is later assigned escort duties for a flotilla of LSTs moving from Okinawa to Sagami Wan in Japan. After that mission is completed, UDT Twenty is ordered to report to Hokkaido, where it accepts the surrender of the city from the Japanese there, becoming the only UDT to officially accept a Japanese surrender. Afterwards, it conducts inspections of the city's dock and landing facilities. Marking the navigational hazards there, UDT Twenty helps guide in the landing craft of the U.S. Army's Seventy-seventh Division, which takes over the occupation of the area.

September 05

1945 (Pacific)—UDTs Eight, Nine, Twelve, Fifteen, Twenty-three, and Twenty-six are assigned to the Seventh Amphibious Force in Okinawa. Immediately after their arrival, they leave Okinawa for operations at Jinsen, Korea, and have to cross a mine-laden East China Sea in the process. Once in Korea, they will conduct recons for suitable landing areas, clear obstacles, and destroy leftover Japanese ordnance.

1951 (USA)—UDT Five is commissioned in Coronado, California. It will be used, in part, to support UDT operations in Korea during the Korean War. The first mission of UDT Five is to build up strength and training so that it can report to the Korean theater in early 1952 and relieve UDT One, which has been assigned to the western Pacific for missions in Korea and elsewhere.

1961 (USA)—The U.S. Army authorizes the wearing of the green beret.

1966 (USA)—UDT Eleven is awarded a Navy Commendation Medal for missions it conducted from January 28, 1964 to September 5, 1966, in South Vietnam. During this time period, operators from UDT Eleven took part in eight major amphibious landings in Vietnam, as well as reconned more than 110 miles of coastline and waterways in South Vietnam. These recons were conducted both in the open and in a clandestine manner as needed.

1990 (Saudi Arabia)—Assets from the U.S. Army's Fifth Special Forces Group begin relieving the SEALs. The SEALs have been manning the listening and observation posts along the Saudi Arabian–Kuwaiti border since August 19.

September 06

1987 (Persian Gulf)—The oil servicing barges *Hercules* and *Winbrown 7* are leased by the U.S. Navy for a period of six months. The barges are set up as floating Naval Special Combat bases in the Persian Gulf for quick reaction assets of the SEALs and boats from Naval Special Boat Units deployed to the gulf. Each barge can house 10 small boats, 3 helicopters, and more than 150 men, along with the necessary ammunition, fuel, food, supplies, and service support for their operations.

September 07

An A/MH-6 Little Bird helicopter flies across the water. The helicopter is armed with a seven-round 2.75-inch rocket pod, visible below the open door.
U.S. SOCOM PAO

September 08

1943 (Southwestern Pacific)—Units from the first class that graduated from the Naval Combat Demolition Unit School at Fort Pierce, Florida, are sent to the southwestern Pacific. Two initial NCDUs are assigned to the U.S. Seventh Fleet. They are later joined by an additional four NCDUs in early January 1944. With a total strength of six officers and thirty enlisted men, the six NCDUs conduct operations for more than a dozen landings during their assignment to the Seventh Fleet. When the other NCDUs are absorbed into UDTs, these six NCDUs retain their organization and remain NCDUs until the end of the war; they are the only such units to do so.

1945 (Korea)—The Seventh Amphibious Force arrives without incident off Jinsen. UDTs Eight, Nine, Twelve, Fifteen, Twenty-three, and Twenty-six are part of the force. UDT Twelve is assigned to scout the Yellow 2 Beaches on the island of Getsubi near Jinsen to determine if the beaches can be used by heavy landing craft. The scout mission shows that the beaches, with long tidal flats that leave huge ranges of mud at low tide, are rendered useless for the heavy landing craft.

1945 (Korea)—UDT Nine, which is on the USS *Laning* (APD 55) is assigned to recon the Blue Beaches off Jinsen for landings by forces from the U.S. Seventh Infantry Division. The twenty-eight-foot tidal variation leaves extremely wide expanses of mud flats exposed at low tide. Only LCTs can use the beaches, and then only for the few hours of high tide, so no landings are conducted at the Blue Beaches.

September 09

BARNDANCE # __3-46__   SEAL TEAM __2__ ; DET. __FA__ ; __3B__ PLT.

DATE(S): __09 SEP 68__   OTHER UNITS: __RIVSEC 552 CTE 116.9.1__
__RSSB LHFT STW 116.4.B__

MSG REF(S): _____

NAMES OF PERS: __LT JG BREWTON, TODD, FOX, BURWELL, McCLURE,__
__WARMACK__

MISSION TASK: __AMBUSH__

INTEL/INFO SOURCE(S): __NONE__

INSERTION: TIME: __092430H__ METHOD: __PBR__   AMS COORD: __YS056919__

EXTRACTION: TIME: __092200H__ METHOD: __PBR__   AMS COORD: __YS056919__

TERRAIN: __OPEN, DENSE NEAR RIVERS & STREAMS, HIGH GRASS__
WEATHER: __CLOUDY WITH RAIN__ TIDE: __HIGH__   MOON: __L 3/4__

BRIEF MISSION NARRATIVE: __INSERTED YS056919. REMAINED IN INSERTION__
__POINT. PBR SIGHTED SAMPAN UPSTREAM FROM POSITION. AT__
__092195 SAMPAN WITH 4 TURNED OFF MAIN RIVER AND__
__BEGAN TO PROCEED UPSTREAM ALONG OPPOSITE BANK FROM__
__AMBUSH. TOOK UNDER FIRE. EXTRACTED FOLLOWING AMBUSH.__
__SEAWOLF PUT STRIKE IN AREA AFTER EXTRACTION.__

RESULTS OF ENEMY ENCOUNTERED: __2 VC KIA (BC), 2 VC KIA (PROB) CAPTURED:__
__1 B40 ROCKET LAUNCHER, 3 ROCKETS, 1 US M1 CARBINE, 1 US M2 GRENADE,__
__DOCUMENTS, PERS EFFECTS, MED SUPPLIES, DESTROYED 1 SAMPAN.__

FRIENDLY CASUALTIES: __NONE__

REMARKS (SIGNIFICANT EVENTS, OPEVAL RESULTS, ETC.): __RECEIVED 2 40MM HE__
__ROUNDS 100-200M SOUTH OF POSITION FOLLOWING INSERTION.__
__MAY HAVE BEEN FROM SAMPAN UPSTREAM FROM POSITION.__
__OBSERVED SEVERAL LIGHTS & 1 RED FLARE SOUTH OF__
__POSITION.__

RECOMMENDATIONS/LESSONS LEARNED: __INSERTION POINTS LIMITED IN AREA.__
__RECOMMEND CAUTION IF PLAN FUTURE OPS IN THIS AO.__
__BOOBY TRAPS POSSIBLE.__

BD COPY DIST: _____

(FORM REV. 8/68)   BARNDANCE # __3-46__

1990 (Saudi Arabia)—A second group of personnel from Naval Special Warfare Group One in Coronado, California, arrives to increase the manpower available to the Naval Special Warfare Task Group already on site, which will eventually have 275 personnel available to it.

September 10

1994 (USA)—General John Shalikashvili, the chairman of the Joint Chiefs of Staff, is ordered by President Bill Clinton to execute Operation Uphold Democracy, the invasion of Haiti, within the next ten days.

September 11

1987 (USA)—The U.S. Army Special Forces Branch is activated as an independent unit.

2001 (USA)—During the midmorning hours the people of New York City witness the greatest individual act of terrorism ever committed. At 0845 hours, hundreds of people see a Boeing 767 of American Airlines Flight 11 smash into the upper floors of the 1,300-foot-tall North Tower of the World Trade Center (WTC).

Eleven minutes after the first plane struck, any question of the incident being a bizarre accident is removed when a second Boeing 767, United Airlines Flight 175, smashes into the South Tower of the WTC.

New York is not the only place hit. At 0938 hours, a Boeing 757, American Airlines Flight 77, smashes into the side of the Pentagon near Washington, D.C.

The flights are hijacked by terrorist members of al Qaeda, followers of Osama bin Ladin. Al Qaeda, bin Ladin, and those who supported, concealed, or sided with the terrorists soon become the targets of the worldwide war on terrorism.

September 12

1944 (France)—Jedburgh Dudley is infiltrated. Meanwhile, the 885th Bomber Squadron flies its last supply drop mission into France.

1944 (Hawaii)—A number of the NCDUs who had been sent to the South Pacific and are not conducting operations there are gathered together with other personnel in Hawaii for the formation of UDT Able. There has never been an official explanation given as to why the UDT is given the unique designator of a letter rather than a number during the war except that the NCDUs so used were from the first graduating class from Fort Pierce, Florida.

UDT Able is given advanced training at Maui. Training is completed so quickly that the team is included for the planned operations at Peleliu. While underway for the invasion of Peleliu, the USS *Noa* (APD 24), with UDT Able aboard, is struck and severely damaged by a U.S. destroyer. UDT Able has to abandon the sinking *Noa* without being able to salvage any of its equipment or explosives. Returning to Hawaii, UDT Able is dissolved and its personnel assigned to six of the newly forming UDTs.

1980 (Middle East)—Iraq launches an attack across the border and into Iran after months of minor skirmishes between the two countries. With the Shah of Iran gone and the unsettling nature of the Ayatollah Khomeini's execution of 500 of the officer corps of the Iranian military and eliminating another 10,000, Saddam Hussein considers the time ripe for a quick action and victory for Iraq. The relatively unskilled but fanatical resistance put up by the Iranian forces proves much more difficult than Hussein expects.

Instead of a quick victory, the Iran-Iraq war runs for eight years, involving many nations beside the two direct combatants. Most nations are not directly involved with the fighting between Iraq and Iran, but they are dependent on oil from the region. To help prevent the Islamic fundamentalism that Khomeini espouses from being exported all through the Middle East and around the world, the United States supports Iraq in the struggle. It is done in a low-key and partially covert manner. To overcome the stalemate between the forces of Iraq and Iran, Hussein employs chemical weapons, both crude and later more sophisticated versions, in combat.

September 13

1969

```
BARNDANCE #  9-67          SEAL TEAM   2  ;  DET.  A  ;  9TH  PLT.

DATE(S):  13 SEPTEMBER 1969    OTHER UNITS:  2 USA SLICKS
                                             12 PRU'S
MSG REF(S):                                  1 LDNN

NAMES OF PERS:  LTJG ELLIS, BMC RABBITT, GMG1 THORNTON, SF1 BRADLEY, PC2 SCHMIDT
STG3 GLASSCOCK, AND LDNN BON


MISSION TASK:   CAPTURE 4 VCI AT SCHEDULED VC CADRE MEETING.


INTEL/INFO SOURCE(S):  PRU AGENT INTELL

INSERTION:    TIME:  13 1650H   METHOD:   SLICK    AMS COORD:  XS 882732

EXTRACTION:   TIME:  13 1730H   METHOD:   SLICK    AMS COORD:  XS 882732

TERRAIN:  RICE PADDY
WEATHER:  FAIR              TIDE/SURF:   N/A     MOON:     NONE

BRIEF MISSION NARRATIVE:   DEPARTED NHA BE BY SLICK AT 13 1635H XXX INSTEAD OF
SCHEDULED TIME OF 13 1600H DEPARTURE TIME. INSERTED AND UPON QUESTIONING PERSONS
AT TARGET DISCOVERED THAT 4 VCI CADRE FROM 1ST BATT. SR-6 HAD CONCLUDED SCHEDULED
MEETING AND DEPARTED AREA 15 MIN PRIOR TO OUR ARRIVAL.



FRIENDLY PERS/MATERIAL CASUALTIES:  NONE



ENEMY PERS/MATERIAL CASUALTIES:    NEG.



REMARKS (SIGNIFICANT EVENTS, OPEVAL RESULTS, ETC.):  SLICKS WERER DIVERTED TO
ANOTHER OPERATION AND WERE 30 MIN. LATE CAUSING SEALS TO MISS VC MEETING AND LOSE
PRISONERS AND INTELLIGENCE FOR FURTHER OPERATIONS.




RECOMMENDATIONS/LESSONS LEARNED:  CO-OPERATION AND SUPPORT AND UNDERSTANDING OF
PRIORITIES IS POOR. XXXXX SLICKS SHOULD ALWAYS BE AVAILABLE TO SEALS OPERATOR.




BD COPY DIST:

(FORM REV. 4/69)                        BARNDANCE #   9-67
```

September 14

1944 (Pacific)—The invasion of the Yap Island group is canceled. The planned actions are abandoned as being too costly and unnecessary for the further advancement of the war. Nevertheless, a number of ships are already underway for the operation. The men of UDT Four aboard the USS *Goldsborough* (APD 132) have prepared their equipment for the Yap landings when the news reaches them.

1944 (Pacific)—UDT Seven decides to go in on a demolition swim to destroy obstacles discovered at Peleliu by a prior reconnaissance swim. Steel tripods (hedgehogs) and rows of wood posts are found about seventy-five yards from the beach. Higher on the beach, about thirty yards above the high water mark, further obstacles in the form of log barriers and concrete cribs are also noted.

The demolition swim is considered a "disappointing" operation by the men and officers of UDT Seven. This is due to the poor planning of the operation. It adds to the problem of excessive manpower being available and causes even more confusion than usual for the night operation. In spite of this, the landing operations take place as planned.

1944 (Pacific)—UDT Eight conducts its first combat operation. The UDT is assigned to support the landings at Auguar Island in the Palau group. After a thirty-minute bombardment by a battleship, two cruisers, and three destroyers and then being covered by the naval gunfire, UDT Eight conducts a recon of the waters off Green Beach on the southeastern shore of Auguar. No mines or serious obstacles for the upcoming landings are found. This operation is actually a feint to distract the Japanese from the real landings at Red Beach on the northern shore of the island. The next morning at Red Beach, UDT Eight discovers jetted rails (steel rails stuck in the ground at an angle). A later demolition swim is planned for their removal.

1962 (South Vietnam)—The Headquarters Detachment (Provisional) of the Fifth Special Forces Group arrives.

September 15

1944 (Pacific)—The invasion of Peleliu begins. UDTs Six and Seven conduct reconnaissance and demolition swims in support of the operation. In addition to its own original assignments, UDT Six takes on the targets that were supposed to have been examined by UDT Able before its transport ship was stricken and forced to return to base.

1950 (Korea)—Operation Chromite, the largest amphibious landing since World War II, is planned to put U.S. and UN troops in Jinsen, Korea, which is within striking distance of Seoul. UDT One conducts a reconnaissance of the beaches and tidal flats; their information is of significant strategic importance to General Douglas MacArthur and his planners. Few man-made obstacles are found, but the area has extensive mud flats at low tide. Operators from UDT One help guide in the first wave of landing craft for the huge operation, which successfully ends up driving the People's Army of North Korea back across the seventeenth parallel for the first time.

1970 (USA)—The Navy Seawolves are one of the units that the SEALs give a lot of credit to for the overall success of their efforts in Vietnam. The valor of the Seawolves has never been in question, as is illustrated by the citation for Lieutenant (j.g.) Robert E. Baratko's Navy Cross. The citation reads:

> For extraordinary heroism on 15 September 1970 while serving as the aircraft commander of an attack helicopter, attached to Helicopter Attack (Light) Squadron THREE, during operations against enemy forces in the Republic of Vietnam. Lieutenant (jg) Baratko participated in a mission to provide cover for a medical evacuation helicopter which had previously attempted to evacuate several seriously wounded personnel in the face of intense enemy fire. As his plane and three others entered the evacuation area, the surrounding treelines erupted with intense fire which downed two aircraft and seriously damaged a third. Lieutenant (jg) Baratko's aircraft sustained several critical hits, including one

through the fuel tank. With the only flyable helicopter on the scene, he provided gun-ship coverage while the medical evacuation helicopter eventually succeeded in rescuing the downed crews. As he was flying this coverage, Lieutenant (jg) Baratko's plane was again subjected to heavy fire and sustained several more hits. After the medical evacuation helicopter departed the area, Lieutenant (jg) Baratko flew to a nearby landing strip with his fuel supply practically exhausted. By his perseverance and great personal valor in the face of almost overwhelming odds, he was directly instrumental in saving the lives of several of his shipmates. His selfless and determined efforts were in keeping with the highest traditions of the United States Naval Service.

★ ★ ★ ★ ★

September 16

1944 (Pacific)—After a thirty-minute bombardment, operators from UDT Eight land on Red Beach at Auguar Island and conduct the only combat demolition operation of the war for UDT Eight. The UDT operators use 120 pounds of tetryl to blast away the obstacles on the beach.

1967 (South Vietnam)—As part of Operation Crimson Tide, the three platoons of SEAL Team Two's Detachment Alfa conduct a day-long island sweep operation. The large operation will destroy a possible VC strongpoint in the Mekong Delta area. The target for the SEALs' sweep is Tan Dinh Island in the Song Hau Giang River at the southern edge of Ving Long Province.

Fourth, Fifth, and Sixth Platoons are inserted into the canal bank behind the island (on the southern side) and proceed to burn structures, destroy bunkers, and capture equipment. After an area is cleared, the SEALs extract and are reinserted at another point. This procedure is repeated during the entire operation, which runs from 0430 to 2000 hours. A total of nine insertions are made.

The results of the operation include 3 VC killed, 1 probably killed, about 100 hooches burned, 75 bunkers destroyed, 100 sampans destroyed, 20 sampan motors captured, 2 kilograms of documents captured, along with two male VC captured. Also, three weapons are taken, an M1 Garand, an M1 Carbine, and a Chicom rifle, as well as ammunition for each weapon. One SEAL is wounded slightly from the fragments of a 40mm M79 grenade, but he is treated and returned to duty quickly.

1994 (Haiti)—A detachment of Navy SEALs conducts a hydrographic reconnaissance of targeted beaches along the coast of Haiti. The beaches near Cap Haitian will be the next landing site for the troops of Operation Uphold Democracy. The waters the SEALs sometimes move through are thick with garbage and refuse. The SEALs also hear drumbeats from the Haitians on shore. At times, there are so many Haitian civilians in areas that the SEALs are supposed to recon that they cannot conduct their full recon without being detected. The SEALs, nevertheless, complete their recons successfully and the information they gather corresponds with intelligence from other sources, verifying the accuracy of their work in spite of the situation.

September 17

1944 (Pacific)—The invasion of Auguar Island takes place as part of the planned island-hopping campaign in the Pacific. For two weeks after the invasion, the men of UDT Eight work for the beachmaster of the invasion, clearing mines and destroying floating hazards.

1994 (Haiti)—Former president Jimmy Carter, Senator Sam Nunn, and retired General Colin Powell broker a last-minute deal to allow the incoming forces of Operation Uphold Democracy to land peacefully and restore order. All invasion forces moving toward Haiti are either aborted, diverted, or reconfigured to land peacefully and unopposed.

September 18

1968

```
BARNDANCE #  ___3-54___        SEAL TEAM  _2_ :  DET. _A_ :  _____ PLT.

DATE(S):  _18SEPT68_           OTHER UNITS:  7 PRU,1 INTERPRETER, 1 POW
                                             RIVDIV 592
MSG REF(S):  _____                 MST-2 DET D
                                             ARMY LIFT 12TH AHC

NAMES OF PERS:  LTJG WOOLARD, LTJG BREWTON, WO1 ATKINSON, GARNETT, TODD, ISHAM,
FOX, BURWELL, MCCLURE, WARMACK, MCCOY, RAMOS, DELAINE

MISSION TASK:  ___SEARCH___

INTEL/INFO SOURCE(S):  _1 POW CAP 15 SEPT68_

INSERTION:  TIME: _181645H_   METHOD: LSSC AND PBR   AMS COORD: XS881729

EXTRACTION: TIME: _181745H_   METHOD:    "          AMS COORD:    "

TERRAIN:  OPEN, THICK NIPA NEAR STREAMS
WEATHER:  CLOUDY            TIDE:  LOW        MOON:  NONE

BRIEF MISSION NARRATIVE:  INSERTED TWICE PREVIOUS TO FINAL INSERTION WITHOUT
RESULTS. REASONS FOR NUMEROUS INSERTIONS AND EXTRACTIONS WAS TO PREVENT HAVING
TO SWIM STREAMS EACH TIME POW TOOK US TO NEW LOCATION. ALL BUNKERS WERE IN SAME
GENERAL AREA. POW LED US TO VERY FINE WEAPONS CACHE LAST TIME. EXTRACTED FOLLOWING
FIND.

RESULTS OF ENEMY ENCOUNTERED:  NO VC ENCOUNTERED. WEAPONS CAP: 1 30 CAL. MG AND
TRIPOD, 2 60MM MORTARS COMPLETE WITH AIMING STAKES,1 RPG-7V ROCKET LAUNCHER AND
8 B-41 rds, 1 RPG-2 ROCKET LAUNCHER AND 19 B-40 RDS,26 B-40/B-41 BOOSTERS, 3 SIGHTS
FOR RPG'S, 2 AK 47 with 7 magazines, 40 ANTITANK PARACHUTE SHAPE HEAD GRENADES
FRIENDLY CASUALTIES: NONE. RED. 850 RDS .45 CAL, 350 RDS 7.62SHORT, 5000 RDS
7.62 HMD, 50 RDS 30 CAL. 3 CHICOM GRENADES, 1 CHICOM STICK-TYPE DEFENSIVE GREN.,
6 SETS WEB GEAR, 1 AMMO BOX DOCUMENTS.

REMARKS (SIGNIFICANT EVENTS, OPEVAL RESULTS, ETC.):  NO CASUALTIES.

RECOMMENDATIONS/LESSONS LEARNED:  PRU'S ARE PROVING TO BE VALUABLE PART OF
OUR OPERATIONS. ESP. GOOD AS INTEROGATORS, INTEND TO USE MORE IN FUTURE WHERE
POSSIBLE.

BD COPY DIST:  _____

(FORM REV. 8/68)                         BARNDANCE #  _XXXXX 3-54_
```

September 19

1994 (Haiti)—The patrol craft USS *Monsoon* (PC 4) becomes the first U.S. ship to enter the harbor of Port-au-Prince. As elsewhere in Haiti, troops land unopposed and peacefully. The landing marines are provided beach security and terminal guidance by the SEALs deployed with the task force.

September 20

1945 (USA)—By Executive Order 9621, signed by President Harry S. Truman, the OSS is disestablished effective October 1.

1964 (Vietnam)—A Montagnard uprising begins in Vietnam.

September 21

1961 (USA)—The Fifth Special Forces Group (Airborne) is officially activated. The unit can trace its lineage directly to the First Special Service Force of World War II.

1961 (USA)—The green beret becomes the official headgear of the U.S. Army Special Forces.

1987 (Persian Gulf)—U.S. Army Task Force 160 Nightstalker helicopters conduct nighttime patrols. Taking off from the frigate USS *Jarrott* (FFG 33), they come across the small Iranian amphibious ship *Iran Ajr* laying mines in the international shipping channels of the gulf. Operating under very strict rules of engagement, while the helicopters wait for radioed permission to open fire, they videotape the *Ajr* laying mines. Once the helicopters receive permission, they stop the *Ajr* with rockets and machine gun fire. When the ship tries to flee the area, further gunfire from the helicopters forces the crew to abandon ship.
A detachment of SEALs from the amphibious assault ship *Guadalcanal*, along with a team of marines and EOD personnel, board the *Ajr*. A number of old

Soviet M-08/39 moored contact mines—each charged with 253 pounds of TNT—are found on board. The Iranian crew is recovered from the water and detained for questioning. The *Ajr* is taken in tow for closer examination after the mines are declared safe by the EOD personnel.

1994 (Haiti)—An unopposed and peaceful landing by U.S. Marines and UN forces on the beaches originally targeted for the invasion of Haiti goes forward. The information gathered by the SEALs during their hydrographic recons of the area weeks before is proven to be very accurate.

September 22

UDT operators work on the recovery of the *Apollo Eleven* space capsule. The operators are wearing protective suits and masks against any possible contamination of the capsule by its exposure to space and the moon. U.S. NAVY

September 23

1945 (Japan)—Navy Task Unit Fifty-four, with several UDTs assigned to it, arrives off Wakayama on September 22 to prepare the way for incoming U.S. occupation forces. In the early morning light of September 23, UDT Three performs a beach reconnaissance and demolitions as needed to clear the way for the Thirty-third Infantry Division of the U.S. Sixth Army. UDT Seventeen also conducts a reconnaissance of 2,000 yards of beach. In the afternoon, UDT Seventeen conducts a hydrographic and photographic survey of the Wakayama boat basin and inner harbor. Meanwhile, UDT Three examines the dock facilities on the Kino River.

Since the Japanese surrender, no organized resistance is expected by the UDT operators or the incoming U.S. forces. Regardless, the recon and landing operations are carried out as an active combat mission, save the prelanding bombardment, in case of possible scattered resistance by local fanatics.

September 24

1945 (Japan)—UDT Three continues operations off the Wakayama landing beaches. Orders from the commander of Task Unit Fifty-four direct the men of UDT Three to accomplish the following:

1. Three hulks of small craft on the landing beaches have to be demolished
2. Wooden pilings in the area of the pier on Yellow Beach have to be cut away with explosives
3. A sea mine just west of Blue 2 Beach has to be blown
4. A string of recons of the beaches from the pier east for 1,500 yards has to be conducted

1945 (Japan)—UDT Seventeen conducts a reconnaissance of Wakanoura Wan and Osaki Wan. The team is locating piers or docks that can be used as unloading facilities by the incoming occupation forces. No hostilities take place between the UDT and the Japanese in the area. No mines or obstacles are found that will block incoming landing craft.

September 25

1945 (Japan)—At about 0830 hours, the first wave of incoming troops of the U.S. Sixth Army begins to come ashore at Wakayama Beach to occupy Japan. No incidents take place between the Japanese population and the occupation troops as they land and take up positions. Landings and the unloading of supplies continue smoothly.

1953 (USA)—The Seventy-seventh Special Forces Group is activated.

1964 (South Vietnam)—After a three-month-long screening process conducted by SEAL advisors, sixty South Vietnamese volunteers, considered to be some of the very best men available, are put in a sixteen-week LDNN training program. The program is established at Nha Trang in Khanh Hoa Province in the Second Corps area and is closely based on the Underwater Demolition Team Replacement training conducted in the United States.

September 26

1944 (Pacific)—At Peleliu, UDT Six is ordered to conduct a daylight reconnaissance mission and then a nighttime demolition operation close to enemy-held beaches. The UDT operators complete their work in spite of being under Japanese machine gun and sniper fire during the majority of the mission.

1966 (USA)—The first two SEAL Team Two platoons scheduled to deploy to South Vietnam begin their extensive predeployment training. The Second and Third Platoons, each with two officers and ten enlisted men, are the first direct-action platoons from SEAL Team Two to make up Detachment Alpha, under the command of an additional SEAL officer from Team Two. They will leave for Vietnam early the next year.

1987 (Persian Gulf)—The *Iran Ajr*, the minelaying ship captured by U.S. forces in the gulf, after having been closely examined and searched for any materials of intelligence or military worth, is taken out and sunk in deep water.

1969 (USA)—The Special Forces Memorial Stone is dedicated at Fort Bragg, North Carolina.

September 27

A group of Iranian prisoners, part of the crew of the minelaying ship *Iran Ajr*, are escorted along the deck of the USS *Guadalcanal*. U.S. NAVY

September 28

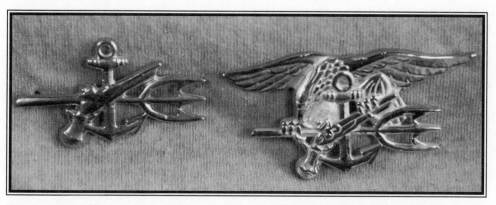

The Naval Special Warfare breast insignia—the Trident, only worn by qualified SEALs and UDT operators. The original second insignia for the UDT operators is on the left. KEVIN DOCKERY

September 29

1952 (Korea)—For eight days, beginning on September 21, UDT Three operating from the USS *Weiss* (APD 135) conducts nine missions off the northeast coast of Korea in support of Operation Fish. Five nets and fish traps and five sampans are destroyed, and forty-four prisoners are captured. The missions become so successful that techniques for conducting Operation Fish missions are suggested by the commanding officer of UDT Three. Suggestions include conducting the operations at night on nets that are spotted during the day or from interrogating prisoners, allowing ninety minutes per net for complete destruction, and issuing the UDTs saw-toothed knives and heavy cable cutters.

September 30

1945 (China)—UDT Nine arrives off Taku to recon landing facilities on the Hai Ho River. It also examines the navigability of the river and its mouth. This mission is to support landings of the First Marine Division, which is to occupy the Tien-tsin area of China from the surrendered Japanese. Landings begin a few days after the recon is completed.

1960 (USA)—The First Special Forces Regiment is established.

1991 (Haiti)—A military coup in Haiti removes the democratically elected Jean-Bertrand Aristide from office.

OCTOBER

A target of US Navy shelling and SEAL boarding parties, this Iranian oil platform burns during part of the action of Operation Praying Mantis. U.S. NAVY

October 01

1969 (USA)—The U.S. Department of the Navy officially adopts the Naval Special Warfare breast insignia. It is to be used by members of the SEAL and UDT units and to be worn on the upper left breast of the uniform, above any other ribbons or decorations. The layout of the insignia quickly earns the official nickname "Trident" among the members of the teams. The unofficial nickname "Budweiser" quickly spreads among the SEAL teams because of its resemblance to the symbol for that popular product line.

The Trident is recognized by many as a symbol associated with the U.S. Navy SEALS. It is, in fact, the one external indicator differentiating qualified SEALs and UDT operators from other uniformed members of the navy. Approval for wear on service dress uniforms is given by the U.S. Department of the Navy in 1970.

The Trident design is composed of four main symbolic elements. Centrally placed is a vertical anchor (representing the branch of service as the navy). A horizontal trident (representing the sea working environment with Neptune's scepter) intersects the anchor, and a diagonally positioned flintlock musket, set at half-cock, indicates a combat force that is always at the ready. Reaching around the anchor to grasp the trident in its right talon and the barrel of the pistol in its left is an American eagle with outstretched wings. The eagle represents both the United States and the aerial medium in which SEALS also operate.

Originally, the Trident insignia is issued in two colors: silver for enlisted men and gold for officers. At first, both the SEAL and UDT units of the Naval Special Warfare Group are issued slightly different insignia. UDT Tridents differentiate by the omission of the eagle. The UDT version, however, is discontinued shortly after the adoption of the device. Subsequently, a decision is made to issue the Tridents in gold to all qualified SEAL and UDT members regardless of rank and the silver color is dropped.

Authorization to wear the Trident is and will always be a very significant moment for each member of the teams. It is not won easily and can only be gained after successfully completing both the grueling BUD/S training and an additional six-month period of advanced training.

1990 (Persian Gulf)—Operation Sea Soldier I begins. The amphibious exercise is conducted for five days. The massive landing exercises are part of General Norman Schwartzkopf's deception plan to convince the Iraqis that a major amphibious landing will be part of his overall attack plan against occupied Kuwait. SEAL detachments take part in the landings as part of their normal operations with Marine Expeditionary Groups and amphibious landings. Witnessing the operations are members of the media who report on the actions.

1992 (Yugoslavia)—Operation Provide Promise, the U.S. airdrop of humanitarian assistance supplies in Bosnia-Herzegovinia, comes to an end as civilian population groups cut off by the surrounding fighting are freed.

October 02

1945 (Japan)—UDT Five arrives off Japan aboard the USS *Hobby* (APD 95). From October 2 to 4, the UDT conducts a reconnaissance of the Kure-Hiro naval station in West Honsue. The UDT operators work with advanced units from the Tenth Army Corps and the senior beachmasters of Transportation Squadron Sixteen.

The area of the Kure-Hiro naval station is divided into three sections for the reconnaissance: the Ondo Strait, the Hiro area, and the Kure area. Port facilities, all types of obstacles, Japanese gun positions, and other information on the areas are gathered, as well as a hydrographic reconnaissance of some locations.

October 03

1943 (USA)—The 5307th Composite Unit (Provisional), nicknamed "Merrill's Marauders," is activated.

1983 (USA)—The Secretary of Defense Casper W. Weinberger puts out a memo to all of the services to "fix Special Operations" correcting their organization and streamlining their command structure. The action is completed by the end of the 1990 fiscal year. The memo helps direct the eventual development of SOCOM.

1993 (Eastern Africa)—In Mogadishu, a joint unit of Rangers, specialized army assets, and SEALs drive out to conduct an assault on a building on Hawlwadig Road near the Olympic Hotel. During the approach to the target site, a SEAL chief is struck by a round from a Somali gunman. The bullet is stopped by shattering the blade of the knife on the SEAL's hip. After the blade fragments are removed and the wound is bandaged, the SEAL chief continues on the operation.

1993 (Somalia)—An Army UH-60 Blackhawk helicopter is shot down in Mogadishu by a Somali gunman armed with an RPG-7. A battle follows in which U.S. forces try to rescue the downed crew and passengers of the Blackhawk. The fire fight lasts into the next day as armed gunmen, U.S. forces, and Somali civilians fill the streets around the crash site. When the battle is over, 18 Americans are dead, 70 are badly wounded, and an estimated 1,000 Somalis are either killed or wounded. The incident finally results in the complete U.S. pull-out of forces under Operation United Shield.

1993 (Somalia)—Units from the Twenty-fourth Special Tactics Squadron take part in the rescue of the downed Army UH-60 Blackhawk helicopter in Mogadishu. This operation becomes known to the public as "Blackhawk Down." In Mogadishu, Master Sergeant Gary Gordon and Sergeant First Class Randall Shugart perform the actions that result in their being awarded the Congressional Medal of Honor posthumously.

October 04

1943 (Europe)—The OSS participates in the expulsion of Germans from Corsica.

1968 (South Vietnam)—SEAL Team Detachment Bravo, which consists of PRU advisors throughout the Fourth Corps Tactical Zone (Mekong Delta) area, is expanded. The original manpower allotment of one officer and twelve enlisted men grows to thirteen officers and twenty-one enlisted men. The manpower for the detachment comes from both SEAL Teams One and Two.

October 05

```
BARNDANCE #    10-30              SEAL TEAM  TWO ;  DET.  A ;  10  PLT.

DATE(S):  05 OCT 69              OTHER UNITS:   MST -2   1 LSSC
                                               RSSZ LHFT
MSG REF(S):                                    2 PBR


NAMES OF PERS:   LTJG BRYSON, CLARK, DILLEY, NOLLEY, PERZANOWSKI, MCDONALD,
   MOORE


MISSION TASK:   CANAL AMBUSH


INTEL/INFO SOURCE(S):    PAST INCIDENT REPORTS

INSERTION:   TIME: 041800H     METHOD:   LSSC      AMS COORD: YS192713

EXTRACTION:  TIME: 042100H     METHOD:   LSSC      AMS COORD: YS192713

TERRAIN:  MUD
WEATHER:   CLEAR              TIDE/SURF:  HIGH      MOON:  NONE

BRIEF MISSION NARRATIVE:       DEPARTED NHA BE 041500H IN PBR.  INSERTED AND
  SET CANAL AMBUSH.  AT 042030 TOOK SAMPAN WITH THREE VC TRAVELING WEST FROM
  SMALL CANAL TO NORTHEAST IN LARGE CANAL UNDER FIRE.  SCRAMBLED LHFT AND
  REQ. EXTRACTION BY LSSC.  EXTRACTED 042100H AND DIRECTED LHFT STRIKE INTO
  POSITION.  TOWED SAMPAN TO GO GIA RIVER AND DESTROYED.  RETURNED TO NHA BE
  051230H


FRIENDLY PERS/MATERIAL CASUALTIES:       NONE


ENEMY PERS/MATERIAL CASUALTIES:      1 VC KIA (BC), 2 VC KIA (PROB)
  CAPTURED: 3 KILOS CLOTHING, 1 KILO DOCUMENTS


REMARKS (SIGNIFICANT EVENTS, OPEVAL RESULTS, ETC.):      NONE




RECOMMENDATIONS/LESSONS LEARNED:     CARRY MANY PARACHUTE FLARES




BD COPY DIST:

(FORM REV. 4/69)                          BARNDANCE #   10-30
```

October 06

1967 (South Vietnam)—While training for operations in the Rung Sat Special Zone, Signalman Third Class Leslie Funk drowns. He is working as part of SEAL Team One's Detachment Golf at the time of the incident.

1968 (South Vietnam)—Following timely intelligence on the location of a VC POW camp, operators from Second Squad of SEAL Team One's Alfa Platoon and a number of PRU members conduct a prison camp raid. The location of the camp according to women who had been allowed by the VC to visit their husbands there is in the Cu Lao Dung Island complex near the mouth of the Bassac River.

Put together quickly and smoothly, the operation is under the leadership of Scott Lyon, a PRU SEAL advisor. With Seawolves for air support and a large number of PBRs for transportation and support, the SEALs and the PRU move out on the operation at 0215 hours.

With some difficulty, the women acting as guides finally locate where the SEALs can insert with a good chance of finding the POW camp. Finally, the SEALs are inserted and patrol to where they can overlook the camp, which is complete with bamboo cages for the prisoners, hooches for the guards, and eight to ten armed VC guards.

Shortly after dawn, the SEALs and the PRU assault the camp with overwhelming, but accurate, fire. The VC guards are stunned by the sudden firepower and quickly surrender. The entire assault lasts for only three minutes, until the SEALs and the PRU gain complete control of the situation. They liberate twenty-four South Vietnamese prisoners but do not find any American POWs. During a search of a VC tax collector's hooch, more than $68,000 (U.S. value) in Vietnamese currency is found. Some of the POWs have been in captivity for extended periods and fall to their knees to kiss the feet of the SEALs who have liberated them. This is something the SEALs are not used to, so they quickly herd the prisoners to the extraction boats and away from the camp.

October 07

1966 (South Vietnam)—SEAL Team One suffers a heavy hit in terms of casualties when the Mike boat being used to transport two SEAL squads in the Rung Sat Special Zone is ambushed by a large number of VC and taken under fire. A mortar round makes a direct hit on the boat and wounds sixteen of the nineteen men aboard. In spite of the severity of the wounds, the SEALs successfully fight their way out of the situation. Three SEALs are medically discharged from the service due to the severity of their injuries. Later intelligence reports state that forty VC were killed in the ambush. The Silver Star is awarded to Chief Petty Officer Churchill of SEAL Team One for his actions during the incident. His is only one of a number of medals given out for actions by the SEALs aboard the Mike boat that day. The citation reads:

> *For conspicuous gallantry and intrepidity in action while accompanying a patrol party of SEAL Team One Detachment GOLF in the Rung Sat Special Zone, Republic of Vietnam on 7 October 1966. Chief Petty Officer CHURCHILL, in self defense, manned a thirty caliber machine gun on an armed LCM when the Viet Cong initiated an ambush with small arms, automatic weapons, machine guns, and mortars. He attempted to return fire from his mount but found his weapon jammed. While attempting to clear his weapon, an enemy mortar round made a direct hit on the LCM approximately six feet from his position. Although seriously wounded and semiconscious, he noticed smoke coming from the boat's mortar position, and discovered that a hot mortar fragment was causing the wooden boxes containing sixty millimeter mortar ammunition to burn. He picked up the hot fragment and threw it overboard, suffering severe burns. Chief Petty Officer CHURCHILL noticed that the gunner on a fifty caliber machine gun was unconscious and not returning fire. Exposing himself to enemy fire, he pulled the gunner from his position and, in defense of the wounded, attempted to man the weapon. When the senior officer present arrived and took over the mount, Chief Petty Officer CHURCHILL began to care for the seriously wounded men around him, even though he was exposing*

himself to direct enemy fire. Chief Petty Officer CHURCHILL's inspiring leadership, sense of responsibility, and courage under fire were in keeping with the highest traditions of the United States Naval Service.

1985 (Mediterranean)—At 0845 hours, four Palestinian passengers on the Italian-owned cruise ship *Achille Lauro* are spotted in their cabins cleaning weapons. They are members of the Palestinian Liberation Front (PLF), planning a suicide raid on the Israeli port of Ashdod. Their discovery, however, changes their plans. The four terrorists suddenly charge into the main dining room of the ship, firing their weapons into the overhead, wounding two of the passengers, and taking the rest hostage. Very quickly, the terrorists take complete control of the cruise ship and its 427 passengers and 80 crew members. The terrorists demand the release of fifty Palestinians being held in Israeli custody. The Israelis refuse and negotiations continue.

2001 (Afghanistan)—Operation Enduring Freedom, the U.S. mission to wipe out al Qaeda, locate Osama bin Laden, and eliminate the Taliban government, begins. With the repeated refusals of the Taliban government to turn over bin Laden to be tried for the September 11, 2001, attacks in the United States, President George W. Bush orders the launch of the first wave of air strikes against military targets in Afghanistan.

October 08

1943 (Australia)—The 5217th Special Reconnaissance Battalion is formed.

1985 (Mediterranean)—Aboard the hijacked cruise ship *Achille Lauro*, negotiations between the four PLF terrorists and the authorities hit an impasse. The terrorists kill Leon Klinghoffer, a sixty-nine-year-old American invalid confined to a wheelchair. The ship is refused docking rights in Syria and sails on toward Port Said, Egypt.

Elements of SEAL Team Six have been notified and prepare to do a takedown of the ship at sea. The SEALs have been training and preparing for years for just such a mission. Their operation is put on hold as negotiations continue for the release of the hostages. At Port Said, Abbu Abbas, the head of the PLF and a senior member of the Palestinian Liberation Organization, persuades the terrorists to surrender to Egyptian authorities. When the terrorists leave the *Achille Lauro* and release the hostages, Egypt refuses to turn them over to the United States for prosecution.

1967 (Bolivia)—Ernesto "Che" Guevara is captured by Special Forces–trained Manchego Number 2 Bolivian Rangers.

1987 (Persian Gulf)—Four Iranian speedboats, manned by Pasdaran crews, are spotted operating fifteen miles southwest of Farsi Island. The armed speedboats have been a consistent threat in the gulf waters. After the speedboats open fire on circling U.S. Army helicopters, the helicopters return fire, sinking one of the boats and damaging the other two. The two remaining speedboats are quickly taken captive.

October 09

1969

```
BARNDANCE #    9-90          SEAL TEAM   2  ;  DET.   A  ;  9TH   PLT.

DATE(S):  9 OCTOBER 1969     OTHER UNITS:  12 PRU'S
                                           CTE 116.6.7.4 (LTJG HAZARD)
MSG REF(S):  _____                 CTU 116.9.8 (LTJG SCOTT)
                                           2 USA SLICKS

NAMES OF PERS:  CWO2 RUTH, ADJ1 JESSIE, AMB3 SMITH, BM3 NAUS, AND LDNN QUOI.



MISSION TASK:  CANAL AMBUSH                                              √


INTEL/INFO SOURCE(S):  PRU'S

INSERTION:   TIME: _____  METHOD: _____  AMS COORD: _____

EXTRACTION:  TIME: _____  METHOD: _____  AMS COORD: _____

TERRAIN:
WEATHER: _____        TIDE/SURF: _____  MOON: _____

BRIEF MISSION NARRATIVE:    INSERTED BY SLICK AND SET AMBUSH AT CANAL JCT. AT 1600
6 PRU EXTRACTED BY SLICK AT 1715 TWO SAMPANS APROACHED AMBUSH SITE, TOOK UNDER
FIRE. 4 VC SWAM TO NEAR BANK (ABOUT 10 METERS) AND EVADED TO SOUTH. SEAWOLF CALLED
SEALS AND PRU PURSUED VC SEAWOLF PUT STRIKE ON SUSPECTED HIDING PLACE RESULTS UNKNOWN


FRIENDLY PERS/MATERIAL CASUALTIES:   NONE


ENEMY PERS/MATERIAL CASUALTIES:    2 VC KIA(BC), 2 SAMPANS CAPTURED ALSO 2 M26
 HAND GRENADES, 8 PACKS PERSONAL GEAR, 1 TRANSITOR RADIO FOOD CONSITING OF FISH
CRABS BREAD, FRUIT, AND VEG. FOR ABOUT 100 MEALS.

REMARKS (SIGNIFICANT EVENTS, OPEVAL RESULTS, ETC.):   PRU OPENED FIRE PREMATURLY.




RECOMMENDATIONS/LESSONS LEARNED:  HAVE SEALS INITIATE FIRE.




BD COPY DIST: _____

(FORM REV. 4/69)                         BARNDANCE #    9-90
```

254

October 10

1968 (South Vietnam)—The actions conducted by the SEALs are often classified and as such cannot be told to the public. Occasionally, however, this causes problems. When a SEAL receives a particularly public award, such as the Navy Cross, citations have to be written to account for the actions that resulted in the award. Yeoman Third Class Gary Gallagher is still performing actions that cause him to be awarded the Navy Cross when he receives it as Detachment Bravo's PRU advisor:

> For extraordinary heroism on 10 and 11 October 1968 while serving with friendly foreign forces engaged in armed conflict in the Mekong Delta region of the Republic of Vietnam. Distinguishing himself by his exemplary leadership and selfless courage, Petty Officer Gallagher, serving in the capacity of Reconnaissance Unit Adviser, led his unit in a capture mission deep into enemy-controlled area. As the operation progressed and the unit began picking up prisoners, the unit split and advanced on both sides of a small canal in an effort to capture additional members of the Viet Cong infrastructure. At this time, an earlier-acquired captive made a warning sound to his comrades in the vicinity. Immediately, heavy fire from a numerically-superior enemy force was encountered by the separated half of Petty Officer Gallagher's patrol unit. In order to prevent his prisoners from escaping, he forced them to lead the way while crossing the canal to assist his stricken troops. Rallying his reconnaissance unit, Petty Officer Gallagher boldly exposed himself to the hostile fire while directing return fire on the enemy. His driving determination to succeed in his mission served to inspire his men and resulted in the temporary neutralization of the enemy attack. Petty Officer Gallagher then led a hasty, yet professionally executed, withdrawal—with his entire unit and all prisoners-of-war intact. Before concluding the extraction phase, he administered lifesaving first aid to a

seriously wounded companion and carried the man over eight kilometers to safety. Petty Officer Gallagher's heroic response while leading this Vietnamese force, his demonstrated initiative and valor, and his selfless dedication under concentrated enemy fire were in keeping with the highest traditions of the United States Naval Service.

★ ★ ★ ★ ★

1985 (Mediterranean)—The Palestinian terrorists who hijacked the cruise ship *Achille Lauro* board an Egyptian Boeing 737 and leave Egypt for Tunisia and freedom. During their evening flight over the waters of the Mediterranean, four F-14 fighters from the aircraft carrier USS *Saratoga* (CV 60) intercept the flight in international airspace. The pilot of the Boeing 737 is convinced in no uncertain terms to turn his aircraft north and land at the NATO airbase at Sigonella, Sicily.

Once on the ground, the aircraft is quickly surrounded by many of the American operators planning the takedown of the *Achille Lauro*. Italian authorities arrive on the scene and surround the aircraft and the American operators. The standoff is tense until the Americans receive orders to stand down and let the terrorists be turned over to Italian authorities.

October 11

1945 (Japan)—UDT Five continues its operations of conducting a reconnaissance of the Mitsuhana waterfront area in Shikoku. The UDT operators again work with advanced units of the Tenth Army Corps. The purpose of the mission is to locate suitable landing and storage areas for the occupation forces.

1945 (USA)—UDT Twenty-five arrives at the Naval Amphibious Base in Coronado, California. It is assigned to the task of assisting Lieutenant Commander Draper Kauffman in setting up and organizing the permanent postwar Underwater Demolition Base to be located at the Coronado facility.

1950 (Korea)—At Wonsan, UDT One personnel conduct minesweeping operations from October 11 to 24. The wooden boats integral to the UDT transport, combined with the skills of the operators, allow them to be used as an interim minesweeping force to clear the approaches to Wonsan Harbor. The mines are located by helicopters that direct the UDT boats toward the mines. UDT operators buoy the mines, marking their locations for later clearance and to indicate a safe passage for the minesweeper ships to fully clear the area. Though the work is hazardous, it does not require any special skills on the part of the UDT operators, though the boats and buoys used are organic to their normal issue of equipment. The UDTs adapt well to the work, locating and marking fifty mines during their first day of operation.

October 12

1945 (China)—UDT Nine receives orders directing it to Tsing Tao. The men of the UDT recon the alternate landing beaches on the south side of the city as well as examine the docks and wharves on the west side of Tsing Tao. The facilities and landing beaches will be used to bring ashore the occupation troops of the Sixth Marine Division. With no further duties, and remaining in the area of Tsing Tao until October 17, the men of the UDT are given liberty to go ashore.

1950 (Korea)—During regular minesweeping operations in Wonsan Harbor, the minesweeper USS *Pirate* (AM 275) strikes a mine and quickly sinks. That afternoon, the minesweeper USS *Pledge* (AM 277) also hits a mine. A large number of the crew of the *Pledge* are injured from the blast and are in no shape to help themselves. Ignoring the danger to itself from the mines, the destroyer USS *Endicott* (DMS 35) moves quickly to provide aid to the men of the stricken minesweeper. UDT operators in their landing craft also rush to the aid of the *Pledge*. Through the efforts of the UDT operators, who refuse to leave the *Pledge* until the last moment before its sinking, more than fifty of its crew are saved with only six men lost.

1961 (USA)—During a visit by President John F. Kennedy to the U.S. Army's Special Warfare School at Fort Bragg, North Carolina, he is presented with a green beret by the members of the Seventy-seventh Special Forces Group. A request is made to the president that he grant the Special Forces permission to wear the green beret as a distinctive part of its military uniform. The request is later granted.

October 13

1944 (Europe)—All American and British Jedburghs are ordered to return to the United Kingdom.

A side view of a Mark II PBR (patrol boat, river) being driven along by its water-jet propulsion system. The water-jet system prevented the need for an exposed propeller that could be quickly fouled in the plant and debris–choked waters of inland streams and canals. U.S. NAVY

October 14

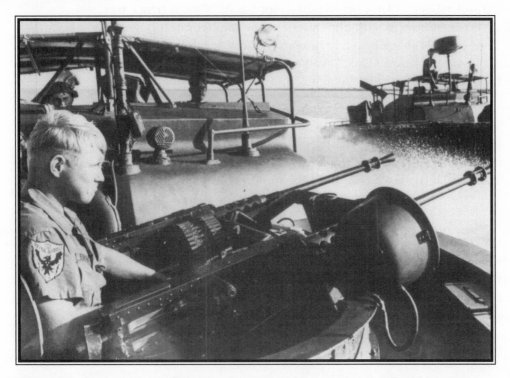

The bow twin-.50 gun turret of a PBR while a pair of the craft are underway in a South Vietnamese waterway. U.S. NAVY

October 15

1993 (USA)—President Bill Clinton orders the U.S. Navy to send six ships to Haiti. Admiral David P. Miller, the commander in chief of the U.S. Atlantic Command, activates the Combined Joint Task Force 120 to conduct Operation Support Democracy, a multinational action to enforce the UN economic embargo in Haiti.

October 16

1987 (Persian Gulf)—A reflagged Kuwaiti oil tanker, the *Sea Isle City*, is struck by a Chinese-made HY-2 Silkworm antiship missile. The Silkworm has been launched from a site on the Fao Peninsula in Iranian territory and hits the tanker on the waters just outside of Kuwait City. Seventeen of the tanker's crew as well as the American captain are injured in the attack.

October 17

1944 (Philippines)—Mucci's Rangers, the Sixth Ranger Battalion, leads the assault on the island of Dinagat, which guards the mouth of Leyte Gulf.

October 18

1977 (Somalia)—The German counterterrorist unit GSG-9 rescues the eighty-six passengers and four crew of Lufthansa Flight LH 181 in Operation Fire Magic. The aircraft has been hijacked by four members of the Popular Front for the Liberation of Palestine–Special Operations Group on behalf of the Red Army Faction and flown to Mogadishu Airport.

October 19

1944 (Philippines)—At 1100 hours, UDT Nine begins reconnaissance of the White Beaches near the Tacloban landing strip on Leyte. The UDT arrives late for its missions because its transport had to skirt a typhoon on its way to Leyte. In addition, the minesweeping operations of the north beach areas have not yet been completed, forcing UDT Nine to concentrate on the White Beaches. Additional recons are being conducted by UDTs Six and Ten in support of the upcoming invasion.

Approaching the beaches, UDT Nine takes a number of casualties when the Japanese forces open fire. The landing craft carrying Platoon One is hit by mortar fire and has to withdraw from the operation. Cover fire support from the offshore fleets is impossible because the water has not been swept clear of mines and the ships cannot draw any closer to shore.

1983 (Grenada)—Prime Minister Maurice Bishop is executed by Deputy Prime Minister Bernard Coard, a hard-line Marxist. As the control of Grenada is seized by the Revolutionary Military Council, a twenty-four-hour curfew is put in place with the warning that anyone breaking it will be shot on sight. This puts nearly 1,000 Americans in Grenada, most of them students at Saint George's Medical College, at great risk. It is the final incident of unrest on the island for the Reagan administration as orders are issued to put Operation Urgent Fury, the invasion of Grenada and the protection of American citizens, into action.

1987 (Persian Gulf)—As retribution for the Iranian Silkworm missile attack on the reflagged Kuwaiti tanker *Sea Isle City*, Operation Nimble Archer is put into effect. Four destroyers, the USS *Hoel* (DDG 13), the USS *Leftwich* (DD 984), the USS *Kidd* (DDG 933), and the USS *John Young* (DD 973), conduct a naval gunfire attack on two Rashadat oil platforms in the Rostam oil field. Used as military outposts, they are the command and control platforms for the Iranian-armed speedboats.

After a fifteen-minute warning is given, the four destroyers fire approximately 1,000 rounds of five-inch high-explosive shells into the two targets. The platforms are effectively destroyed from the waterline up. Later, a SEAL platoon is sent aboard to search for intelligence materials. Demolition charges set by the SEALs complete the destruction of one of the platforms. In addition to the two shelled platforms, the SEALs board and search a third platform two miles away. On that platform, the SEALs locate and remove intelligence documents and communications equipment.

2001 (Afghanistan)—As part of Operation Enduring Freedom, more than 100 U.S. Army Rangers are brought in to conduct a raid near Kandahar.

October 20

1944 (Philippines)—U.S. forces go ashore to continue the liberation of the Philippines. After what UDT observers consider one of the most devastating shore bombardments to be seen in the Pacific to date, U.S. troops land on Leyte. The UDTs are sent a dispatch from Admiral Thomas C. Kinkaid:

> X FOR EMBARKED UNDERWATER DEMOLITION TEAMS X YOU HAVE REASON TO BE PROUD OF THE PART YOU PLAYED IN THE LEYTE OPERATION X WELL DONE AND GOOD LUCK X

1945 (USA)—At the Amphibious Training Base in Oceanside, California, UDT Four is dissolved as part of the postwar cutbacks. One of the first UDTs formed eighteen months earlier, UDTs One and Two had proved the value of Rear Admiral Richmond Kelly Turner's idea.

October 21

1956 (South Vietnam)—While operating as an instructor for indigenous Special Forces personnel in South Vietnam, Captain Harry G. Cramer is killed by enemy action. Captain Cramer was part of the Fourteenth Special Forces Operational Detachment of the Seventy-seventh Special Forces Group. He became the first U.S. combat loss in Vietnam and his name is the first engraved on the wall at the Vietnam Veteran's War Memorial in Washington, D.C.

October 22

1944 (Pacific)—The third letter from D. M. Logsdon, the commanding officer of UDT Six, is written to the team:

UNDERWATER DEMOLITION TEAM NO. 6

22 October 1944

From: The Commanding Officer

To: The Officers and Men of U.D.T. No. 6

Subject: Palau and Leyte Island Operations—Performance of Team Personnel

1. Upon completion of the underwater demolition work required in the retaking of Guam, this team was ordered to join the task force which was then being assembled for the attack on Palau. Pending departure from the staging area the team was reorganized, additional personnel were obtained and a full outfit of battle equipment was procured.

2. Military intelligence indicated that the Peleliu phase of the Palau operation would entail difficult and dangerous work for the team, but it was not until the reconnaissance data was assembled that the real character of the work became known. The three beaches and the LST landing area which were assigned to this team were found to be littered with large coral boulders which would prevent the passage of tanks, DUKW's and vehicular equipment. Furthermore, the enemy had erected lines of heavily braced posts near the shore abreast these beaches. The reconnaissance showed that passages had to be blasted through these boulders and obstacles before landings could be made, and it showed how effectively the enemy had emplaced its heavy machine guns covering those beaches.

3. The attack plan assigned two of the beaches to this team and a third beach and the LST area to another team. An operational

casualty in the early morning of the day on which the work was to begin, however, made the employment of that other team impossible and necessitated the assignment of all the work of both teams to Team No. 6.

4. The reconnaissance, made three days before the assault, was accomplished under heavy machine gun and sniper fire. On the two following days the operating platoons were engaged in blasting boulders on the reef where all hands were exposed to constant enemy fire. On the second night before the assault eight demolition groups from this team proceeded across the reef under cover of darkness and placed over a thousand demolition charges with fifty yards of the enemy machine guns and rifle pits; these charges cleared the obstacles to the beaches. A happy combination of good fire support, coolness and battle-wisdom on your part and rare good luck enabled you to accomplish these dangerous tasks without a casualty

5. On the twelfth day of the battle for Peleliu when the marines had driven the enemy to the northern end of that island, this team and Team No. 8 were directed to conduct a daylight reconnaissance of the narrow straight between Peleliu and Ngesebus Islands. The reconnaissance parties were required to swim a total distance of three miles; over a great part of this distance they were under constant mortar, machine gun and sniper fire from both shores.

6. The excellent work you did in that operation, under conditions which were worse than those ever before experienced by an underwater demolition team, aroused the unstinted praise of all fair-minded observers. The commander of the demolition group, in his action report on the Peleliu operation, commended this team for its "outstanding performance in action requiring extraordinary courage and endurance while working with high explosives on an exposed reef without natural cover, while under enemy machine gun and sniper fire, for a daylight reconnaissance under fire on 12 September 1944 and 24 September 1944 and night demolition work close to enemy-held beaches."

7. Upon completion of the Ngesebus reconnaissance the team was ordered to join the task force which was then assembling for the long awaited attack on the Philippine Islands. In this campaign, however, the conditions were far different from those to which you had become accustomed. The attacking force had such a wide choice of islands and beaches that the enemy was unable to prepare adequate beach defenses. Your task was therefore far easier than it had ever been in the earlier operations. Since there were no man-made obstacles nor coral to be removed, your only task consisted of reconnoitering the assault beaches and searching for mines. The enemy was able to give you a moderately warm reception with its mortars, machine guns and sniper fire but you did your job quickly and well.

8. This war will go on for many months more, but the extent to which beach reconnaissance and underwater demolition work will be necessary in those future theaters of action remains to be seen. Of this, however, you can be fairly sure—no team will ever be required to do a more difficult and dangerous job than this team did at Peleliu, nor will it be able to do it better.

9. You can now look back on four successful operations, operations in which you carried out your dangerous missions with superb courage and skill. You have won the respect and admiration of those fighting men for whom this work was done.

10. In congratulating you for what you have already done I feel sure that in the performance of those duties that lie ahead you will show the same courage and competence that you have in the past.

D. M. LOGSDON

1983 (USA)—SEAL Team Six receives word about the situation on Grenada. The team is told that its initial mission will be to put some members of an air force unit into Grenada, recon the airport facilities there, and determine if they would accept landings from U.S. C-130 and C-141 aircraft.

October 23

1945 (USA)—UDT Five returns to the Naval Amphibious Base at Coronado, California, after completing its mission in Japan clearing the way for the incoming occupation forces. It is then formally decommissioned on this date.

1983 (Lebanon)—A suicide truck bomb drives through the perimeter defenses of the barracks for the Twenty-fourth Marine Amphibious Unit in Beirut. The huge blast from what is later estimated to be several tons of military-grade high explosives kills 241 marines and navy personnel, as well as wounding another 80. In an almost simultaneous attack, another huge suicide truck bomb is detonated at the French troops' barracks in Beirut. Fifty-eight French soldiers are killed in the attack.

1983 (Grenada)—Eight SEALs are in-flight to conduct an air drop into the waters near Grenada. The SEALs jump with their Boston Whaler powerboats rigged out for a daylight drop. The air force crews aboard the C-130s do not know that the SEALs' mission is part of an active combat drop. The aircraft arrive at the zone much later than expected and the sun has gone down. The SEALs decide to go ahead with the operation and two four-man SEAL teams and two boats exit their aircraft into the darkness.

A sudden squall below the parachuting SEALs forces them away from the drop zone by several miles. Instead of landing in calm seas, the SEALs smash into six- to eight-foot waves. One boat is capsized and lost. As the rest of the SEALs struggle with their equipment and parachutes in twenty-knot winds and high waves, four of them are lost and never recovered. They are the first combat losses to the teams since 1972 and the end of the Vietnam War.

October 24

1983 (Grenada)—A detachment of SEALs from SEAL Team Four, which is attached to the Twenty-second Marine Amphibious Unit ordered to Grenada, conducts a standard hydrographic reconnaissance operation at 2200 hours local time. In spite of driving rain and poor visibility making the conditions bad for their operation, the SEALs recon beaches at the north end of Grenada. Inserting from rubber boats launched from Seafox boats, which transport them from the ship, the SEALs are close enough to the shore to overhear the conversations of Grenadian workers. The recon determines that the offshore waters are unacceptable for anything but very shallow-draft vessels. The marines change their plans and conduct a helicopter-borne landing instead.

1994 (Haiti)—The new Cyclone-class patrol craft leaves the waters off Haiti. During Operation Support/Uphold Democracy, the new craft demonstrate their abilities to be both effective military craft as well as operational SEAL launching platforms.

October 25

1983 (Grenada)—Invasion forces begin to move in on Grenada at 0520 hours local time. Echo Company of the Twenty-second Marine Amphibious Unit lands by helicopter near the Pearls Airport, while Fox Company lands nearby at Grenville. Detachments of SEALs move in after dawn to secure the Radio Free Grenada transmitting site, as well as to secure and protect Governor General Sir Paul Scoon at his government house mansion. Specialized army units go on to other targets, securing the island in a matter of days.

1983 (USA)—President Ronald Reagan goes on television to announce that the United States has invaded the island country of Grenada in the southern Caribbean. This announcement is the first time the public hears about Operation

Urgent Fury. In his explanation, the president states that the operation is being conducted by a joint force of the U.S. military backed by a small military contingent from several Caribbean nations. Cuban workers and military advisors have been on Grenada for several years, most recently enlarging the island's major airfield to accept Soviet bombers and cargo planes heading on to Nicaragua. Additionally, Moscow has been sending large shipments of arms, ammunition, and military supplies for stockpiling on the small island.

October 26

A UDT swimmer attempts to meet some friendly locals. The thin rubber dry suit the operator is wearing over insulating clothing protects him from the frigid Antarctic waters that would otherwise kill an unprotected swimmer in a few minutes. U.S. Navy

October 27

BARNDANCE # ___9-110___   SEAL TEAM _2_ ; DET. _A_ ; _9TH_ PLT.

DATE(S): _28 OCTOBER 1969_   OTHER UNITS: _SEAL STAB BOAT_
6 PRU'S

MSG REF(S): _____

NAMES OF PERS: _GMG1 THORNTON, PC2 SCHMIDT, EM2 NAUS_

MISSION TASK: _DISTRICT LEVEL CADRE MEETING_

INTEL/INFO SOURCE(S): _PRU'S_

INSERTION: TIME: _27 2400H_   METHOD: _STAB_   AMS COORD: _XS 887626_

EXTRACTION: TIME: _28 0600H_   METHOD: _STAB_   AMS COORD: _SAME_

TERRAIN: _RICE PADDY_
WEATHER: _CLEAR_   TIDE/SURF: _HIGH_   MOON: _FULL_

BRIEF MISSION NARRATIVE: ___INSERTED BY STAB PATROLLED TO G/P AT XS 885629 BETWEEN 28 0100H & 28 0300H OBSERVED 7 VC ENTER NIPP PALM APPROX. 100M ACROSS CANAL WEST OF G/P. AT 28 0430H ONE SAMPAN COMING FROM UP STREAM BEACHED AT NIPP PALM AND TOOK ON 3 VC AND PROCEEDED BACK UP CANAL(NOT TAKEN UNDER FIRE DUE TO DISTANCE INVOLVED AT 0530H BROKE G/P AND SEARCHED NIPP PALM. NEG RESULTS. EXTRACTED FROM INSERTION PT. AND RETURNED TO NHA BE.___

FRIENDLY PERS/MATERIAL CASUALTIES: _NEG._

ENEMY PERS/MATERIAL CASUALTIES: _NEG._

REMARKS (SIGNIFICANT EVENTS, OPEVAL RESULTS, ETC.): _LUCKY BASTARDS!!!_

RECOMMENDATIONS/LESSONS LEARNED: _I WORK TO HARD. I NEED A VACATION._

BD COPY DIST: _____

(FORM REV. 4/69)   BARNDANCE # ___9-110___

October 28

A very memorable class gift to the staff stands duty at the Basic Underwater Demolition/SEAL training center. This *Creature from the Black Lagoon* statue was from BUD/S Class 63 and wears a sign reading: "So you wanna be a Frogman?" KEVIN DOCKERY

October 29

1945 (USA)—UDT Twenty-seven is decommissioned at Coronado, California. Formed February 15 the same year it has only been commissioned as a UDT since June 2.

1963 (South Vietnam)—Special Forces Captain J. N. "Nick" Rowe is captured by the VC.

October 30

1990 (Saudi Arabia)—Operation Sea Soldier II begins in the Persian Gulf. This is another series of amphibious exercises to aid General Norman Schwartzkopf's deception plan against the Iraqis. The aim of the landing exercises, beginning this date and running until November 8, is to show the world news media and through them the Iraqi command that a major amphibious landing will be part of his overall attack plan against occupied Kuwait. The same elements of Amphibious Ready Group Two and the Fourth Marine Expeditionary Group, along with their assigned SEAL elements, take part in the landings during both exercises Sea Soldier I and II.

October 31

1972 (USA)—Petty Officer Michael E. Thornton earns the Congressional Medal of Honor for his actions in Vietnam. The presidential citation from Richard Nixon reads as follows:

> *For conspicuous gallantry and intrepidity at the risk of his life above and beyond the call of duty while participating in a daring operation against enemy forces in the Republic of Vietnam on October 31, 1972, Petty Officer Thornton, as assistant U.S. Navy advisor, along with a U.S. Navy lieutenant serving as senior advisor, accompanied a three-man Vietnamese Navy SEAL patrol on an intelligence gathering and prisoner capture operation against an enemy-occupied naval river base. Launched from a Vietnamese Navy junk in a rubber*

boat, the patrol reached land and was continuing on foot toward its objective when it suddenly came under heavy fire from a numerically superior force. The patrol called in naval gunfire support and then engaged the enemy in a fierce firefight, accounting for many enemy casualties, before moving back to the waterline to prevent encirclement. Upon learning that the senior advisor had been hit by enemy fire and was believed to be dead, Petty Officer Thornton returned through a hail of fire to the lieutenant's last position, quickly disposed of two enemy soldiers about to overrun the position and succeeded in removing the seriously wounded and unconscious senior naval advisor to the water's edges. He then inflated the lieutenant's lifejacket and towed him seaward for approximately two hours until picked up by support craft. By his extraordinary courage and perseverance, Thornton was directly responsible for saving the life of his superior officer and enabling the safe extraction of all patrol members.

NOVEMBER

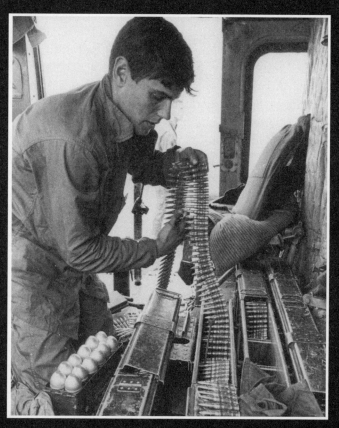

A crewman loads the long ammunition boxes for the mounted outboard 7.62mm machine guns of this Seawolf helicopter gunship. The 600-round long belts of ammunition are just part of the heavy loads of ordnance carried by the Seawolves during their operations.
U.S. Navy

November 01

1945 (Japan)—The proposed launching date for Operation Olympic, the first invasion of the Japanese main islands. Olympic will put Allied forces on the southernmost Japanese home island of Kyushu. In preparation, twenty UDTs will work in the cold waters off the more than fifty proposed landing beaches, including the eighteen landing beaches on the outlying Koshiki Islands. Recon and demolition swims will also be made against the fanatical resistance of the Japanese who are expected to turn any Allied landing into a bloodbath.

Fourteen divisions—766,700 troops—are readied for Operation Olympic. Casualties among the Allies are conservatively estimated at 25,000 killed in action and 132,000 wounded. Admiral Chester W. Nimitz estimates Allied casualties will reach 49,000 within the first thirty days of fighting. Estimates of Japanese casualties are between a quarter and half a million people.

The second main invasion, Operation Coronet, will land Allied troops on the island of Honshu near Tokyo. Coronet is estimated to see Allied casualties of up to 40,000 killed in action, 150,000 wounded, and 3,500 missing. Losses among the Japanese are expected to be between 500,000 and 1 million people killed.

The atomic bombs at Hiroshima and Nagasaki will prevent this, however. And their use is praised by the men of the UDTs who would have had to open the doors to the main islands of Japan, at a possible cost to them of up to 75 percent of their numbers.

1959 (USA)—The First Special Forces Group (Airborne) forms Special Forces Operational Companies 101, 202, 303, and 404.

1963 (South Vietnam)—President Ngo Dinh Diem is assassinated during a military coup and the government of the country threatens to fall. This begins years of political turmoil within the country.

1980 (USA)—SEAL Team Six, the U.S. Navy's specialized counterterrorist team, is commissioned. The enlisted men and officers of the new team are divided into two operational groups: Blue Team and Gold Team. The very ambitious and rugged training schedule put forward by Richard Marcinko, the team's first commander and founder, allots only six months before the unit is expected to be operationally capable.

1992 (Yugoslavia)—Operation Maritime Guard is put into action by the North Atlantic Treaty Organization to prevent unauthorized ships from entering the waters of former Yugoslavia. The action is an attempt to choke off military supplies entering and supplying the warring factions in the area and to cut back on the civilian suffering and strife caused by the fighting.

November 02

1945 (USA)—The bulk of the World War II UDTs have been decommissioned. Members either leave service or return to the fleet navy. Six new teams are designated to maintain the UDT mission into the postwar years.

November 03

Engineman First Class Michael E. Thornton, SEAL Medal of Honor recipient. Thornton received his medal for saving his "senior SEAL advisor," as it was stated in his citation. That advisor was Lieutenant Tom Norris—not mentioned by name in the citation due to the security classification of the operation at the time. This situation resulted in a Medal of Honor recipient being awarded the medal for saving another Medal of Honor recipient— the only time that has happened in the entire history of the award. U.S. NAVY

November 04

1979 (Iran)—Militant Iranian students overrun the U.S embassy in Teheran, taking the diplomats and their staff hostage. Fifty-two Americans are held captive by followers of the Ayatollah Khomeini, who as head of the Islamic fundamentalist government has overthrown the Western-leaning Shah of Iran.

November 05

1959 (USA)—The 329th Special Forces Operational Detachment is activated.

November 06

Sliding a high-explosive rocket into a launcher mounted on a Seawolf helicopter gunship, this aviation ordnanceman reloads the M158A1 2.75-inch rocket pod. Two of the seven-round pods are carried by the Seawolf, one on either side of the bird. At the end of the mount can be seen the left-side pair of M60C mounted machine guns. U.S. NAVY

November 07

Caught by the camera, the dark-tipped white rod passing the nose of this Seawolf gunship is a just-fired 2.75-inch high-explosive aircraft rocket. U.S. NAVY

November 08

1942 (North Africa)—Operation Torch is the first major U.S. and Allied amphibious operation of World War II. The mission will prevent the Axis forces from having an operational base on the Atlantic shore of North Africa, as well as to reinforce the British forces already in place.

While British forces land in the Mediterranean at Oran and Algiers in Algeria, U.S. forces land at three primary locations in Morocco: Fedala near Casablanca, Safi to the south, and Mahdia and Port Lyautey to the north. Prior to the landings and without support, Scout and Raider personnel successfully locate their assigned beaches and mark locations of the invasion beaches for the incoming landing craft. Of the ten scout boat officers who take part in the landings, eight are recommended for and later receive the Navy Cross for their part in Operation Torch. The eight Scout and Raider chief specialists taking part in the Torch actions are later commissioned as ensigns.

The primary mission of the Northern Attack Group going in at Mahdia is to secure intact the Port Lyautey landing field. Located several miles inland from the Atlantic beaches, the Port Lyautey landing field is close to the shore of the winding Wadi Sebou River. The plan to secure the landing field for immediate use by the U.S. forces requires the destroyer USS *Dallas* (DD 199) to transport an army raiding party upriver to capture the airfield intact.

A heavy steel cable boom, supported by floats, blocks the passage of river traffic in the Wadi Sebou. A specialized Navy Demolition Unit (NDU) of two officers and fifteen enlisted men gathers in Little Creek, Virginia, and trains for this specific operation. This is the first specialized navy demolition unit of the war.

During its attack against the cable boom, the two landing craft transporting the NDU attempt to penetrate the mouth of the Wadi Sebou and traverse the 4,000 yards upriver to attack the cable boom. The intense machine gun and cannon fire from the Vichy French manning a stone fort overlooking the river, combined with extremely rough seas, drive the NDU men back out to sea before their craft are sunk.

1962 (South Vietnam)—The Headquarters of the U.S. Army Special Forces Command, Vietnam, is established in Saigon.

November 09

Demolition Crew—The Marianas by Robert Benny. This painting depicts a group of men preparing a variety of beach obstacles for demolition. The man lying down *(center right)* is working on a J-13 anti-boat mine. Very early in their operations, the UDTs still wore uniforms and steel helmets on operations.

November 10

1942 (North Africa)—The destroyer USS *Dallas* (DD 199) moves upriver to unsuccessfully ram through the steel cable boom blocking its way. At 2130 hours on November 9, the landing craft transporting the NDU move away from their transport craft, the USS *George Clymer* (APA 27). This time, both boats are armed with a pair of .30 caliber light machine guns while the men carry small arms. Fire is returned from the French fort as the boats move into the mouth of the Wadi Sebou and continue upriver. Fire is extremely heavy but the small craft push on and reach the target cable. At 0230 hours, the boom is cut and the demolition party withdraws. The *Dallas*, with its raiding troops on board, enters the Wadi Sebou at 0530 hours and the airfield is officially held by U.S. troops at 0800 hours. A number of the men from the first NDU go on to join the Naval Combat

Demolition Unit School at Fort Pierce, Florida. One of the enlisted men from this unit, William Freeman, goes on to receive the Navy Cross and a commission as an officer for his actions at Normandy as part of a GAT.

1952 (USA)—The first Special Forces training course, 1-53, at the U.S. Army Psychological Warfare School begins.

November 11

1945 (USA)—Aboard the USS *Laning* (APD 55), UDT Nine returns to the United States by way of Okinawa, Guam, Eniwetok, and Pearl Harbor. At the Naval Amphibious Base at Coronado, California, after nearly eighteen months of service, UDT Nine is redesignated as postwar Team Baker. The bulk of the UDT Nine personnel receive their discharge from the navy, get reassigned, or reenlist into the regular navy.

1953 (USA/West Germany)—A labor uprising in East Germany has the U.S. Army Special Forces reacting to the situation by sending half of the Tenth Special Forces Group to West Germany. After the failure of the uprising, half of the available manpower of the Tenth is permanently stationed at Bad Tolz, West Germany. The remaining half of the group stays in the United States at Fort Bragg, North Carolina, and is redesignated the Seventy-seventh Special Forces Group.

BARNDANCE # 9-121   SEAL TEAM 2   DET A   9TH

DATE(S): 11 NOVEMBER 1969   OTHER UNITS: 1 LDNN/CTE 116.6.7.4 MST2/NAVY LHFT
                                          CTE 116.9.8/ 2 PBR'S, 2 USN OV 10
MSG REF(S):   NAVY LAFT 116.4.9/USAF KENNY FAC FM 19th
                                          TASS/ USAF TAC AIR FM 35TH TFW PHANG RANG

NAMES OF PERS: LTJG ELLIS, CWO 2 RUTH, HM1 O'BRYAN, PC2 SCHMIDT, QM2 VEASEY,
STG2 GLASSCOCK, LDNN QUOI.

MISSION TASK: CANAL AMBUSH

INTELL/INFO SOURCE(S): AGENT INTELL

INSERTION: TIME 10 1600H   METHOD LSSC   APS CORD: YS 066787

EXTRACTION: TIME 10 1700H   METHOD LSSC   ANI CORD: YS 066787

TERRAIN: NIPP PALM MUD
WEATHER: CLEAR   TIDE: HIGH   MOON: N/A

BRIEF MISSION NARRATIVE: SET AMBUSH AT 10 1630H. HEARD SIGNAL SHOT NW OF G/P
NEAR SUSPECTED BASE CAMP, HEARD ANSWERING SHOT EAST OF G/P. AT 10 1645H OBS.
ONE SAMPAN W/2 VC TRAVELING W TORWARD SMALL CANAL AND TOOK UNDER FIRE. SEARCHED AREA
RECIEVED LIGHT AUTO WEAPONS FIRE RESULT 1 SEAL WIA. CALLED MEDIVAC, SCRAMBLED
SEAWOLFS WHO PLACED STRIKES AND MEDIVACD WIA. SCRAMBLED BLACK PONY'S/OV 10 WHO
PLACED STRIKES AND RECIEVED GROUND FIRE. USAF TAC ARRIVED AND PALCED STRIKES RESULT
IN 4 SECONDARY'S. EXTRACTED BY LSSC AND RETURNED TO NHA BE.
RESULTS OF ENEMY ENCOUNTERED: 2 VC KIA(BC), CAPTURED 1 AK 47,1 KILO DOCUMENTS,
AK AMMO WEB GEAR, MIS CLOTHING, DESTROYED 1 SAMPAN.

FRIENDLY CASUALTIES: 1 SEAL WIA,(MEDIVAC TO 3RD FIELD HOSP. SGN.)

REMARKS (SIGNIFICANT EVENTS, OPEVAL RESULTS, ETC.) NONE

RECOMMENDATIONS/LESSONS LEARNED: ONCE AGAIN NAVY LHFT/ SEAWOLFS DID AN OUTATANDING
JOB; DUMPING GEAR AND AMMO AND IMMED LANDED OUR POSIT. TO MEDIVAC WIA.

RD COPY LIST:

(FORM ... 68)   BARNDANCE # 9-121

November 12

1968—

FPO SAN FRANCISCO 96627

ST-1/GOLF/SSM/jt

1650

Ser:

12 November 1968

From: Officer in Charge, SEAL Team Detachment GOLF

To:

Subj: Letter of Commendation

ref: (a) CTG 115.5 MSG 0816152 NOV 68

1. Reference (a) was received from Commander Special Task Group 115.5 and is quoted for your information.

SEAL TEAM DET GOLF, ALFA AND HOTEL PLATOONS CONDUCTED UNCONVENTIONAL WARFARE AGAINST THE VIET CONG ENEMY AS THE PRINCIPAL UNIT OF SPECIAL OPERATIONS GROUP (TG 115.5) FROM 27 OCT 68 TO 8 NOV 68. THE PERFORMANCE OF DUTY BY EACH MAN IN THOSE PLATOONS WAS SUPERIOR. EACH MAN PARTICIPATED IN DAILY, CONTINUOUS, HAZARDOUS DUTY IN THE FIELD. EACH MAN WAS EXPOSED TO ENEMY FIRE AND RESPONDED WITH THE COOL, EFFECTIVE, PROFESSIONAL REACTION WHICH IS THE TRADEMARK OF SEALS.

THESE OPERATIONS CONTRIBUTED IMPORTANT INTELLIGENCE INFORMATION REQUIRED TO DETERMINE ENEMY INTENTIONS IN A SENSITIVE AREA OF OPERATIONS. SIGNIFICANT PERSONNEL CASUALTIES WERE INFLICTED ON HIM. EVEN MORE IMPORTANT THE

ABILITY OF SEALS TO STRIKE HIM IN AREAS WHERE HE HAD TRADITIONALLY BEEN SAFE CAUSED A MAJOR DISRUPTION IN VIET CONG ACTIVITIES. THAT THESE RESULTS WERE ACHIEVED WITH NO CASUALTIES IS A FURTHER TRIBUTE TO THE TEAMWORK AND PROFESSIONALISM OF EVERY SEAL WHO PARTICIPATED IN THESE OPERATIONS.

2.   As Officer in Charge, SEAL Team Detachment Golf it gives me great pride to present this commendation to you for a job well done. Your hard work and professionalism under very hazardous conditions is commendable and upheld the highest traditions and reputations of the SEAL Teams.

3.   A copy of this letter will be made a permanent part of your service record.

STANLEY S. MESTON

Copy to:

BUPERS

SERVICE RECORD

FILES

★ ★ ★ ★ ★

November 13

1945 (USA)—UDT Twenty returns from Japan and unloads its equipment at the Naval Amphibious Base at Coronado, California. It is redesignated UDT Charlie, one of the six immediate postwar teams.

1965 (South Vietnam)—Australian Warrant Officer Second Class Kevin A. Wheatley, attached to the Fifth Special Forces Group, performs actions that later result in his receiving the Victoria Cross posthumously.

BARNDANCE #   10-67   SEAL TEAM TWO   DET A   10

DATE(S):   14 NOV 69   OTHER UNITS: 1 LDNN, 2 SLICKS, LHFT, LAFT
                                          USA H/K TEAM

REC REP(S):

NAMES OF PERS: LTJG BRYSON, DILLEY, NOLLEY, CLARK, PERZANOWSKI, MACDONALD,
MOORE, LDNN LONG

MISSION TASK: TRAIL AMBUSH

INTELL/INFO SOURCE(S):   NONE

INSERTION: TIME: 140915H   METHOD SLICK   AMB COORD   YS180785

EXTRACTION: TIME: 141330H   METHOD SLICK   AMB COORD   YS178790

TERRAIN: DENSE UNDERBRUSH BORDERING RICE FIELD
WEATHER: HOT   TIDE: NA   MOON: NA

BRIEF MISSION NARRATIVE: DEPARTED NHA BE BY SLICK. INSERTED AND PATROLED WEST
TO YS173783 AND SET TRAIL AMBUSH.   AT 141200H BROKE AMBUSH AND PATROLED
SE TO YS178781. HEARD VC COUGHING/TALKING APPOX 25 METERS TO NORTH.
USING HELO NOISE FOR COVER, PATROL MOVED BACK TO YS175782 AND SCRAMBLED
H/K TM TO LOCATE VC AND PROVIDE COVER. AT 141232H DIRECTED LOH INTO
POSITION OVER VC AND MOVER TO VC POSITION YS178782 USING LOH NOISE
AS COVER. OPENED FIRE ON FOUR VC. RESULTS 4 KIA (BC). RECEIVED A/W
RETURN FIRE RESULTING IN ONE SEAL WIA (SLIGHT). WHILE PROVIDING COVER
LOH RECEIVED A/W FIRE RESULTING IN TWO USA WIA (SLIGHT). SCRAMBLED
DUSTOFF AND PATROLED NORTH. SCRAMBLED LAFT AND LHFT WHO PLACED STRIKES
ON ENEMY POSITION. BOTH LAFT AND LHFT RECEIVED GROUND FIRE. RESULTS
4 VC KBA (BC).   EXTRACTED BY SLICK AND RETURNED TO NHA BE.

US CAS: 1 USN SEAL WIA, 2 USA WIA
EN CAS: 4 VC KIA (BC), 4 VC KBA (BC)
CAPTURED: 1 AK-47, 1 BKS, 1 K-54 PISTOL, 1 KILO DOCUMENTS, 1 BLASTING CAP
           WEB GEAR, MISC CLOTHING

RECOMMENDATIONS/LESSONS LEARNED: NONE

BD COPY DIST:

(FORM NO.   60)   BARNDANCE #   10-67

As he waves to the cameraman, Astronaut Edwin R. Aldrin rides in a life raft with his partner James A. Lovell after their 1966 splashdown in the *Gemini 12* space capsule.

SEAL teams conduct a great deal more missions than just those of combat and demolition. From the first flight of the Mercury program to the last splashdown of an Apollo moon shot, the men of the SEAL and UDT teams are there to greet every returning astronaut.

In this picture, specially trained volunteers from the UDTs and the SEAL teams not only make sure that the astronauts are safely taken from their space capsule, but also that the capsule itself is secure. The large, inflatable flotation collar around the Gemini capsule is attached, secured, and inflated by the men of the teams after they are sure about the astronauts' safety.

November 16

```
BARNDANCE #  9-131        SEAL TEAM  2  : DET  A  :  9TH  PLT

DATE(S): 16 NOVEMBER 1969   OTHER UNITS: CTE 116.6.7.4 (LTJG HAZARD MST 2)
                                          CTU 116.9.8 (NAVY LHFT)
MSG REF(S):


NAMES OF PERS: LTJG ELLIS, HM1 O'BRYAN, QM2 VEASEY, STG2 GLASSCOCK, BM2 NAUS



MISSION TASK: CANAL AMBUSH


INTELL/INFO SOURCE(S): AGENT INTELL

INSERTION:   TIME: 16 1900H    METHOD  LSSC    AMS COORD:  YS 034793

EXTRACTION:  TIME: 16 2200H    METHOD  LSSC    AMS COORD:  YS 036794

TERRAIN: MUD - NIPPA PALM
WEATHER: CLEAR                 TIDE: HIGH          MOON: 1/2

BRIEF MISSION NARRATIVE: WHILE PROCEEDING SOUTH ON CANAL JUST PRIOR TO INSERTION
OBERVED 4 VC WALKING TORWARD WATER ON SOUTH BANK AND TOOK UNDER FIRE. SEAWOLFS
PLACED STRIKES, SEARCHED AREA. LCM PLACED .50 CAL M/G FIRE IN AREA AND DEPARTED
SET STAY BEHIND AMBUSH. AT 16 2030H HEARD 2 SIGNAL SHOTS NORTH OF POSIT. AND
ANSWERED IT WITH AK 47 FROM OUR POSIT.. NEG. MOVEMENT AND EXTRACTED AND RETURNED
TO NHA BE.

RESULTS OF ENEMY ENCOUNTERED: 4 VC KIA(PROB)



FRIENDLY CASUALTIES: NONE



REMARKS (SIGNIFICANT EVENTS, OPEVAL RESULTS, ETC.): NONE





RECOMMENDATIONS/LESSONS LEARNED: WATERPROOF BINOCULARS (T&E) ITEM EXCELENT
USED TO SPOT VC IN THIS OP APPROX. 100M AWAY.




BD COPY DIST:

(FORM REV 2/63)                            BARNDANCE #9-131
```

November 17

A surfaced Mark IX SEAL delivery vehicle (SDV). Hidden from view by the water and its low, flat design, this two-man SDV can conduct covert recons and studies of an area. U.S. NAVY

November 18

These UDT operators manhandle a Mark VIII SDV along the deck of the submarine *Grayback*. Seen here on its launching and recovery cradle, the SDV will be housed in one of the bow hangars of the submarine *(upper right)*. U.S. NAVY

November 19

1977 (USA)—Authority is granted to activate a new Special Forces unit assigned to the specific mission of counterterrorism. The unit is officially known as the First Special Forces Operational Detachment, Delta, more commonly known as Delta Force. The commander of the new unit is Colonel Charles Beckwith, who has worked for more than a year to create the new unit. Basing his vision of Delta on his own experiences with the British Twenty-second SAS, Colonel Beckwith is given two years in which to get his new organization up and running. After a very arduous selection process and against the initial reluctance from other Special Forces commanders to allow their best men to volunteer for the new unit, two complete squadrons of Delta conduct their evaluation exercises during the first three days of November 1979.

November 20

1943 (Pacific)—The invasion of Tarawa Atoll in the Gilbert Islands begins. Part of Operation Galvanic, it is ordered by the Joint Chiefs of Staff and led by Vice Admiral Richmond Kelly Turner as part of the central Pacific campaign against the Japanese. Vice Admiral Kelly is responsible for the final decision to make the assault on Tarawa and the Gilbert Islands.

The plan is to have the first troops (marines) land via Landing Tracked Vehicles (LTVs), with the next wave of personnel arriving in LCVPs (flat-bottomed Higgins boats). However, information on the islands and their surrounding coral atolls is limited. According to the sparse intelligence available, there should be as much as five feet of water above the reefs. In spite of heavy fire from the Japanese, the LTVs are able to traverse the reefs.

However, unpredicted tidal conditions make it too shallow for the LCVPs to follow suit as they run aground. The stranded marines attempt to wade into shore. Many fall into holes that have been blasted into the coral by the initial bombardment and, weighed down by their burden of supplies and ammunition, drown. More men drown during the assault on Tarawa than are killed in the fighting.

The terrible cost of Tarawa convinces Vice Admiral Turner to develop specialized scouting/reconnaissance and demolition units to measure the waters off invasion beaches, find any obstacles or mines, and blast them out of the way. The result of this decision is that Amphibious Force Fleet Directives will be issued for the establishment of two UDTs. Also, the Naval Combat Underwater Demolition Training and Experimental Base at Maui will be created for their training. Experienced demolition personnel, such as Seabees and NCDUs, are already at Maui developing coral blasting techniques, among other skills. Vice Admiral Turner will look to these men to be the core of his new UDTs. Two Teams, UDT One and Two, are quickly organized to take part in the upcoming Operation Flintlock, the invasion of Kwajalein Atoll in the Marshall Islands.

November 21

1970 (North Vietnam)—Six helicopters fly over Laos into North Vietnam in the early morning hours, thereby launching Operation Kingpin, the raid on the Son Tay POW camp. As air attacks take place throughout North Vietnam to distract the enemy from the incoming helicopters, Special Forces operators assault the prison where the POWs are thought to be kept. The first helicopter intentionally crashes into the center of the prison to put the first assault group in place as quickly as possible. In spite of the fact that no prisoners are recovered, the operation is considered a success in at least one way. The North Vietnamese begin treating the American POWs with much greater care as they realize that the American public will be seriously angry at the treatment their POWs have been receiving, to the point that they might increase their direct actions against North Vietnam.

1973 (USA)—SEAL Team Two receives the second of its two Presidential Unit Citations from President Richard Nixon for its actions during the Vietnam War. The citation reads:

By virtue of the authority vested in me as President of the United States and as Commander-in-Chief of the Armed Forces of the United States, I have today awarded

THE PRESIDENTIAL UNIT CITATION (NAVY)
FOR EXTRAORDINARY HEROISM TO
SEAL TEAM TWO

For extraordinary heroism and outstanding performance of duty in the conduct of unconventional warfare against enemy forces in the Republic of Vietnam from 1 July 1969 to 30 June 1971. While conducting swift and daring operations into enemy strongholds and sanctuaries located in and about the riverine environment of the Mekong Delta, SEAL Team TWO accounted for large numbers of enemy casualties, enemy troops captured, weapons, ammunition and documents of significant intelligence value. Characteristic of the courage, professionalism and dedication of SEAL Team TWO's personnel were their actions during the morning hours of 22 August 1970. While units of the U.S. Army and Australian Air Force provided blocking force air strikes, a SEAL Team platoon successfully liberated twenty-eight South Vietnamese prisoners of war from a prisoner of war camp deep inside the violently hostile Dam Doi District of the Mekong Delta. On another occasion, a SEAL Team squad engaged a platoon of prisoner of war camp guards in a firefight during which the guards fled, leaving four casualties and six individual weapons behind. On a third occasion, U.S. Navy helicopter gunships and destroyer fire, reacting to intelligence received from a SEAL squad, resulted in eighty enemy casualties. The exceptionally distinguished combat record achieved by the officers and men of SEAL Team TWO reflected the highest credit upon themselves and the United States Naval Service.

Richard Nixon

November 22

1968 (South Vietnam)—Electronics Technician Third Class James Sanders of SEAL Team One dies while in Saigon, though not by enemy activity.

November 23

Ebb Tide, Tarawa by Kerr Eby. This charcoal sketch depicts some of the terrible cost of taking Tarawa. It was to minimize this loss of life during the landing phase of amphibious operations that Admiral Richmond Kelly Turner directed the creation of the underwater demolition teams. NAVY HISTORICAL CENTER COLLECTION

Struggling to pull ashore a rubber boat filled with their equipment, explosives, and wounded or injured comrades, these men land on Normandy Beach, June 6, 1944. U.S. NAVY

November 25

1963 (USA)—During the funeral ceremony for President John F. Kennedy, one member of the graveside honor guard, Sargent Major Francis J. Ruddy, removes his green beret and places it on the president's grave. The action is done in respect for the president, who personally authorized the wearing of the headgear by the Special Forces.

1965 (North Vietnam)—Six Nasty-class patrol boats conduct an Oplan 34A maritime mission against targets on Gio Island, just north of the seventeenth parallel. The six boats stay offshore and fire into the targets with 57mm recoilless rifles, 81mm mortars, and automatic weapons before withdrawing back south of the DMZ.

1967 (South Vietnam)—The Fifth Platoon of SEAL Team Two's Detachment Alpha runs into what it considers a "hot time" according to the after-action report of its mission. Having established an observation post between two deserted hooches, the SEALs later conduct a patrol of the area. Hailing a Vietnamese the SEALs spot working near a house in the early morning hours, the unit takes the man under fire as he runs from the area. A second Vietnamese is seen running toward the hooch after the SEALs set up a quick security perimeter. He is taken under fire and killed.

The SEALs begin hearing voices coming from the jungle on three sides of their position. An estimated fifteen VC are speaking as they begin surrounding the SEALs. Fifth Platoon immediately calls in a Seawolf air strike as it leaves. At the same time, it calls in the extraction boat. As the extraction boat enters a nearby canal, fire erupts from an estimated fifteen to twenty automatic weapons from three flanks around the SEALs. Sporadic fire begins coming in to the SEALs as they move to the canal for extraction after the arrival of their boat.

While they move to the canal, the SEALs come across a bunker with four VC inside. Immediately, the SEALs take it under fire, killing the occupants. Even after reaching the extraction boat, the SEALs and their craft remain under constant sniper fire. There are no U.S. casualties during the operation and six VC are known to have been killed.

November 26

During a training operation, combat swimmers place a limpet mine on the keel of a target ship.
U.S. NAVY

November 27

1951 (Korea)—During mid-October, General Douglas MacArthur, the supreme allied commander in Korea, is informed about the presence of thirty-eight Chinese divisions located in Manchuria. None of them, however, is in a position to cross the border into North Korea. This is also the same time period when the Chinese begin moving six armies toward North Korea. Moving primarily on foot with relatively light equipment, the Chinese have huge numbers of men at the North Korean border, in close proximity to UN troops in Korea, at the end of October.

With the apparent defeat of the North Korean People's Army close at hand, all of the plans of MacArthur's and the UN forces are changed on November 27 when the Chinese government sends 200,000 troops across the Yalu River into North Korea. The UN forces are quickly redistributed along the front to face this new threat from the Chinese People's Army. The U.S. and UN forces are soon driven south, back along territory gained only months before.

1965 (North Vietnam)—Nasty-class boats continue maritime operations against targets in North Vietnam in support of Oplan 34A. A number of PTFs return to Cape Ron and shell North Vietnamese military facilities there from offshore positions.

1990 (USA)—The U.S. Army Special Operations Command is reorganized to align all Special Forces Civil Affairs and Psychological Operations units under the new U.S. Army Civil Affairs/Psychological Operations Command.

1969

```
BARNDANCE #  9-144              SEAL TEAM   2  ; DET   A   ;   9TH   PLT.
DATE(S):  28 NOVEMBER 1969   OTHER UNITS:  6 PRU'S, 2 USA SLICKS, TACT AIR(F 100'S)
                                            _CTE 116.6.7.4 (LTJG HAZARD MST 2)
MSG REF(S):                                 _CTU 116.9.8 (NAVY LHFT)
                                            _2 USN OV-10 (BLACK PONEY'S)

NAMES OF PERS:  LTJG ELLIS, CWO2 RUTH, BMC RABBITT, GMG1 THORNTON, SF 1 BRADLEY,
BM2 CYRUS, STG2 GLASSCOCK, ADJ1 JESSIE, HM1 O'BRYAN, QM2 VEASEY, BM2 NAUS.

MISSION TASK:  PATROL/TRAIL AMBUSH

INTELL/INFO SOURCE(S):  AGENT INTELL

INSERTION:     TIME: 28 0800H     METHOD  SLICK     AMS COORD: YS 106787

EXTRACTION:    TIME: 28 1800H     METHOD  SLICK     AMS COORD: YS 109794

TERRAIN:  FIELD, RICE PADDY
WEATHER:  CLEAR                  TIDE:  N/A         MOON:  N/A

BRIEF MISSION NARRATIVE:  INSERTED AND SET TRAIL AMBUSH. OBSERVED 2 INDIVIDUALS
AT YS 108788, MOVED TO POSIT AND TOOK INTO CUSTODY. OBSERVED 2 VC AT YS 109794
AND FOLLOWED. VC EVADED TO WESTERN TREE LINE, TAKEN UNDER FIRE AND PURSUED
INTO UNDERGROWTH. RECIEVED AUTO WEAPONS FIRE, RESULT IN 1 SEAL WIA. NAVY LHFT
PLACED STRIKES ON TARGET. CALLED NAVY LAFT WHO DIRECTED STRIKES. SEAWOLFS AGAIN
PLACED STRIKES AND RECIEVED FIRE. XXXXXX TACT AIR PLACED IN AREA AFTER EXTRACTION
BY SLICK.
RESULTS OF ENEMY ENCOUNTERED:  2 VC KIA (BC), CAPTURED 2 SUSPECTS, M16 MAGS,
FIRING WIRE, MISC. GEAR.

FRIENDLY CASUALTIES:  1 SEAL WIA (SL)

REMARKS (SIGNIFICANT EVENTS, OPEVAL RESULTS, ETC.):  NONE

RECOMMENDATIONS/LESSONS LEARNED:  QM2 VEASEY DID AN OUTSTANDING JOB IN ALERTLY
SPOTING AND RECOGNIZING VC FROM LONG DISTANCE AWAY.

BD COPY DIST:

(FORM REV. 9/68)                        BARNDANCE # 9-144
```

November 29

1990 (USA)—The United Nations adopts Resolution 678, which states "to use all necessary means" to remove Iraqi forces from Kuwait, unless it withdraws on or before January 15, 1991. This UN sanction allows for war in the Persian Gulf. It does not extend to an overthrow or elimination of Saddam Hussein or the Baathist Party in Iraq, only to the use of force to liberate Kuwait.

November 30

Underway at high speed in the Pacific is a Nasty-class fast patrol craft. A number of these Norwegian-built craft were purchased by the U.S. Navy and supplied to South Vietnam for operations against North Vietnam in the mid 1960s. U.S. NAVY

DECEMBER

During the land warfare phase of this Basic Underwater Demolition/SEAL (BUD/S) student training cycle, an instructor points out one of the details of cleaning an M16A1 rifle to this student.

December 01

As part of a classic beach demolition operation, this UDT operator is towing a haversack packed with high explosives in to the beach.
U.S. NAVY

December 02

1943 (Europe)—The First Special Service Force attacks Monte La Difensa, Italy.

1992 (Somalia)—Operation Restore Hope is put into action by order of General Colin Powell. The action is to support the United Nations' relief efforts in Somalia. The nation has been suffering from internal civil war, lack of an effective single government, and widespread starvation because of drought. An amphibious squadron is made up of the USS *Tripoli* (LPH 10), USS *Juneau* (LPD 10), and USS *Rushmore* (LSD 47). The Marine Expeditionary Unit on board the squadron, as well as the SEAL platoon detachment from SEAL Team One, are to secure transportation facilities in Mogadishu.

December 03

1966 (South Vietnam)—From December 3 to 4, SEAL Team One personnel volunteer to conduct reconnaissance patrols in support of a U.S. Army unit conducting Operation Charleston, an extensive series of sweeps against VC positions in the Rung Sat Special Zone. One of the patrols conducted by the SEALs, a six-

An aerial view of the Rung Sat Special Zone.

man fire team captures a 57mm recoilless rifle, 2 machine guns, 2 carbines, and 10,000 rounds of assorted ammunition. Intelligence provided by these SEAL patrols leads to the location and capture of numerous other weapons and supplies by the army unit.

1966 (USA)—As a member of the West Coast Underwater Demolition Team Replacement Training Class 36, Ensign Theodore Roosevelt IV has a stand-out family background. It doesn't matter at UDTR (later BUD/S) training. The soft-spoken Roosevelt, a twenty-three-year-old great-grandson of President Theodore Roosevelt, has this illustrious ancestor to thank for the three-foot-long tree branches that the instructors insist he carry at all times. Instructors are not known for their gentle approach to seeing if a student has the heart to make it to the teams. Any piece of information about an individual and his background are fair fodder for the instructors to make life miserable for the student. The Harvard-educated officer takes it in stride and completes the course, graduating with his class in December.

December 04

1981 (USA)—President Ronald Reagan signs Executive Order 12333. The order further restricts covert activity by any of the government's intelligence agencies. It works in conjunction with President Gerald Ford's Executive Order 11905 (signed on February 18, 1975) to eliminate the use of assassination as a tool of U.S. foreign policy.

December 05

1945 (France)—The First Special Service Force stands down from active combat.

December 06

1992 (Somalia)—In preparation for the U.S. Marines to land, the SEAL detachment assigned to the amphibious squadron conducts a classic UDT beach recon. During the evening hours of December 6, the SEALs conduct a string reconnaissance, that is, measure the water's depth with lead-weighted fishing lines that have knots at regular intervals. The system was first developed by Lieutenant Commander Draper Kauffman during World War II. The simple technique adds important details to the SEALs' beach reconnaissance and cartographers are able to draw detailed charts from the information. Besides noting the water depths, details of the beach, including any man-made or natural obstacles, the shore gradient, and the composition of the beach itself are gathered by the SEALs through a close investigation.

December 07

1941 (Hawaii)—At 0755 hours local time, 423 Japanese aircraft launch from six aircraft carriers to attack the U.S. Naval Base at Pearl Harbor. The base is surprised by the attack with the Japanese maintaining tactical and strategic superiority throughout the mission's two waves. A total of 188 U.S. aircraft are lost, while the Japanese lose 29. By the end of the day, the bulk of the U.S. Pacific Fleet is damaged or sunk at Pearl Harbor, though none of the U.S. aircraft carriers are in port during the attack.

1971 (South Vietnam)—At 1400 hours, Mike Platoon, the last platoon of SEAL Team One's Detachment Golf, leaves Vietnam along with the MST detachments. This ends five years of direct Naval Special Warfare involvement in Southeast Asia. SEALs remain active in Vietnam after this date, but they are small units with specific missions other than direct combat.

1992 (Somalia)—SEALs from the amphibious squadron swim into Mogadishu Harbor to examine the area for landing sites, to determine if any direct threats are present, and to see if the port facilities are intact or sufficient to offload supplies from ships. In spite of the lack of enemy fire acting as a threat, the mission is a difficult one. The warm waters and strong current in the harbor soon exhaust the SEALs. Furthermore, raw sewage in the water poses a long-term threat of illness to them. Nevertheless, the SEALs locate good landing beaches as well as facilities for offloading ships.

December 08

1941 (USA)—Following the devastating attack on the U.S. Naval Base at Pearl Harbor, the United States declares war on the Japanese empire. Great Britain joins the United States in the declaration of war.

1965 (North Vietnam)—The last maritime operation of the year in support of Oplan 34A takes place as four Nasty-class boats attack the Mach Nuoc radar facility in North Vietnam.

1992 (Somalia)—The actual landing of marines from the amphibious squadron in support of Operation Restore Hope begins. The landings take place at night to aid in security. Both SEALs and the marine's own Force Reconnaissance units supply swimmer scouts going in to the beaches ahead of the landing forces. The swimmer scouts meet a new threat on the beach, however, one their military training had not quite prepared them for.

On the shore in the darkness are a number of media press corps reporters from around the world, complete with cameramen and bright lights. A number of very bewildered Force Reconnaissance swimmer scouts, thinking they are going in for a landing on a possibly hostile beach, are caught in the sudden glare of the camera lights. The SEAL detachment conducts its portion of the prelanding scout about a quarter of a mile away.

December 09

With the nose of their ASPB (assault support patrol boat) nosed into the mud of the riverbank, these SEALs insert for a village search operation in the Kien Hoa province of South Vietnam. U.S. NAVY

December 10

1951 (Korea)—The 8086th Army Unit becomes the Far East Command, 8240th Army Unit, Korea.

1956 (USA)—The U.S. Army Psychological Warfare Center in Fort Bragg, North Carolina, is renamed the U.S. Army Special Warfare School.

December 11

1941 (USA)—Nazi Germany declares war on the United States. The U.S. Congress responds with its own declarations of war and votes that President Franklin D. Roosevelt may send U.S. forces to any part of the world.

1961 (USA)—The term "SEAL Unit One" is being used on initial orders for men to report to what will become SEAL Team One.

December 12

Holding his Stoner Mark 23 machine gun well clear, this SEAL sinks into hip-deep mud during an insertion in Vietnam.
U.S. NAVY

December 13

Slipping in from the water, silent and undetected, just one of the skills of the Navy SEALs. U.S. Navy

December 14

1995 (France)—A formal peace agreement between the Bosnian Serbs and the other factions fighting in Bosnia-Herzegovinia is signed in Paris. The agreement is based on the Dayton Peace Accords worked out in Dayton, Ohio, between representatives of the various fighting factions from October to November 1995. Operation Joint Endeavor is put into place to implement the peace agreement. During Joint Endeavor, North Alliance Treaty Organization (NATO) forces will conduct peace enforcement, including separating warring factions, maintaining security, and establishing demilitarized zones.

1995 (Europe)—The U.S. Special Operations Command Europe establishes the Special Operations Command Implementation Force (SOCIFOR) and includes its manpower with the Joint Special Operations Task Force Two (JSOTF Two). JSOTF Two was established at the San Vito Air Station near Brindisi, Italy, in February 1993 to conduct combat search and rescue missions, fire support, air drops, and visit, board, search, and seizure operations. The addition of SOCIFOR is to provide special operations forces to NATO and non-NATO forces in Bosnia, among other missions.

December 15

1963 (USA)—Defense Secretary Robert McNamara issues Oplan 34A. The mission of Oplan 34A is to make a series of covert attacks against North Vietnam beginning on February 1, 1964. The attacks will provide maximum pressure against the North Vietnamese government with minimum risk to the mission personnel (through planning, training, and high-speed boats). Oplan 34A leads directly to the creation of the Military Assistance Command, Vietnam—Studies and Observations Group, the largest clandestine military unit of the Vietnam War.

1964 (South Vietnam)—The first daylight missions are conducted by a new form of flying weapons platform created by members of the U.S. Air Force. The new weapon is the venerable C-47 cargo plane fitted out with three 7.62mm miniguns aiming out the left side of the aircraft. Each minigun can fire up to 6,000 rounds per minute, spraying the ground with a rain of rifle-caliber projectiles. Newly named the FC-47, FC for Fighter Cargo, the gunship will fire on enemy trails, buildings, sampans, and suspected staging areas where the enemy forces will gather in the jungle.

1989 (Panama)—The National People's Assembly, made up primarily of Manuel Noriega appointees, declares that a state of war now exists between Panama and the United States.

December 16

1966 (South Vietnam)—SEAL Team One, Detachment Golf, aids the U.S. Army in Operation Charleston in the Rung Sat Special Zone by performing additional reconnaissance missions combined with ambush operations. While conducting one of these patrols, the SEALs find a VC base camp. Calling back over the radio for explosives, the SEALs demolish the camp and extract by helicopter. All SEAL personnel participating in Operation Charleston are recommended for the U.S. Army Commendation Medal by the army unit commander.

1989 (Panama)—Panamanian troops shoot and kill a U.S. Marine. The officer has been driving with a group of his fellow marines looking for a local restaurant. Another marine officer and his wife who witness the shooting are arrested by Panamanian authorities.

December 17

1992 (Somalia)—Operating off the French frigate *Dupleix*, SEALs from the marine amphibious unit in Mogadishu scout and survey the port of Kismayu. Somali snipers take the SEALs under fire, but none of the operators are hit.

December 18

1961—(USA)—Earlier orders for men to report to "SEAL Unit One" are corrected to read "SEAL Team One" to reflect the name of the new organizations.

1989 (USA)—The execution order is issued for Operation Just Cause—the invasion of Panama and arrest of Noriega. It begins December 20.

December 19

1989 (Panama)—Twenty-one men from SEAL Team Two make up the reinforced platoon of Task Unit Whiskey. It arrives in Panama at about 0800 hours local time. The primary mission of the task unit is to destroy the Panamanian patrol boat *Presidenti Porras*, which is secured to Pier 18 in Balboa Harbor. Destruction of the patrol boat will prevent its use as an escape means by Panamanian dictator Manuel Noriega.

Two swimmer pairs from the task unit will approach the pier underwater and attach two Mark 138 demolition charges, each charge being a haversack filled with twenty pounds of C-4 plastic explosive, to the underside of the target's hull. The two pairs of SEALs will effectively conduct the exact same mission along slightly different routes to ensure that at least one pair will successfully attack the target.

Around 2300 hours, two rubber boats leave the Rodman Naval Station in Panama and transport the combat swimmer pairs to within swimming range of their target. During their underwater operation, Draeger LAR-V rebreathers are used to keep from leaving a trail of bubbles in the water. The swimmer pairs are conducting the first-ever U.S. combat swimmer limpeteer attack—the attack and destruction of a ship by swimmers with Limpet mines. The demolition charges are both set to detonate at the same time: 0100 hours on December 20. The blasts are planned to be the opening strike of Operation Just Cause.

1989 (Panama)—In the evening, Task Unit Charlie, a joint unit consisting of eight SEALs, twelve soldiers, two riverine patrol boats, and a pair of landing craft, blocks all shipping from entering the Panama Canal from the Caribbean side. The task unit also prevents any Panamanian Defense Forces (PDFs) from fleeing the country by boat or sabotaging the canal. The task unit patrols the shipping channel near Colon throughout the night.

1989 (Panama)—The largest SEAL element of the Naval Special Warfare Task Group is Task Force White, made up of the SEAL detachments who will be actively conducting operations during Operation Just Cause. The largest single task unit of Task Force White is Task Unit Papa, made up of Bravo, Delta, and Golf Platoons from SEAL Team Four, along with additional assets. With sixty-two SEALs, Task Unit Papa will conduct the single largest mission for the SEALs in Panama: securing the Paitilla Airfield and destroying Manuel Noriega's personal Lear jet that is stored there.

At 1930 hours local time, Task Unit Papa launches from the beach at Howards Air Force Base using fifteen rubber boats. It takes the SEALs about four hours to cover the fifteen miles between their launch site and the target beach near Paitilla. Arriving at their target at 2330 hours, the SEALs send out swimmer scouts to check the landing site and then guide the rest of the unit in. At 0045 hours, December 20, Task Unit Papa begins landing.

December 20

1970 (USA)—As in most actions where significant acts of valor take place, the individuals involved are reacting to an overwhelming situation. The citation for the last Navy Cross of the Vietnam War to be awarded to a U.S. Navy SEAL, Radioman Second Class Harold L. Baker, is an example of the tenacity of a Navy SEAL in the support of his teammates. The citation reads:

> *For extraordinary heroism in action on the night of 20 December 1970 while serving as the rear security for a five-man SEAL patrol on an interdiction mission deep within enemy territory in the Republic of Vietnam. Immediately after inserting ashore, the patrol came under withering enemy fire from automatic weapons, grenades, and rockets, mortally wounding the patrol leader and the automatic weapons man, and critically wounding the patrol's radioman and Vietnamese guide. Although he was not wounded, Petty Officer Baker found himself in the river waters struggling to keep his head above the surface. Through sheer determination, he pulled himself and the body of a fallen comrade onto the bank and then returned a heavy volume of automatic weapons fire toward the enemy in an effort to stave off an assault on the squad's position. Subsequently, Petty Officer Baker administered lifesaving first aid to the two wounded members of the patrol and directed the recovery of the bodies of the patrol leader and the automatic weapons man. By his great personal valor and fighting spirit in the face of heavy enemy fire, he upheld the highest traditions of the United States Naval Service.*

★ ★ ★ ★ ★

1989 (Panama)—After landing on the beach just outside of Paitilla Airfield, the SEALs of Task Unit Papa form into platoons and cut through the fence securing the airfield. By 0105 hours, the leading SEAL platoon, Golf, arrives at a point just outside the hangar where the Lear jet is known to be stored. At this point, Golf Platoon runs into a group of PDF fighters who open fire on the SEALs on the tarmac. Caught in the open, eight SEALs are wounded, five of them seriously. Fifteen minutes later, at 0117 hours, the PDF fighters withdraw. The SEALs report the airfield secure at 0146 hours. By 0205 hours, a medevac helicopter arrives to recover the wounded. The SEALs establish a secure perimeter and settle down to wait for their relief. The SEALs, who planned for the mission to last five hours, will not be relieved for another thirty-seven hours.

1989 (Panama)—At 0100 hours, the two demolition charges secured underneath the Panamanian patrol boat *Presidenti Porras* at Pier 18 detonate, heaving the boat out of the water and dropping it back down, broken and immobilized. The two swimmer pairs make their way back to their pickup boats without injury. The balance of Task Unit Whiskey assists in the seizure of Manuel Noriega's private yatch at the Balboa Yacht Club. While securing the yacht, the SEALs also secure the club.

1989 (Panama)—Task Unit Foxtrot secures the Pacific approaches to the Panama Canal, conducting patrols during the night and into the next day.

1989 (Panama)—At 0930, after having conducted patrols the entire night, the joint force of SEALs and army soldiers of Task Unit Charlie are told that as many as thirty PDF troops have boarded the German merchant ship *Asian Senator* in Cristobal. Arriving near the ship, the men of Task Unit Charlie see men in civilian clothes running along the pier and the ship. The men on the ship are tossing weapons over the side, down to the men on the pier. Three of the boats of Task Unit Charlie open fire across the bow of the *Asian Senator*. Seeing the firepower that can be brought to bear on them, the PDF forces aboard the seized boat quickly surrender.

1989 (Panama)—Operation Acid Gambit goes into action as men from Special Forces Operational Detachment Delta (Delta Force) raid the Modelo Prison, where Kurt Muse is being held to await trial and probable execution. Muse had conducted broadcasts that undermined the government of Panamanian dictator Manuel Noriega. Delta Force operators snatch up Muse just as a Panamanian guard is about to shoot him. They extract from the prison under the covering fire of a Specter gunship circling overhead.

December 21

1964 (South Vietnam)—For the first time, a forward air controller calls in a gunship attack on a ground target by the new FC-47 aircraft. The FC-47 opens fire on a structure that a number of VC were seen running in to. After the attack, twenty-one enemy bodies are found and the building is reported to look like a sieve.

1989 (Panama)—The SEALs of Task Unit Papa are finally relieved at their position at the Paitilla Airfield. The operation has cost four SEALs their lives and eight are wounded. The CH-47 helicopters bringing in the U.S. Army Rangers to relieve the SEALs are the same helicopters that take the SEALs out.

1989 (Panama)—Task Unit Foxtrot secures and searches two of Manuel Noriega's personal yachts, the *Passe Porte Tout* and *Macho de Monde*. The SEALs capture eighteen Panamanians as well as a large quantity of small arms and ammunition.

December 22

1970

```
BARNDANCE #   9-26    SEAL TEAM TWO, DET ALFA, NINTH PLATOON
DATES  22 DEC 1970    OTHER UNITS:  4 SEALS (10TH PLT)  SHOTGUN .45
MSG REF:                            2 AUSTRAILANDS    CTU 116.7.5 (SEAWOLF)
                                    4 INTELL PLT      NILO CA MAU (LT ROBERT
                                    LT YEAW-LT1c BENTLY
                                    175 AVIATION CO.
NAMES OF PERSONS PARTICIPATING  LT MORAN, GALLAGHER, MONCRIEF, NEIDRAUER,
  OSBORNE, MYERS, KEITH, ROGUES, BARON, CYRUS, SQUIRES, FALLON.
MISSION TASK:  BODY SNATCH
INTEL/INFO SOURCES:  INFORMANT INTELL
INSERTION:     TIME: 220745H DEC    METHOD: SLICK    COORD: VR 959109
EXTRACTION:    TIME: 221030H DEC    METHOD: SLICK    COORD: VR 955109
BRIEF OF MISSION NARRATIVE:  REACTING ON INTELL, DEPARTED CA MAU 220730H
AND PROCEEDED TO INSERTION POINT. AFTER INSERTING, PROCEEDED 400 M
WEST WHERE ALFA SQUAD SEARCHED SUSPECTS HOOTCH AND BRAVO SQUAD SEARCHED
HOOTCHES IN NEARBY TREE LINE. AT SUSPECTS HOOTCH, 150 RDS OF AK-47
AMMO, 1 VC GRENADE, VC PICTURES, AND ½ KILO OF DOCUMENTS. THE GUNSHIPS
REPORTED THAT ON INSERTION, THEY SHOT 3 VC WHO FLEEING THE SCENE.
SCOUTING PARTY DETAINED ONE MALE. GUIDE SAID THAT THE MALE WAS A FARMER
SO HE WAS RELEASED. AT 221015 PLT CALLED FOR AND EXTRACTION AND EX-
TRACTED, RETURNING CA MAU 221050H.

RESULTS OF ENEMY ENCOUNTERED: 150 RDS AK-47 AMMO, 1 VC GRENADE, ½ KILO
  3 VC KBA (PROB)              OF DOCUMENTS, SOME VC PICTURES CIA

FRIENDLY CASUALTIES:           NONE


REMARKS:            NONE



RECOMMENDATIONS/LESSONS LEARNED:   NONE



COPY DIST:  NAVSPECWARGRUV, SEAL DET ALFA, SEAL TEAM 2, SEAL TEAM 1.
SIGNATURE OF PERSON MAKING REPORT:
                                      LT R F MORAN
BARNDANCE # 9-26
```

December 23

1942 (USA)—A Joint Chiefs of Staff directive authorizes the OSS to form Detachment 101 and the Jedburghs.

1943 (England)—NCDUs arrive at Falmouth, Cornwall, at 2000 hours. The next morning, the officers of the NCDUs receive word that they will have the Officer of the Day watch for the next seven days and will conduct "collateral duties as directed by the executive officer." The secret nature of the NCDUs' operations, combined with a total lack of knowledge of just what to do with such highly trained men in England, results in a terrific waste of time. The men and officers of the NCDUs conduct what specialized training they can in England, in addition to their "collateral duties."

1989 (Panama)—SEALs from Task Unit Whiskey help repel PDF boarders who try to board the merchant ship *Emanuel B* in the Panama Canal.

December 24

1942 (Tunisia)—Two C-47 Skytrain aircraft drop thirty-two paratroopers well behind enemy lines to destroy the El Djem Bridge. The target is destroyed as the German forces close in. Only 8 paratroopers manage to complete the 110-mile march across the desert to reach friendly forces. The rest of the force was killed or captured. This is the first true special operations jump of World War II.

1979 (Scotland)—Naval Special Warfare Unit Two (NSWU Two) is reestablished in Macrihanish, Scotland. NSWU Two is a forward operating unit that will support SEALs deployed to Europe or the Arctic areas of NATO countries. The unit gives the SEALs a much faster response time in dealing with quickly rising actions in the region.

December 25

1943 (Italy)—The First Special Service Force captures Hill 730.

1989 (Panama)—Naval Special Warfare Task Group's Task Unit Whiskey seizes Manuel Noriega's beach house on Culebra Island. It does not locate the missing dictator after a detailed search of the house and its surrounding area. This is the last active mission of Task Unit Whiskey during Operation Just Cause.

December 26

1989 (Panama)—During Operation Just Cause, Task Unit Charlie of the Naval Special Warfare Task Group is deactivated after only a short service life. Task Unit Charlie's mission was to secure the Caribbean side of the Panama Canal and prevent shipping from entering and leaving the canal during the hostilities.

1989 (Panama)—Task Unit Foxtrot conducts maritime patrols along the waters near the Papal Nunciature, a property having both a diplomatic and religious status. It is known that Manuel Noriega has taken refuge inside the building.

December 27

1962 (USA)—Rear Admiral Allen L. Reed, the assistant chief of naval operations issues Naval Warfare Information Publication (NWIP) 29-1. The forty-page document outlines the mission parameters and capabilities intended for the new SEAL teams. Updated and reissued a number of times over the years, NWIP 29-1 still remains classified except for portions of the original document. One of those portions is as follows:

THE SEAL MISSION PROFILE (NWIP 29-1)

    (1)   *Primary:* To develop a specialized capability to conduct operations for military, political, or economic purposes within an area occupied by the enemy for sabotage, demolition, and other clandestine activities conducted in and around restricted

waters, rivers, and canals, and to conduct training of selected U.S., allied and indigenous personnel in a wide variety of skills for use in naval clandestine operations in hostile environments.

(2) *Secondary:* To develop doctrine and tactics for SEAL operations and to develop support equipment, including special craft for use in these operations.

(3) *Tasks:* Tasks may be overt or covert in nature

    (a) Destructive tasks—These tasks include clandestine attacks on enemy shipping, demolition raids in harbors and other enemy installations within reach; destruction of supply lines in maritime areas by destruction of bridges, railway lines, roads, canals and so forth; and the delivery of special weapons (SADM) to exact locations in restricted waters, rivers or canals.

    (b) Support tasks—The support tasks of SEAL Teams include protecting friendly supply lines, assisting or participating in the landing and support of guerrilla and partisan forces, and assisting or participating in the landing and recovery of agents, other special forces, downed aviators, escapees and so forth.

    (c) Additional Tasks:

        1. Conduct reconnaissance, surveillance and intelligence collection missions as directed.

        2. In friendly areas train U.S. and indigenous personnel in such operations as directed.

        3. Develop equipment to support special operations.

        4. Develop the capability for small boat operations, including the use of native types.

December 28

1952 (Korea)—The 8240th Army Unit Jesse James I radio team infiltrates into North Korea.

1968 (North Korea)—The eighty-two surviving crewmen and one set of remains from the USS *Pueblo* (AGER 2) are repatriated back to the United States through P'anmunjom by the North Koreans. The men are being released after eleven months of captivity following the U.S. government admitting to having conducted espionage in the coastal waters of the Sea of Japan. The *Pueblo* itself, however, is never returned to the U.S. government.

1992 (Somalia)—U.S. Army Special Forces assets in Kenya move to join with other U.S. forces in Somalia. The mission of the Special Forces, Operation Restore Hope, is to work with local Somalis to build intelligence on the local situation and prevent dangerous situations from arising among the various rebel groups.

December 29

1952 (Korea)—The 8240th Army Unit Jesse James II radio team infiltrates into North Korea.

December 30

1952 (Korea)—The 8240th Army Unit Jesse James III radio team infiltrates into North Korea.

December 31

The thumbs-up sign is given by a fully equipped SEAL from
SEAL Team Eight during VBSS training aboard the *Joshua
Humphries* during Desert Storm. His primary weapon is an
MP-5N submachine gun fitted with a removable flash hider
and loaded with a double set of 30-round magazines. With
this arrangement, the empty magazine can be removed and
the loaded magazine quickly slipped into place. U.S. NAVY

Glossary

AGER The Navy code designation for an Environmental Research Ship. These are former Army cargo ships that have been converted into electronic intelligence gathering platforms. The AGER-2 was the USS *Pueblo*.

AH-6 A variant of the McDonnell Douglas MD520/530 helicopter. This small teardrop-bodied helicopter has a five-bladed rotor powered by a jet engine. The AH-6 variations are generically known as "Little Birds" and they are used in an armed configuration by the 160th Special Operations Aviation Regiment.

APD High speed transport. During World War II, these were often converted obsolete "four-stacker" destroyer escorts. They could carry an entire UDT, its equipment, and explosives.

APL A barracks ship supplying living quarters and support for personnel.

APSS Amphibious transport submarine. This was the conversion of World War II *"Balao"* class diesel-electric submarines to act as underwater transports for troops and for covert operations. This craft was known as the *"Sealion"* type for the first ship converted (APSS 315). Other such submarines were the *Perch* (APSS 313), and *Tunny* (APSS 282). The subs could transport seven officers and eighty enlisted troops in addition to the ship's normal complement of six officers and sixty-eight enlisted men. The room for the additional personnel came from removing all of the torpedo tubes and half of the diesel engines from the original design. The APSS designation was changed to LPSS in January 1969.

ASPB (assault support patrol boat)   A heavily armored and armed shallow water craft for operations in rivers and inshore waters.

BUD/S (basic underwater demolition/SEAL)   The name of the twenty-six week long training course today conducted at the Naval Amphibious Base in Coronado, California. Passing this course is the only way to become a SEAL.

C3 (Composition 3)   An earlier formulation of plastic explosive based on RDX that was developed toward the end of World War II and used through the end of the Vietnam War.

C4 (Composition 4)   The standard plastic explosive used today. The explosive formulation is plastic at normal temperatures and very stable. It can be formed and shaped by hand to fit to a target and is relatively waterproof. C4 and the earlier C3 can only be detonated by the explosive shock from a blasting cap, primercord/detonating cord, or other detonator.

CIA   The Central Intelligence Agency, post-World War II replacement for the OSS.

CSAR   Combat search and rescue.

DDG   Guided missile destroyer.

Det (detachment)   The designation for a group of SEALs assigned to a specific area or mission. A det can be as small as just a couple of SEALs or UDT operators, or as large as a number of platoons.

EOD (explosive ordnance disposal)   The military unit assigned to disarm or render safe unexploded ordnance including mines, bombs, and artillery shells.

Fast carrier force   A World War II task force organization implemented and used in the Pacific theater. A fast carrier force had at least two fleet carriers and two light carriers as well as a number of capital ships, destroyers, and support craft. Each fleet carrier included in its air group close to forty fighter planes, thirty-five dive bombers, and eighteen torpedo bombers. The light carriers maintained around twenty-three fighter planes and 10 torpedo bombers. The capital ships in the force could include battleships as well as heavy and light cruisers.

FAV (Fast Attack Vehicle)   This is more correctly called the DPV, for Desert Patrol/Light Strike Vehicle. It is a development of the Chenowth dune buggy racing vehicle. The vehicle can carry a number of SEALs for over 200 miles across desert terrain and mount an assortment of machine guns, grenade launchers, and recoilless weapons for heavy support.

GAT (gap assault team)   An organization made up of Navy Combat Demolition Unit personnel, Army engineers, and Navy volunteers. The mission of the GATs was to blow open fifty-yard-wide gaps through the obstacles on Utah and Omaha beaches during the Normandy invasion.

HSSC (heavy SEAL support craft)   A converted Mark 6 LCM landing craft for use as a support craft for SEAL operations in Vietnam. The craft were heavily armored and armed, carrying an assortment of fifty-caliber machine guns as well as a 106mm recoilless rifle, and 81mm mortar, automatic grenade launchers, 7.62mm machine guns, and a selection of small arms. Only a very few of the heavy, slow HSSC craft were converted, and they operated in Vietnam from the earliest years of the SEALs' active combat involvement there.

Jedburgh teams   A World War II result of the combined efforts of the American OSS and the British Special Operations Executive (SOE). Jedburgh teams were three-man units made up of an American, an Englishman, and a third trained operative who was a native of the country the Jedburgh was intended to operate in.

Klick   A kilometer, 1,000 meters.

LCM   Landing craft, medium.

LCPL   Landing craft, personnel, large.

LCPR   Landing craft, personnel, ramped. The earlier World War II version of this craft was known as a *Higgins boat*.

LDNN   South Vietnamese SEALs/UDTs. The name underwent some changes, though the initials remained the same. Originally LDNN stood for *Lien Doc Nguoi Nhai* (soldiers who fight under the sea). *Doc* was later changed to *doi*, which means team, then finally changed to *doan*, which means group.

Limpet mine   An explosive device intended to be attached by hand to the hull of a ship.

LPSS   Amphibious transport submarine.

LSSC   Light SEAL support craft.

LST (landing ship, tank)   A heavy oceangoing transport ship that could land vehicles and tanks onto a beach through its large bow doors.

MACV   Military Assistance Command–Vietnam (also written *MAC-V*).

MH-47E Chinook   This is a special operations version of the twin-rotored CH-47 Chinook medium-lift helicopter. The MH-47E can transport more than a platoon of special operations personnel over 700 miles on an operation. The aircraft has specialized navigation and electronic countermeasure equipment to aid it in its mission.

Mike boat   A smaller armed and armored conversion of landing craft for use by the SEALs in Vietnam.

NAB   Naval amphibious base.

Nasty boat   These were the Norwegian-built PTF boats purchased by the U.S. Navy. The Nasty-class boats were modern versions of the World War II torpedo (PT) boats, though not normally used by U.S. forces armed with torpedoes. The Nasty boats mounted a variety of automatic weapons including 20mm and 40mm cannon.

NCDU (naval combat demolition unit)   A six-man unit of five enlisted men and an officer trained to conduct demolition operations to clear obstacles from the water. The six-man size of the NCDU was based on their operating from seven-man inflatable rubber boats—the space for the seventh man being taken up by the unit's explosives. The primary mission of the NCDUs was to blast open the beaches for the invasion of Europe. These were the direct ancestors of the UDT.

NVA   The North Vietnamese Army, also called *NVA regulars*. These were the uniformed military forces of North Vietnam.

OG   During World War II, the Operational Groups branch of the OSS was established to provide trained soldiers who would form the nucleus of a native guerrilla force inside of enemy occupied territory. The basic organization of an OG was four officers and thirty enlisted men. Successful field operations were conducted with OG units as small as one officer and two enlisted men. The OGs acted as commandos on many operations.

OH-58   The Bell model 406 "Kiowa" scout helicopter.

Oplan (operational plan)   The overall plan including the allowance of manpower, equipment, support, and expenditures for conducting an extensive military or intelligence operation.

OSS   The Office of Strategic Services, America's World War II organization tasked with collecting and analyzing intelligence from all theaters as well as conducting unconventional warfare against the enemy.

PBR Mk I (patrol boat, river)   A thirty-one foot fiberglass-hulled small boat propelled by a waterjet pump. The PBRs were very maneuverable and extremely heavily armed for their size. In the bow was a sunken gun tub that was usually armed with twin fifty-caliber Browning machine guns. A single-stand mount at the stern was also usually armed with a fifty-caliber machine gun. The midships station usually had a 7.62mm M60 machine gun and a belt-fed Mark 18 40mm grenade launcher. The boats were fast when new, but very lightly armored.

PBR Mk II   An improved version of the original PBR Mk I. Armed with the same compliment of weapons, the Mark II PBR was more strongly built and had other improvements based on experience with the earlier version.

PCF (patrol craft, fast)   This was the official designation for the Swift boat.

PRU (provincial reconnaissance unit)   An organization of mercenaries and local forces assigned to local provinces in South Vietnam, specifically, to attack the Viet Cong infrastructure of leaders and cadre. The PRUs were paramilitary units armed and paid by U.S. intelligence services and advised by U.S. military personnel. They were extremely effective in eliminating the Viet Cong as functioning units in many areas of South Vietnam.

PTF (patrol boat, fast)   This was the official designation for the Nasty-class boat.

Riverine   An area of land, either inland or coastal, characterized by limited land lines of communication and by extensive waterways.

SAS   The Special Air Service, a name used by both the British, Australian, and New Zealand units. The British SAS began the operations of the first unit during World War II and are considered to have set the standard that many special operations units have tried to meet ever since.

SDV (swimmer [now SEAL] delivery vehicle)   A small wet-type underwater vehicle that can carry a number of SEALs and their equipment underwater over long distances. Because the vehicles are of the wet type, they are flooded with water when operating, and the crew and passengers must all wear breathing equipment.

SDVT (SEAL delivery vehicle teams)   These are specialized teams manned by fully qualified SEALs who operate the SEAL delivery vehicles (SDV) and dry deck shelters (DDS) for the rest of the teams.

SEAL   The name of the Navy special warfare units taken from the three environments they operate in: Sea, Air, and Land.

SF   Special Forces, commonly known to the public as the "Green Berets." This is the largest Army contingent of U.S. special operations forces.

SF Group   A large organization of Special Forces troops. A Group is often assigned to a specific geographical area, and their training and language skills reflect this assignment.

SOG (special operations group)   In Vietnam, this was later changed to mean "studies and observation group" for added security.

STAB Mk I (SEAL team assault boat)   A converted commercial Powercat Trimeran boat. The conversion of the boat, which included placing mounting points for weapons and armoring some of the hull and the twin outboard motors that powered the craft, was conducted at SEAL Team Two at the NAB in Little Creek. The boats were a great success in Vietnam and were used until they were literally worn to pieces.

STAB Mk II   Also known as the Mark II LSSC, this was a Navy small boat designed by the Grafton Boat Company for use by the SEALs in Vietnam starting in 1969. The boats were powered by inboard Chevrolet engines that drove a water-jet pump.

Swift boat   A metal-hulled fifty-foot PCF converted from a crew boat originally used to service offshore oil rigs.

Teams   The name used by operators to refer to the SEAL teams and UDTs.

UDT   Underwater demolition team.

UDTR (underwater demolition team replacement)   The course of training that had to be passed in order to join the UDTs or SEALs as an operator. This course was later renamed *BUD/S*.

UH-1B   The workhorse helicopter of the Vietnam War. This is the B model of the Bell Model 204 helicopter first flown in 1956. Originally designated the HU-1 (for helicopter, utility) after acceptance, the bird was most often known by its nickname, "Huey." Even after the designation was changed to UH-1 in 1962, the nickname stuck. The aircraft was much more rarely called its official Army designation, *Iroquois*.

USS   United States ship.

VC   The Viet Cong, the communist insurgent guerrilla forces fighting in South Vietnam and elsewhere in Southeast Asia.

ZU-23mm   A fully automatic, belt-fed cannon developed by the Soviets primarily for antiaircraft use. The guns are sometimes found mounted singly but more commonly in double or quadruple mounts. They are also used as the main armament of some light armored vehicles.

Index

About the Authors

KEVIN DOCKERY has been a professional writer for over a decade, concentrating his efforts on recording the history of the Navy SEALs and their predecessors. Presently a noted historian, Dockery has completed over a dozen works on the history of the SEALs, biographies of individual operators, and a number of unique firearms references. His hobbies of blacksmithing, knife and sword making, and fencing keep him active away from the keyboard.

ELAINE ABBRECHT is a historical researcher and a financial assistant in southeast Michigan, where she also indulges her passion for ballroom dancing. This is her first book.